T0144513

Wireless and Mobile Networking

Mahbub Hassan

School of Computer Science and Engineering
The University of New South Wales, Sydney, Australia

CRC Press is an imprint of the
Taylor & Francis Group, an **informa** business

A SCIENCE PUBLISHERS BOOK

First edition published 2022
by CRC Press
6000 Broken Sound Parkway NW, Suite 300, Boca Raton, FL 33487-2742

and by CRC Press
2 Park Square, Milton Park, Abingdon, Oxon, OX14 4RN

CRC Press is an imprint of Taylor & Francis Group, LLC

Library of Congress Cataloging-in-Publication Data (applied for)

ISBN: 978-0-367-48735-5 (hbk)
ISBN: 978-1-032-27007-4 (pbk)
ISBN: 978-1-003-04260-0 (ebk)

DOI: 10.1201/9781003042600

Typeset in Times New Roman
by Radiant Productions

Preface

Why this Book was Written

Our modern way of life is critically dependent on wireless and mobile networking technology which enables citizens to communicate with each other and access all types of information and services from anywhere anytime. To meet the growing demand and diversified requirements of new applications and services, wireless networking technology has advanced at a rapid pace in recent years introducing many new features and concepts. These developments range from adding new features to previous versions of the technology to developing completely new paradigms for wireless networking. While it is important for the next generation students to gain a good understanding of these latest developments, it is rare to find a text that covers them in a compact form. This book fills this gap by covering not only the latest developments in Bluetooth, WiFi, and Cellular networks, but also the emerging wireless networking paradigms including Internet of Things (IoT) networking with LoRa, Artificial Intelligence (AI) assisted wireless networking, wireless sensing with WiFi and millimeter wave radars, and aerial networking with drones. Presenting the fundamental wireless concepts in a less mathematically intensive manner is another key feature of this book, which makes it accessible to readers from a wide range of backgrounds.

Who can Benefit from this Book

This book would be an ideal text for a one semester course on Wireless and Mobile Networking suitable for both undergraduate students in their 3rd or 4th year and postgraduate students from a range of disciplines including Computer Science, Information Technology, Information Systems, Mechatronics, and Electrical Engineering. Instructors using the book as a text for classroom teaching can obtain from the author power point slide decks as well as additional multiple-choice questions for each chapter. Professionals working in the industry as well as hobbyists can use the book to keep themselves abreast with the latest developments in popular and emerging wireless networking technologies.

Organization of the Book

The book is organized into six parts including the first one that introduces the book. Part II is a review of the fundamentals of wireless communications that are critical to understand the wireless technologies covered in the rest of the book. These fundamental wireless concepts are explained without resorting to intensive mathematics, which makes them accessible to readers from a wide range of background. Chapter 2 covers the basic theories of **coding and modulation**, which is the fundamental technique to map digital information to the underlying signal so that a receiver can retrieve the information from the signal using appropriate decoder and demodulator, while Chapter 3 explains the fundamentals of **wireless signal propagation.**

Part III covers **WiFi**, which is one of the most widely used wireless networking technologies today, especially for indoor and local area applications. WiFi has been primarily used as a networking technology for enterprise and residential domains, as well as connecting personal mobile devices, such as mobile phones, tablets, laptops, etc., to the Internet in homes, cafes, airports, and university campuses. These mainstream WiFi predominantly used the ISM bands 2.4 GHz and 5 GHz, with the new versions aiming to use the 6 GHz band. In addition to these mainstream WiFi, IEEE has also released several 802.11 amendments that target some niche applications. These niche WiFi standards operate outside the mainstream bands, both at the very low end of the spectrum, i.e., below 1 GHz, as well as at the very high end, i.e., 60 GHz. For example, 802.11af is targeting the exploitation of 700 MHz spectrum recently vacated by TV stations due to their digitization, 802.11ah using 900 MHz to connect emerging Internet of Things operating at low power, and 802.11ad/ay at 60 GHz to support multi-gigabit applications at short range. To systematically cover these developments, this part breaks the treatment of WiFi into three chapters. Chapter 4 covers the **basics of WiFi** that are common to all WiFi versions. Chapter 5 covers the **mainstream WiFi**, while Chapter 6 focuses on **niche WiFi**.

Part IV is dedicated to **cellular networks**, which are designed to provide wide area coverage to both static and mobile users. Cellular network is the oldest communications network technology, which has now gone through several generations of evolution with the fifth generation currently being deployed. Chapter 7 covers the fundamental concepts of cellular networks with a brief examination of the advancements brought forth by each generation up to the fourth. While the previous four generations mainly sought to improve the data rate and capacity of the cellular systems, 5G is designed to improve several other aspects of communications and connectivity beyond the data rates. Chapter 8 discusses the new applications promised by 5G and some of the key networking technologies behind them.

Part V is devoted to **Internet of Things (IoT)**, which is an emerging networking paradigm to connect all types of objects to the Internet, making it possible to digitize every phenomenon and processes of interest. Chapter 9 introduces **IoT** discussing the business opportunities and the recently standardized wireless networking technologies to support the need of IoT. Chapter 10 explains **Bluetooth**, the oldest and the most pervasive technology to connect a wide range of devices and 'things' around us. This chapter covers its history, markets, and applications, followed by the core technologies behind the three generations of Bluetooth including versions 5.0 and 5.3. Pervasive IoT deployments demand low-power wide area networking (LPWAN) solutions that can connect hundreds of thousands of sensors and 'things' over a large area with minimal infrastructure cost. While Bluetooth is certainly low-powered, it works only for short ranges. Cellular networks are designed for wide area coverage, but they consume too much power which requires large batteries and frequent battery recharging for the end nodes. Consequently, there is a significant momentum in standardizing new networking solutions for LPWAN. New developments are emerging from both cellular and WiFi standard bodies, i.e., from the 3GPP and IEEE/WiFi-alliance, respectively, to fill this gap, but there is a third momentum that is proving very successful. It is called LoRa Alliance (LoRa stands for *long range*), which is an industry alliance committed to accelerate the development and deployment of LPWAN networks. Chapter 11 examines the details of the **LoRa** technology.

Part VI covers some of the latest developments in wireless and mobile networking. As wireless networks get more and more complex to deal with the ever-growing demand for capacity and quality of service, artificial intelligent (AI) is being explored as a potential aid to wireless networking in the future. Chapter 12 examines what, why, and how questions for **AI in wireless**. While wireless has revolutionized mobile data communications, it also plays a major role as a sensing technology. Recently, scientists are discovering techniques to monitor human activities and even vital signs, such as heart and breathing rates, simply by analyzing the wireless signals reflected by the human body. These advancements have created the potential for wireless to penetrate the growing mobile and IoT sensing market. Chapter 13 explains the working principles of the popular wireless sensing tools and techniques targeted at the IoT market. Finally, miniaturization of electronics has created an opportunity to fit wireless communications equipment into the payload of various aerial platforms such as drones and aerostats. Aerial wireless networks can be deployed quickly and cost-effectively to provide coverage in remote areas where terrestrial infrastructure is difficult to build, in disaster zones with damaged cellular towers, and even in urban areas to absorb sudden peaks in data traffic. The final chapter of the book, Chapter 14, examines options, characteristics, and design considerations for such **aerial wireless networks**.

Acknowledgements

This book could not be written without the caring mentorship and help from Professor Raj Jain while the author spent his sabbatical at the Washington University in Saint Louis. The author also acknowledges sabbatical leaves, a.k.a. Special Studies Program, granted by the University of New South Wales.

Mahbub Hassan

Contents

Preface   iii

Part I: Introduction

1. Wireless and Mobile Networking: From Past to Present   3

Part II: Physical Layer Fundamentals

2. Wireless Coding and Modulation   11

3. Wireless Signal Propagation   35

Part III: WiFi and Wireless Local Area Networks

4. WiFi Basics   59

5. Mainstream WiFi Standards   78

6. Niche WiFi   104

Part IV: Cellular Networks

7. Cellular Networks   141

8. 5G Networks   164

Part V: Internet of Things

9. Internet of Things   175

10. Bluetooth   187

11. LoRa and LoRaWAN   218

Part VI: Next Frontiers in Wireless Networking

12. Artificial Intelligence-assisted Wireless Networking   233

13. Wireless Sensing   245

14. Aerial Wireless Networks   260

Index   **271**

Part I
Introduction

1

Wireless and Mobile Networking
From Past to Present

‹‹‹

Wireless networking has a long and rich history of innovations. Many significant developments have taken place in the past decades making the wireless technology more affordable, effective, reliable. In this chapter, we will take a brief look at the history of wireless networking, survey the growth forecasts of various categories of wireless and mobile networks, and provide an outline of the book.

1. Wireless History

Today's wireless industry is built on a long and rich history of significant discoveries and innovations over many decades. Figure 1 captures the major developments in wireless history, which started back in 1880's with the discovery and experimental verification of the existence of electromagnetic waves. In the middle of the 19th century, Maxwell derived equations that explained how electric and magnetic fields interact to produce electromagnetic waves. A few years later, in 1886, Hertz experimentally validated successful transmission of radio waves and discovered that all electromagnetic waves travel at a constant speed having the same velocity as light.

While Hertz discovered the most fundamental ingredient of wireless communications that we enjoy today, there was no specific commercial goal behind the discovery. Ten years later, in 1896, Marconi invented wireless telegraph [MARCONI], which enabled transmission of telegraphic messages completely wirelessly, without having to rely on any cables or wires between the sending and receiving stations.

Early to middle 20th century saw the development of audio and video broadcasting using radio and TV technologies including launching of communications satellites to achieve global coverage.

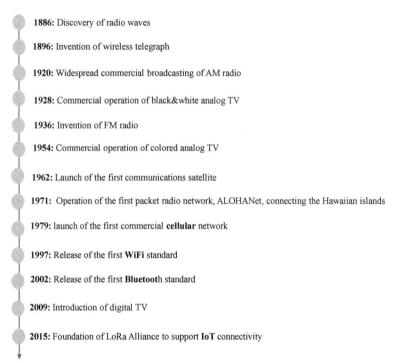

1886: Discovery of radio waves

1896: Invention of wireless telegraph

1920: Widespread commercial broadcasting of AM radio

1928: Commercial operation of black&white analog TV

1936: Invention of FM radio

1954: Commercial operation of colored analog TV

1962: Launch of the first communications satellite

1971: Operation of the first packet radio network, ALOHANet, connecting the Hawaiian islands

1979: launch of the first commercial **cellular** network

1997: Release of the first **WiFi** standard

2002: Release of the first **Bluetooth** standard

2009: Introduction of digital TV

2015: Foundation of LoRa Alliance to support **IoT** connectivity

Fig. 1. Key discoveries and innovations in wireless history.

In terms of data transmission, the first packet radio network, called ALOHAnet [ALOHANET], was deployed in 1971, to provide connectivity between Hawaiian Islands. A major innovation used to operate this network was the medium access control (MAC) protocol, called ALOHA, which allowed wireless packets from different stations to automatically avoid using the wireless channel at the same time in a distributed fashion. Modern communication networks, including WiFi and cellular networks, use MAC protocols that are inspired by ALOHA. Few years later, the first cellular networks, retrospectively called the first generation (1G) networks, were deployed in 1979 to support mobile telephony over large coverage areas.

While cellular networks enabled mobile telephony, WiFi was introduced in 1997 operating at 2 Mbps [WIFI, 1997]. Today it is possible to transmit at close to Gbps over WiFi and hundreds of Gbps speed is within reach.

Introduced in 2002, Bluetooth [BLUETOOTH] is another major development in wireless history that enables many objects to directly connect and transfer data with each at short distances without having to go through a central base station. Bluetooth helped flourish many commercial products and applications including wireless keyboards and mouse, wireless headsets and earbuds, wireless speakers and so on.

The power of Bluetooth to give communications capability to everyday objects has inspired a trend in connecting all types of things to the Internet, so the environment can be digitally monitored 24×7. This new evolution in mass connectivity is referred to as Internet of Things (IoT). A new type of communication networks, called LoRaWAN, became commercially available from 2015 to connect millions of objects and sensors at long distances with minimal energy consumption.

2. Growth in Wireless and Mobile Networking

Since the introduction of WiFi in 1997, there have been phenomenal uptake of wireless and mobile networking technologies. When laptops became widely popular in the late 1990's, they were almost exclusively connected to the Internet via Ethernet cables. Today, all laptops are fitted with WiFi. Tablets and mobile phones are fitted with multiple wireless technologies including WiFi, Bluetooth and cellular. As illustrated in Fig. 2, cables and wires have slowly moved to the backbone, while the access is now almost exclusively dominated by wireless. With the IoT revolution, billions of sensors are also being connected using wireless networking. These trends are fueling massive growths in wireless and mobile networking. For example, in the largest economy of the world, i.e., in the USA, wireless industry alone accounts for close to 3% of its GDP [ACCENTURE].

According to the latest CISCO reports [CISCOREPORT], there will be approximately 628 million public WiFi hotspots by 2023, up from 169 million in 2018. Similarly, 6.2 billion Bluetooth devices are expected to be shipped in 2024, a twofold increase from 2016 [BT-SIG2020]. With increasing investment in IoT-powered Industry 4.0 as well as smart homes and cites, LoRa and LoRaWAN devices' market is estimated to grow at a CAGR 36.5% during 2021–2026, reaching $6.2 billion by 2026.

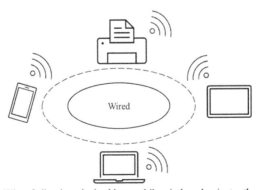

Fig. 2. Wires fading into the backbone while wireless dominates the access.

3. Book Outline

The book is organized into six parts, including the first one that basically provides an introduction to the book. Each of the remaining five parts focuses on a specific broad topic or wireless technology while the subtopics within it are organised into multiple chapters.

Part II provides a review of the fundamentals of wireless communications that are critical to understand the wireless technologies covered in the rest of the book. This part contains two chapters. Chapter 2 covers the basic theories and terminologies of 'coding and modulation', which is the fundamental technique to map digital information to the underlying signal, so that a receiver can retrieve the information from the signal using appropriate decoder and demodulator. Chapter 3 explains the fundamentals of 'wireless signal propagation' and discusses mathematical models used to capture such propagation dynamics.

Part III covers 'WiFi', which is one of the most widely used wireless networking technologies today, especially for indoor and local area applications. WiFi has been primarily used as a networking technology for enterprise and residential domains, as well as for connecting personal mobile devices, such as mobile phones, tablets, laptops, etc., to the Internet in homes, cafes, airports, and university campuses. These mainstream WiFi predominantly used the ISM bands 2.4 GHz and 5 GHz, with the new versions aiming to use the 6 GHz band. In addition to these mainstream WiFi, IEEE has also released several 802.11 amendments that target some niche applications. These niche WiFi standards operate outside the mainstream bands, both at the very low end of the spectrum, i.e., below 1 GHz, as well as at the very high end, i.e., 60 GHz. For example, 802.11af is targeting the exploitation of 700 MHz spectrum recently vacated by TV stations due to their digitization, 802.11ah using 900 MHz to connect emerging Internet of Things operating at low power, and 802.11ad/ay at 60 GHz to support multi-gigabit applications at short range. To systematically cover these developments, this part breaks the treatment of WiFi into three chapters. Chapter 4 covers the 'basics of WiFi' that are common to all WiFi versions. Chapter 5 covers the 'mainstream WiFi', while Chapter 6 focuses on 'niche WiFi'.

Part IV is dedicated to 'cellular networks', which are designed to provide wide area coverage to both static and mobile users. Cellular network is the oldest communications network technology, which has now gone through several generations of evolution, with the fifth generation currently being deployed. Chapter 7 covers the fundamental concepts of cellular networks with a brief examination of the advancements brought forth by each generation up to the fourth. While the previous four generations mainly sought to improve the data rate and capacity of the cellular systems, 5G is designed to improve several other aspects of communications and connectivity beyond the data rates. Chapter 8 discusses the new applications promised by 5G and some of the key networking technologies behind them.

Part V is devoted to 'Internet of Things (IoT)', which is a new networking vision to connect all types of objects to the Internet, making it possible to digitize every phenomenon and processes of interest. Chapter 9 provides an 'introduction to IoT', discussing the business opportunities and the recently standardized wireless networking technologies to support the need of IoT. Chapter 10 explains 'Bluetooth', the oldest and most pervasive technology to connect a wide range of devices and 'things' around us. This chapter covers its history, markets and applications, followed by the core technologies behind the three generations of Bluetooth. Pervasive IoT deployments demand low-power wide area networking (LPWAN) solutions that can connect hundreds of thousands of sensors and 'things' over a large area with minimal infrastructure cost. While Bluetooth is certainly low-powered, it works only for short ranges. Cellular networks are designed for wide area coverage, but they consume too much power which requires large batteries and frequent battery recharging for the end nodes. Consequently, there is a significant momentum in standardizing new networking solutions for LPWAN. New developments are emerging from both cellular and WiFi standard bodies, i.e., from the 3GPP and IEEE/WiFi Alliance, respectively, to fill this gap, but there is a third momentum that is proving very successful. It is called LoRa Alliance (LoRa stands for *long range*), which is an industry alliance committed to accelerate the development and deployment of LPWAN networks. Chapter 11 examines the details of the 'LoRa' technology.

Part VI covers some of the latest developments in wireless and mobile networking. As wireless networks get more and more complex to deal with the ever-growing demand for capacity and quality of service, Artificial Intelligence (AI) is being explored as a potential aid to wireless networking in the future. Chapter 12 examines the what, why, and how questions for 'AI in wireless'. While wireless has revolutionized mobile data communications, it also plays a major role as a sensing technology. Recently, scientists are discovering techniques to monitor human activities and even vital signs, such as heart and breathing rates, simply by analysing the wireless signals reflected by the human body. These advancements have created the potential for wireless to penetrate the growing mobile and IoT sensing market. Chapter 13 explains the working principles of the popular wireless sensing tools and techniques targeted at the IoT market. Finally, miniaturization of electronics has created an opportunity to fit wireless communications equipment into the payload of various aerial platforms, such as drones and aerostats. Aerial wireless networks can be deployed quickly and cost-effectively to provide coverage in remote areas where terrestrial infrastructure is difficult to build, in disaster zones with damaged cellular towers, and even in urban areas to absorb sudden peaks in data traffic. The final chapter of the book, Chapter 14, examines options, characteristics, and design considerations for such 'aerial wireless networks'.

References

[ALOHANET] N. Abramson, The ALOHAnet–surfing for wireless data. *IEEE Communications Magazine*, Dec. 2009, pp. 23–25.

[ACCENTURE] How the wireless industry powers the U.S. economy. Accenture. https://www.accenture.com/_acnmedia/PDF-74/Accenture-Strategy-Wireless-Industry-Powers-US-Economy-2018-POV.pdf [accessed 28 Sep. 2021].

[BLUETOOTH] 802.15.1-2002 - IEEE Standard for Telecommunications and Information Exchange between Systems - LAN/MAN - Specific Requirements - Part 15: Wireless Medium Access Control (MAC) and Physical Layer (PHY) Specifications for Wireless Personal Area Networks (WPANs). pp. 1–473. *In*: *IEEE Std 802.15.1-2002*. 14 June 2002.

[BT-SIG2020] *2020Bluetooth Market Report*, Bluetooth SIG. https:www.bluetooth.com.

[CISCOREPORT] *Cisco Annual Internet Report* (2018–2023) white paper, 9 March, 2020.

[LORAMARKET] LoRa and LoRaWAN Devices Market – Forecast (2021–2026). https://www.industryarc.com/Report/19424/lora-and-lorawan-devices-market.html#:~:text=LoRa%20and%20LoRaWAN%20Devices%20Market%20Overview,36.5%25%20during%202021%2D2026 [accessed 28 Sep. 2021].

[MARCONI] Guglielmo MarconiBiographical. https://www.nobelprize.org/prizes/physics/1909/marconi/biographical/ [accessed 28 Sep. 2021].

[WIFI, 1997]. IEEE standard for Wireless LAN medium access control (MAC) and physical layer (PHY) specifications. pp. 1–445. *In*: *IEEE Std 802.11-1997*. 18 Nov. 1997.

Part II
Physical Layer Fundamentals

2
Wireless Coding and Modulation

Coding and modulation provide a means to map digital information to the underlying signal so that a receiver can retrieve the information from the signal, using appropriate decoder and demodulator. As coding and modulation directly affect the achievable capacity and data rate of the communication system, new coding and modulation techniques are constantly proposed and implemented to keep up with the demand for mobile data. This chapter will cover the basic theories and terminologies of coding and modulation in digital wireless communications.

1. Frequency, Wavelength, Amplitude, and Phase

Signal waveforms are the fundamental carriers of all types of data that we send over a communication system. It is therefore important to understand the basic properties of such waveforms. Figure 1 shows the waves that are created when a rock is thrown into water. Similar waves are also created in wireless networking for communication purposes, but these are called *electromagnetic waves* and special electronic circuits are used to generate and receive them.

In the simplest form, a wave is mathematically represented by a sine wave, $A \sin(2\pi f t + \theta)$, where A = Amplitude, f = frequency, θ = phase, and t is

Fig. 1. Waves in the water.

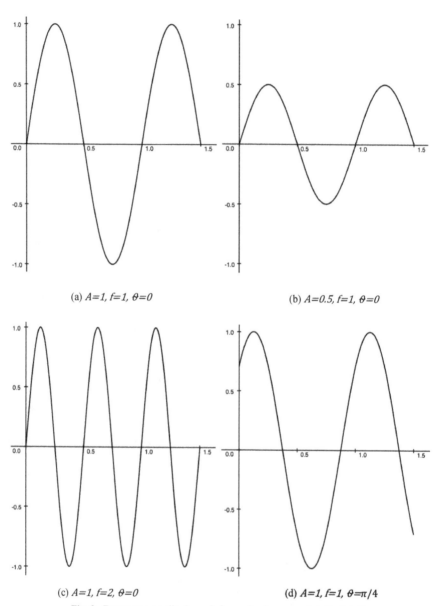

(a) *A=1, f=1, θ=0*

(b) *A=0.5, f=1, θ=0*

(c) *A=1, f=2, θ=0*

(d) *A=1, f=1, θ=π/4*

Fig. 2. Frequency, amplitude, and phase of a sine wave $A \sin(2\pi f t + \theta)$.

the current time, which allows us to obtain the value of the wave at any time using this formula. The period, T, of the wave is obtained as T = 1/f.

Figure 2 illustrates the frequency, amplitude, and phase of a sine wave. Amplitude is the height of the wave, measured from zero to the maximum value, either up or down. Note that the sine wave is cyclic, i.e., it keeps repeating the pattern. One complete pattern is called a *cycle*.

Frequency is measured in cycles/sec or Hertz or simply Hz. For example, if a wave completes 1 cycle per sec, like the wave shown in Fig. 2(a), then it has a frequency of 1 Hz. On the other hand, the wave in Fig. 2(c) has a frequency of 2 Hz.

Phase is the amount of shift from a given reference point. For example, if we consider zero amplitude as our reference point, then the waves that start at zero while gaining their amplitudes, like most of the cases in Fig. 2, then their phase is zero. The maximum phase shift is 360°, i.e., if the wave is shifted by 360°, then its phase is back to zero again. For example, in Fig. 2(d), the phase is shifted by 45°. Usually, the phase is measured in *radians*, where 360° = 2π radian. Therefore, a 45° phase in radian would be π/4.

1.1 2D Representation of Phase and Amplitude

The phase can be represented on a 2D graph. A sine wave can be decomposed into its *sine* and *cosine* parts. For example, a sine wave with a phase of 45°, can be written as the summation of two parts:

$$\sin(2\pi ft + \frac{\pi}{4}) = \sin(2\pi ft)\cos(\frac{\pi}{4}) + \cos(2\pi ft)\sin(\frac{\pi}{4})$$

$$= \frac{1}{\sqrt{2}}\sin(2\pi ft) + \frac{1}{\sqrt{2}}\cos(2\pi ft)$$

(1)

The first part is called the *In-phase component I*, and the second part, the *Quadrature component Q*. In this case, we have $I = \frac{1}{\sqrt{2}}$ and $Q = \frac{1}{\sqrt{2}}$. I and Q are then plotted in a 2D graph as shown in Fig. 3. In this figure, the *x*-axis

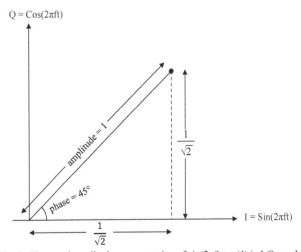

Fig. 3. Phase and amplitude representation of sin(2πft + π/4) in I-Q graph.

is sine and the *y*-axis cosine. With $I = \dfrac{1}{\sqrt{2}}$ and $Q = \dfrac{1}{\sqrt{2}}$, we get a single point in the graph, which has a length (amplitude) of 1 $(= \sqrt{I^2 + Q^2})$, and an angle (phase) of 45°.

1.2 Wavelength

Waves propagate through space and cover distances over time. The distance occupied by one cycle is called the *wavelength* of the wave and is represented by λ. This is the distance between two points of corresponding phase in two consecutive cycles, as shown in Fig. 4.

In the air or space, all electromagnetic waves, irrespective of their frequencies, travel at the speed of light, which is a universal constant of 300 *m/μs*. Given that it takes T sec for the wave to complete a cycle (T is called the period of the wave) and that T = 1/f, we have

$$\lambda = cT = c/f \tag{2}$$

Now we see that the wavelength is inversely proportional to its frequency.

Equation (2) is a universal formula that can be used to derive the wavelength for any type of communication medium. For example, for acoustic communications, which use sound waves to transmit data, the parameter *c* in Equation (2) should represent the speed of sound, which is only 343 m/s in dry air at 20° Celsius. Table 1 lists the wavelengths for some of the popular electromagnetic frequencies.

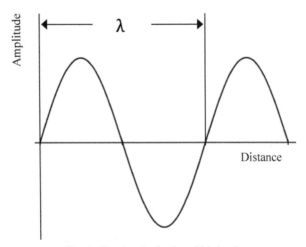

Fig. 4. Wavelength of a sinusoidal signal.

Table 1. Wavelengths of popular electromagnetic frequencies.

Wireless Technology	Frequency	Wavelength
IoT	915 MHz	32.7 cm
Bluetooth/WiFi	2.4 GHz	12.5 cm
Advanced WiFi	700 MHz	42.8 cm
	5 GHz	6 cm
	60 GHz	5 mm
Celluar (3G/4G/5G)	1.7 GHz	17.6 cm
	2.1 GHz	14.2 cm
mmWave and Terahertz for 5G and beyond	28 GHz	1 cm
	73 GHz	4 mm
	140 GHz	2.1 mm
	1 THz	0.3 mm
	10 THz	0.03 mm

Example 1

What is the wavelength of a 2.5 GHz electromagnetic signal propagating through air?

Solution

$$\text{Wavelength} = \lambda = \frac{c}{f}$$

$$= \frac{300 \, m/\mu s}{2.5 \times 10^9}$$

$$= 120 \times 10^{-3} = 120 \, mm = 12 \, cm$$

Example 2

What is the frequency of a signal with 5 mm wavelength?

Solution

Wavelength $= \lambda = 5$ mm

Frequency $= f = c/\lambda$

$= (3 \times 10^8 \text{ m/s})/(5 \times 10^{-3} \text{ m})$

$= (300 \times 10^9)/5 = 60$ GHz

---

2. Time and Frequency Domains

So far, we have seen how to represent waves in time domain. It turns out that every wave can be represented in both time and frequency domains. Given the time domain representation, we can convert it into its frequency domain representation, and vice versa.

Using three different sine waves, Fig. 5 illustrates the conversion from time domain representation (*left hand side*) to frequency domain (*right hand side*). The top sine wave has a frequency 1 (f) and amplitude 1 (A). In the frequency domain, it is therefore just a pulse at frequency $f = 1$ (*x*-axis) having a height A = 1 (*y*-axis). The second sine wave has three times the frequency as the original one, but one-third its amplitude. Therefore, in the frequency domain, its pulse is located at 3 and has a height of 0.5.

The third sine wave is actually a combination of the first and the second waves. One can actually just add the wave values at each time instant to derive the third one. In the frequency domain, it therefore has pulses at two frequencies. The pulse at frequency 1 has a height of 1 and the pulse at 3 has 0.5.

The transformation of a wave from time domain to frequency domain is called *Fourier transform* and from frequency domain to time domain is

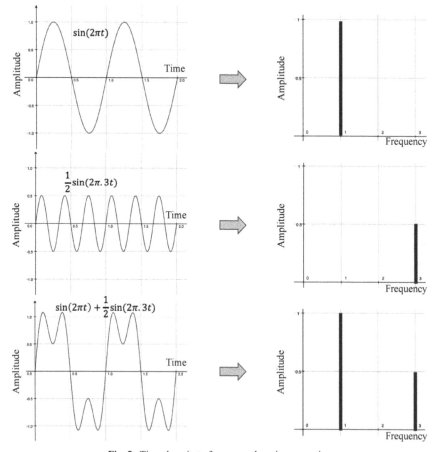

Fig. 5. Time domain to frequency domain conversion.

called *inverse Fourier transform*. There are fast algorithms to do this, such as Fast Fourier Transform (FFT) and Inverse FFT (IFFT). Most mathematical packages, such as MATLAB, has library functions for FFT and IFFT. In recent years, general purpose programming languages, such as Python, are also offering library functions for FFT and IFFT.

3. Electromagnetic Spectrum

Wireless communications use the airwaves, which are basically electromagnetic waves that can propagate through the air or even in a vacuum. Any electricity or current flow will generate these electromagnetic waves. Therefore, many things we use generate or utilize some forms of electromagnetic waves. TV, power supply, remote control, microwave oven, wireless router, etc., all use or generate electromagnetic waves of different frequencies. Even light is basically electromagnetic waves as we use electricity to generate light.

Electromagnetic waves can have a frequency of just 10 Hz, or 300 THz! The *spectrum* is all of the 'usable' frequency ranges. It is a natural resource and like most natural resources, it is limited. Spectrum use is therefore highly regulated by government authorities, such as the FCC in the US or ACMA in Australia.

A large portion of the spectrum is reserved for various government use, such as radar, military communications, atmospheric research, and so on. The rest of the spectrum is often licensed to competing network operators, which give the operators exclusive rights to specific parts of the spectrum. For example, different TV channels or radio stations license different frequencies. Interestingly, part of the spectrum is also allocated for use without having to license it. Such spectrum is called license-exempt and sometimes referred to as 'free' spectrum. The spectrum used by Wi-Fi, such as the 2.4 GHz band, is a good example of such license-exempt spectrum. Table 2 lists some of the currently available license-exempt bands.

It is important to note that although manufacturers of any product can use license-exempt frequencies for free, they are subject to certain rules, such as power limitation for transmitting the frequencies. For example, the maximum transmit power of Wi-Fi products is often limited to about 100 mW, depending on the region of operation.

Table 2. Examples of license-exempt spectrum and their use.

License-exempt Spectrum	Example Use
433 MHz	Keyless Entry
900 MHz	Amateur Radio, IoT (e.g., LoRaWAN)
2.4 GHz	WiFi, Microwave Oven
5.2/5.3/5.8 GHz	WiFi, Cordless Phone

Given the diverse needs of spectrum, spectrum-allocation authorities must follow a set of principles when allocating spectrum. These principles include maximizing the spectrum utilization, adapting to market needs by promoting new technologies that may require some specific spectrum, promoting market competition by strategically making certain spectrum license-exempt, ensuring fairness in licensing spectrum among competing operators, as well as allocating spectrum to satisfy core national interests, such as public safety, health, defense, scientific experiments and so on.

Certain services use specific *bands of frequencies*. For example, the basic Wi-Fi services use a frequency band of 2.4 GHz, which contains frequency in the range of 2.4 GHz to 2.5 GHz. Figure 6 shows the spectrum uses for different services. As we can see, historically wireless communications mostly use the spectrum between 100 kHz to 6 GHz. To meet the exponential demand for mobile data, the industry is now exploring spectrum beyond 6 GHz. For example, 60 GHz is now used in some Wi-Fi standards and the fifth-generation (5G) mobile networks are targeting spectrum beyond 60 GHz.

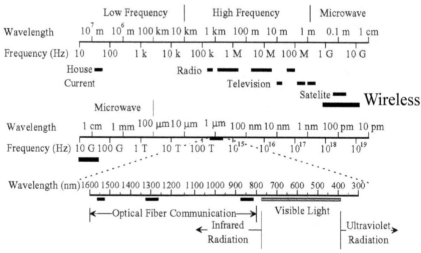

Fig. 6. Spectrum allocation for different services. Wireless communication mostly uses 100 kHz to 6 GHz.

4. Decibels

When waves travel, they lose power. We say that the power is *attenuated*. The question that arises is what would be a practical unit to measure power attenuation that is universal in all wireless communication systems?

Power loss for electromagnetic waves can be many orders of magnitude. For example, Wi-Fi chipsets can decode signals as weak as pico Watts, which allows them to offer reasonable communication coverage and range around the house or office building. Now imagine a signal that was transmitted by the Wi-Fi access point at full power of 100 mW but was received at a distant laptop with only 1 pW of power. The loss is one trillion-folds!

Because the power loss can be many orders of magnitude, the attenuation is measured in logarithmic units. After the inventor Graham Bell, power attenuation was originally measured as *Bel*, where $Bel = \log_{10}(P_{in}/P_{out})$ with P_{in} representing the transmitted powered and P_{out} the attenuated power.

Bel was found to be too large for most practical systems. Later, a new quantity called *decibel*, written as dB, was introduced to measure power loss, where

$$dB = 10\log_{10}(P_{in}/P_{out})$$

Example 3

What is the attenuation in dB if the power is reduced by half (50% loss)?

Solution

Attenuation in dB $= 10\log_{10}(2) = 3$ dB

Example 4

Compute the loss in dB if the received power of a 100 mW transmitted signal is only 1 mW

Solution

Power is reduced by a factor of 100. Attenuation $= 10\log_{10}(100) = 20$ dB

The concept of decibel is also used to measure the *absolute* signal power, i.e., decibel can be used to measure the strength of a transmitted or received signal. In that case, it is a measure of power *in reference to* 1 mW and the unit is dBm. In other words, dBm is obtained as:

dBm $= 10\log_{10}$(power in milliwatt)

Example 5

Convert 1 Watt to dBm.

Solution

We have $10\log_{10}(1 \text{ W}/1 \text{ mW}) = 10\log_{10}(1000 \text{ mW}/1 \text{ mW}) = 30$ dBm

---

Example 6

Express 1 mW in units of dBm

Solution

$10\log_{10}(1) = 10 \times 0 = 0$ dBm (ZERO dBm does not mean there is no power!)

Now we have a way to convert various electrical measurements, which are measured in Watts, into 'networking measurements', which are in dB and dBm. Another important networking measurement is *noise*, which is often produced at the receiver due to the movement of electrons in the electronic circuits. The presence of such noise can make it difficult to decode data from the received signal if the signal-to-noise (SNR) is too low. Because decibel (dB) is basically a method to measure a ratio, it is also used to measure the SNR in wireless communications.

Example 7

With 100 μW of noise, what would be the SNR in dB if the received signal strength is 1 mW?

Solution

P_{signal} = 1 mW (received signal strength), P_{noise} = 100 μW
$SNR = 10\log_{10}(1000/100) = 10\log_{10}(10) = 10$ dB

Example 8

Received signal strength is measured at 10 mW. What is the noise power if SNR = 10 dB?

Solution

$SNR = 10dB = 10\log_{10}(10\ mW/P_{noise})$
$P_{noise} = 1\ mW$

Now we can see that decibel is a versatile method to measure three different wireless communication phenomena: path loss, signal strength, and SNR. We have also seen that transmission or received power is measured in dBm, while path loss or antenna gain is measured in dB. It should be noted that dB can be added to or subtracted from dBm, which would produce dBm again. For example, for a transmission power of 20 dBm and a path loss of 25 dB, the received power can be calculated as 20 dBm–25 dB = –5 dBm. Similarly, if there was a 5 dBi antenna gain for the previous example, the received power would be calculated as 20 dBm + 5 dBi–25 dB = 0 dBm.

It *does not,* however, make any sense to add dBm with dBm. For example, given P1 = 20 dBm and P2 = 20 dBm, it would be incorrect to say that P1 + P2 = 20 dBm + 20 dBm = 40 dBm. The correct way to add powers would be to add them in linear scale and then convert the final value back to dBm. For the previous example, we have P1 = 100 mW and P2 = 100 mW, so P1 + P2 = 100 mW + 100 mW = 200 mW, which is only 23 dBm!

5. Coding Terminology

The following terminology is often used to explain the coding of digital data on the carrier signal:

Symbol is the smallest element of a signal with a given amplitude, frequency, and phase that can be detected. Shorter symbol duration means that more signal elements carrying bits can be transmitted per second, and vice versa.

Baud rate refers to the number of symbols that can be transmitted per second. It is the inverse of symbol duration and hence, sometimes referred to as the symbol rate. It is also called the modulation rate because this is how fast the property of the signal, i.e., its amplitude, frequency, or phase, can be changed or modulated.

Data rate, measured in bits per second, is the number of bits that can be transmitted per second. For example, for a binary signal, only 1 bit is transmitted for a given signal status, i.e., only 1 bit is carried over a baud and hence baud rate and data rate are equivalent. However, an M-ary signal has M distinct symbols and hence can carry $\log_2 M$ bits per baud or symbol. As we will see shortly, most modern wireless modulation techniques transmit multiple bits per symbol.

6. Modulation

Carrier waves are usually represented as sine waves. Data can be sent over a sine carrier by modulating one or more properties of the wave. As we have learned earlier in this chapter, there are three main properties of a wave—*amplitude*, *frequency*, and *phase*, that we can modulate.

Figure 7 shows how 0's and 1's can be transmitted over a sine carrier by modulating one of these three properties. When amplitude is modulated, it is called Amplitude Shift Keying (ASK). Similarly, we have Frequency Shift Keying (FSK) and Phase Shift Keying (PSK). In such modulations, the value of amplitude, frequency, and phase remains constant during a fixed period, called *bit (or symbol) interval*. The receiver observes the signal value during this bit interval to demodulate the signal, i.e., extract the bit or bits transmitted during that interval. Note that the bit interval is essentially the inverse of the baud rate.

In Fig. 7, we used only *two* different values of the amplitude, frequency, or phase to represent 0's and 1's. Therefore, we can send only 1 bit per different value of the signal, i.e., 1 bit per baud. In practical communication systems, usually more than 1 bit is transmitted per baud. For example, if we can modulate the amplitude in a way so that we have four different values of the amplitude, then we need 2 bits to represent each amplitude, enabling us to transmit two bits per baud.

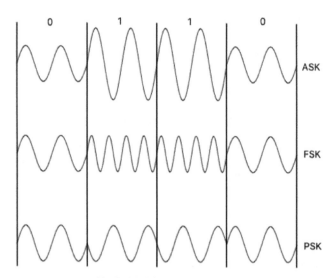

Fig. 7. Modulation of a sine wave.

For PSK, the phase values can be *absolute*, or the *difference in phase* with respect to the previous phase. In Fig. 8, the top graph shows that when there is no change in phase from the previous bit-interval to the next, it is treated as a 0 and when there is a change, it is a 1. This is called *differential* BPSK. With differential, the receiver does not have to compare the phase against some pre-established value, but rather observe the change only, which is easier to implement.

The top graph in Fig. 8 also shows that the phase is shifted by 180° and there is only one value to change. The corresponding 2D (I-Q) graph shows that the two dots are 180° apart. The bottom graph shows that the phase can switch to any of the four different values, which is called Quadrature Phase

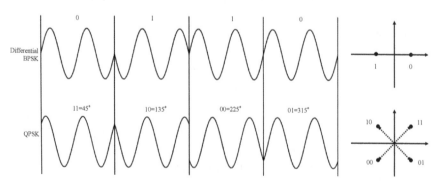

Fig. 8. Differential BPSK and QPSK.

Shift Keying (QPSK). In QPSK, 2 bits can be sent per baud. Here in the I-Q graph, there are four dots and they are separated by 90 degrees.

7. QAM

To push the data rate even higher, we can combine amplitude and phase modulations together, and it is called Quadrature Amplitude and Phase Modulation (QAM).

Note that in QPSK, the amplitude was kept constant. However, we could vary amplitude and get more than 2 bits per baud. A *constellation diagram* is often used to visually represent a QAM. Using constellation diagrams, Fig. 9 shows three examples of amplitude and phase combinations to achieve different levels of QAMs. In the left most graph, we have constant amplitude, but 2 different phases. In total we have $1 \times 2 = 2$ combinations, so we get 1 bit per baud or 1 bit per symbol.

In the middle graph, we have four different phases, but just 1 amplitude. This is actually QPSK, but we could call it 4-QAM. It has a total of $1 \times 4 = 4$ combinations, so we have 2 bits per symbol. In the third graph (16-QAM), we have 3 different amplitudes; there are 4 different phases for each of the smallest and the largest amplitudes while the medium amplitude has 8 different phases. Thus, from 3 different amplitudes and 12 different phases, we use a total of $4 + 4 + 8 = 16$ combinations of amplitudes and phases, which allow us to transmit 4 bits per symbol.

It is clear that we can increase the bit rates by going for higher QAMs. Table 3 lists the use of different QAMs in practical wireless networks, showing that latest wireless standards employ as high as 1024 QAMs. As hardware and signal processing technology improves, we can expect even higher QAMs in the future.

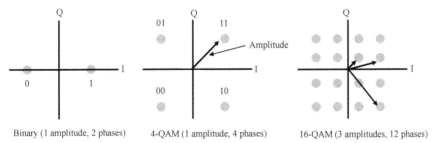

Binary (1 amplitude, 2 phases)   4-QAM (1 amplitude, 4 phases)   16-QAM (3 amplitudes, 12 phases)

Fig. 9. Constellation diagrams illustrating 2, 4, and 16 QAMs.

Table 3. QAMs used in practical wireless technologies.

Wireless Technology	Supported QAM Technique
4G	256-QAM
5G	1024-QAM
WiFi 802.11n	16-QAM, 64-QAM
WiFi 802.11ac	256-QAM
WiFi 802.11ax	1024-QAM

8. Channel Capacity

The capacity of a channel basically refers to the maximum data rate or the number of bits that can be reliably transmitted over the channel. There are two basic theorems that explain the capacity, one by Nyquist and the other by Shannon. Both provide formulae to calculate channel capacity in terms of bits per second, but in slightly different contexts.

8.1 Nyquist's Theorem

Nyquist defines channel capacity under *noiseless* environment. In the absence of noise, receiving hardware can easily differentiate between a large number of different values of the symbol. As such, channel capacity according to Nyquist theorem is mainly constrained by the channel bandwidth, which defines the number of Hertz available in the channel. The higher the bandwidth, the more data rate can be achieved. Nyquist capacity is also dependent on the number of signal levels, i.e., the number of distinct symbols used in encoding. More precisely, Nyquist capacity is obtained as:

Nyquist data rate = 2 × B × $\log_2 M$ bps

where B is the channel bandwidth (in Hz) and M is the number of signal levels.

Example 9
Assume that you have discovered a novel material that has negligible electrical noise. What is the maximum data rate that this material could achieve over a phone wire having a bandwidth of 3100 Hz if data was encoded with 64-QAM?

Solution
We have
B = 3100
M = 64
Data rate = 2 × 3100 × $\log_2 64$ = 37,200 bps

8.2 Shannon's Theorem

Nyquist's theorem is valid for perfect noiseless channel. With perfect channel, we can get an infinite number of bits per Hz by coding data with an infinite number of signal levels. However, in reality, channels are noisy, which makes it difficult for the receiver to confirm exactly what signal value was transmitted. The noise, therefore, puts an upper limit on the number of bits we can transmit reliably. This *upper limit* is called Shannon's capacity and is obtained as:

Shannon's capacity = $B \log_2(1 + S/N)$ bps

where B is the bandwidth of the channel, S is the received signal strength in Watt and N is the noise power in Watt.

Example 10
For an SNR of 30 dB, what is the maximum data rate that could be achieved over a phone wire having a bandwidth of 3100 Hz?

Solution
$10 \log_{10} S/N = 30$
$\log_{10} S/N = 3$
$S/N = 10^3 = 1000$
Shannon's Capacity = $3100 \log_2(1 + 1000) = 30,894$ bps

---

9. Hamming Distance and Error Correction

When data is transmitted over a noisy channel, there is the possibility of receiving the data in error. Using appropriate algorithms, such errors can be detected and even corrected. Hamming distance is a fundamental concept used by these error detecting and correcting algorithms. It is defined as the number of bits in which two equal-length sequences disagree. This can be easily obtained by applying the XOR operator between the two sequences.

Example 11
What is the Hamming distance between 011011 and 110001?

Solution

Sequence 1:	011011
Sequence 2:	110001

Difference (XOR)   101010 → Hamming distance = 3 (i.e., number of 1's in XOR output)

Data is usually *coded* and the codeword, which is longer than the data, is sent for error detection and correction purposes. Let us have a look at some examples.

Table 4 shows the codewords for the data bits where 2-bit words are transmitted as 5-bit words. Now let us assume that the receiver has received 00100, which is not one of the valid codewords. This means there was an error in the transmission.

Now let us look at the hamming distance between the received sequence and each of the valid codewords.

Distance (00100,00000) = 1   Distance (00100,00111) = 2
Distance (00100,11001) = 4   Distance (00100,11110) = 3

It is clear that most likely 00000 was sent, because it has the smallest hamming distance. Hence, the received sequence is corrected to data 00.

Now let us assume that the received sequence was 01010. We have, Distance (01010,00000) = 2 = Distance (01010,11110). There are two codewords at equal distance from the received sequence. In this case, error is detected but cannot be corrected.

Three-bit errors will not even be detected. For example, a 3-bit error could convert the transmitted codeword 00000 to 00111, which is also a valid codeword!

The lesson is, if we want to detect x-bit errors, any two codewords should be apart by a Hamming distance of at least $x + 1$. Similarly, to correct x-bit errors, the minimum Hamming distance required is $2x + 1$. These rules provide valuable guidelines for designing codewords.

Table 4. Coding example for error correction.

Data	Codeword
00	00000
01	00111
10	11001
11	11110

10. Multiple Access Methods

When the communication resources, such as a given frequency band, has to be shared by many devices, there have to be some rules to be followed, so all can enjoy interference-free communication. These rules constitute *medium access control*.

There are three fundamentally different medium access methods. They are based on *time*, *frequency*, or *code*. As such, they are called time division multiple access (TDMA), frequency division multiple access (FDMA), or code division multiple access (CDMA). Using an analogy of communicating groups of people, Fig. 10 illustrates how these three multiple access methods differ from each other. At the top, we can see that the groups take turn, so they do not collide with each other. This is TDMA because time is used to separate them. In the middle, the groups are located at different rooms, i.e., using different frequencies, so they do not collide with each other despite talking at the same time. Interestingly, at the bottom of the figure, all groups are

(a) TDMA: Communicating groups are taking turns

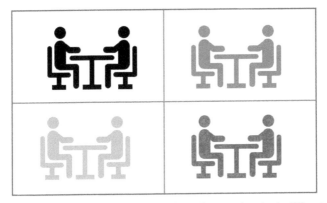

(b) FDMA: Communicating groups are all talking at the same time, but in different rooms

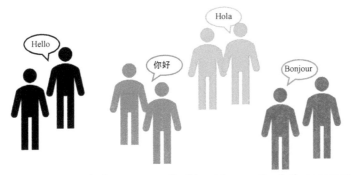

(c) CDMA: Communicating groups are all talking at the same time in the same room

Fig. 10. Multiple access methods.

talking at the same time in the same room, yet they do not really interfere with each other! This is possible because different groups are talking in different languages where people can still pick up their conversations because other languages simply appear as noise to them. Language is the *code* here to avoid interference.

11. Spread Spectrum

Spread spectrum refers to techniques that spread an original narrow bandwidth signal over a much wider bandwidth. There are many purposes for spread spectrum, including improving security by making the signal harder to detect with a narrowband receiver, increasing resistance to interference, noise, and jamming, and to achieve CDMA. *Frequency hopping* and *direct sequence* are two popular spread spectrum techniques used in many communications systems.

11.1 Frequency Hopping Spread Spectrum

In frequency hopping spread spectrum (FHSS), both the transmitter and the receiver use a specific random sequence to switch frequency within the band at every small interval as shown in Fig. 11. Because the transmitter and the receiver use the same seed and random number generator, they have the exact same sequence, so they can change the frequency at the right time to the right frequency and hence decode each other without any problem.

Because FHSS never stays on the same frequency for long, it is hard to jam the transmission using a particular frequency. For the same reason, it is also difficult to eavesdrop, using a narrowband receiver that monitors a particular frequency. It can also be used for CDMA because the random seed for switching frequency becomes a code and those who do not have the code cannot decode the communication.

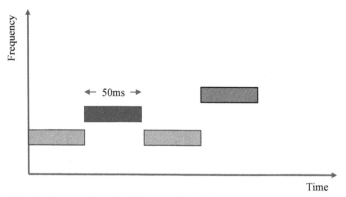

Fig. 11. Frequency hopping. The transmitter switches frequency every 50 ms.

The most common and widespread use of FHSS is in Bluetooth, which switches frequency 1600 times per second or stays only 625 micro second over one particular frequency to avoid interference with nearby Wi-Fi devices that also use the same frequency band. FHSS is also used in military communications due to its anti-jamming and security features. Previous generations of cellular systems used FHSS to share the same frequency over many users at the same time.

Interestingly, FHSS was patented by an actress, Hedy Lamarr, who conceived the idea when she was playing on piano, where the tone is changed all the time. The patent, however, was not widely known until it was used in wireless communications.

11.2 Direct-Sequence Spread Spectrum

Another way to achieve spread spectrum is to use a technique called Direct-Sequence Spread Spectrum (DSSS). The idea, as shown in Fig. 12, is to expand a '0' or '1' by long series of 0's and 1's by applying a secret code to them. Then the resulting codeword is transmitted in place of a '0' or '1' in the data bit sequence.

The receiver knows the secret code used by the transmitter; hence it can retrieve the data bits from the codewords transmitted. In the example of Fig. 12, a 10-bit code is used to create the codewords by applying the operation XOR to the data bits. In this case, 10 bits are actually transmitted over the channel to transmit a single data bit.

Spreading factor is defined as number of code bits per 0 or 1. FCC mandates that the minimum should be 10, but for better privacy, much larger, such as hundreds are used. Military may choose to use thousands. The signal bandwidth therefore has to be orders of magnitude higher than the data bandwidth.

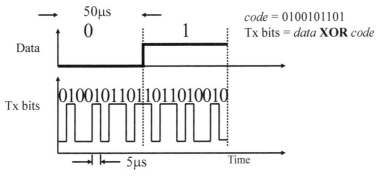

Fig. 12. Direct-sequence spread spectrum.

12. Doppler Shift

The Doppler effect says that if the transmitter or receiver or both are mobile, the frequency of the received signal changes or shifts. This principle is named after Christian Andreas Doppler, an Austrian mathematician and physicist who first proposed the principle in 1842. If the transmitter is moving towards the receiver, then the receiver will receive higher frequency, i.e., the frequency is shifted to a higher value than originally transmitted. If the transmitter is moving away, the effect is opposite. This effect is illustrated in Fig. 13, where a car is approaching a pedestrian, who is hearing higher frequency than what was generated by the car.

The next question is: how much does the received frequency increase or decrease compared to the transmitted frequency? It turns out that this shift in frequency is a function of the relative velocity, v, between the transmitter and the receiver as well as the transmitter frequency or wavelength, which is obtained as follows:

Doppler shift = velocity/Wavelength = v/λ = vf/c **Hz**

Example 12
Assume that a car travelling at 120 km/hr is transmitting a packet to a roadside access point (AP) using 2.4 GHz Wi-Fi. If the car is approaching the AP (i.e., the AP is directly in front it), what is the frequency received by the AP?

Solution
The wavelength of the frequency is: $3 \times 10^8/2.4 \times 10^9 = 0.125$ m
The velocity of the car is: 120 km/hr = $120 \times 1000/3600 = 33.3$ m/s
Freq diff (Doppler shift) = $33.3/0.125 = 267$ Hz
Therefore, the receive frequency at the AP is 2.4 GHz + 267 Hz = 2.400000267 GHz

---

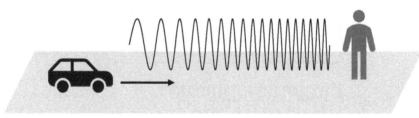

Fig. 13. Effect of Doppler shift.

13. Doppler Spread

Besides receiving the signal from the original source, such as a base station, a mobile object also receives signals reflected from other objects. Thus, a mobile

Fig. 14. Illustration of Doppler spread experienced by a motorist.

object experiences Doppler shifts in both positive and negative directions, as illustrated in Fig. 14 in case of a moving vehicle. Thus, the received frequency is spread equally on both sides of the original frequency. Hence the Doppler spread is obtained as:

Doppler Spread = 2 × Doppler shift = 2vf/c = 2v/λ

14. Coherence Time

Coherence time refers to the time interval during which the channel does not change. This interval is important in optimizing many communication parameters. For example, during packet transmissions, usually there are some preamble signals used to probe the channel. Channel statistics gathered from this probe are then used to optimize the transmission parameters for the rest of the bits in the packet. Obviously, in this case, the packet size has to be optimized so that it can complete within the channel coherence time, otherwise part of the packet will experience a different channel. Conversely, for long packets, multiple probes must be inserted within the packet to obtain the most up-to-date channel information.

Doppler spread is a frequency domain measure that influences the coherence time in a reciprocal relationship as follows:

Coherence time = 1/Doppler spread = λ/2v

Therefore, higher the Doppler spread, shorter the coherence time, and vice versa. For example, doubling the frequency of transmission would halve the channel coherence time.

Example 13
What is the coherence time for a 2.4 GHz Wi-Fi link connecting a car travelling at 72 km/hr?

Solution
V = (72 × 1000)/3600 = 20 m/s
Doppler spread = $2vf/c$ = (2×20×2.4×10⁹)/(3×10⁸) = 320 Hz
Coherence time = 1/320 = 0.003125 s = 3.125 ms

---

15. Duplexing

Duplexing attempts to answer the following question: how the resource should be allocated between the transmitter and the receiver so that they both can exchange information with each other, i.e., both can transmit and receive? Figure 15 shows that there are two ways to achieve this: one way is to allocate different frequencies for different directions. In this case both can talk at the same time, achieving full-duplex communications. This is called frequency division duplexing (FDD). The other method is to use the same frequency for both directions, but only one entity can talk at a given time. For example, when the base station talks, the subscriber listens and when the subscriber talks, the base station listens. This method is called time division duplexing (TDD). Clearly, TDD cannot achieve full-duplex, but provides only a half-duplex communication. Despite this, many cellular deployments use TDD because it allows more flexible sharing of downlink (base station to subscriber) and uplink (subscriber to base station) resources without requiring paired spectrum allocation, which is wasteful if data is asymmetric in these two directions.

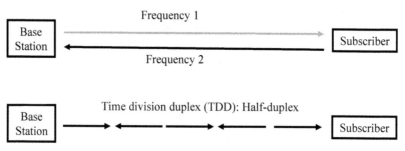

Fig. 15. Frequency division vs time division duplexing.

16. Summary

1. Electric, Radio, Light, X-Rays, are all electromagnetic waves.
2. Wavelength and frequency are inversely proportional ($\lambda = c/f$).
3. Historically, wireless communications mostly used frequencies below 6 GHz, but beyond 6 GHz is actively explored in modern wireless networks.
4. Hertz and bit rate are related by Nyquist and Shannon's Theorems.
5. Nyquist's theorem explains capacity for noiseless channels.
6. Shannon's capacity takes SNR into consideration.
7. Power is measured in dBm and path loss or antenna gain in dB.
8. dB can be added or subtracted to dBm to produce dBm, but dBm cannot be added or subtracted with dBm.

9. By spreading the original signal bandwidth over a much wider band, spread spectrum can provide better immunity against interference and jamming as well allowing multiple parties to communicate over the same frequency at the same time.

10. FHSS and DSSS are two fundamental methods of realizing spread spectrum.

11. Doppler effect explains the shift in frequency experienced by mobile objects.

12. Doppler spread is twice the Doppler shift.

13. Channel coherence time is inversely proportional to Doppler spread.

14. FDD and TDD are two fundamental methods of resource allocation between the transmitter and the receiver so that they both can exchange information with each other.

Multiple Choice, True/False, and Fill-in-Blanks Questions

Q1. The higher the frequency, the more ___ we have.
   A. pass loss   B. noise   C. received power   D. security

Q2. 10 W is equivalent to ___ dBm.
   A. 10   B. 20   C. 30   D. 40

Q3. −50 dB refers to a ratio of 0.00001.
   A. True   B. False

Q4. It is impossible to send 3000 bits/second through a wire which has a bandwidth of 1000 Hz.
   A. True   B. False

Q5. A 200 Hz Doppler shift would cause a 400 Hz Doppler spread.
   A. True   B. False

Q6. For a Doppler shift of 50 Hz, we have a 10 ms coherence time.
   A. True   B. False

Q7. The received signal power is always lower than the transmitted power because of noise.
   A. True   B. False

Q8. TDD requires paired spectrum for uplink and downlink.
   A. True   B. False

Q9. FDD allows more flexible sharing of DL/UL data rate.
   A. True   B. False

Q10. Frequency Hopping and Direct Sequence are two methods of spread spectrum as well as CDMA.
   A. True   B. False

Q11. 64-QAM has 16 bits per symbol.
  A. True   B. False

Q12. QAM combines frequency and phase modulations.
  A. True   B. False

Q13. QPSK combines amplitude and phase modulations.
  A. True   B. False

Q14. You have designed a QAM which has 4 different phases and 2 different amplitudes. How many bits can we transmit per symbol if all phase-amplitude combinations are used?
  A. 2   B. 3   C. 4   D. 5

Review Exercises

Q1. What is the wavelength of a signal operating at the frequency of:
  A. 2.4 GHz   B. 5.2 GHz   C. 1.5 GHz   D. 1.8 GHz   E. 300 GHz

Q2. What is the frequency of a signal having a wavelength of:
  A. 1 meter   B. 50 cm

Q3. Represent the following powers in dBm:
  A. 100 kW   B. 500 mW   C. 2.5 mW   D. 1 mW   E. 100 pW

Q4. Represent the following powers in dBW:
  A. 1 kW   B. 100 mW   C. 1 μW   D. 1 nW   E. 1 pW

Q5. How many Watts of power is:
  A. 30 dBm   B. 10 dBm   C. 30 dBW

Q6. Received signal strength is measured at 10 mW. What is the noise power in dBm, if SNR = 10 dB?

Q7. A telephone line is known to have a loss of 20 dB. The input signal power is measured at 1 Watt, and the output signal noise level is measured at 1 mW. Using this information, calculate the output signal to noise ratio (SNR) in dB.

Q8. What is the maximum data rate that can be supported on a 10 MHz noise-less channel if the channel uses eight-level digital signals?

Q9. Do some search on the Internet and give five examples of license-exempt spectrum.

Q10. Assume that you can measure power only in Volts. What would be the value of parameter a in the following formula? $dB = a \log_{10}(V_{in}/V_{out})$ [*Note*: The original dB formula is used when power is measured in Watts. Think about the relationship between Watt and Volt.]

3
Wireless Signal Propagation

In the previous chapter, we learned how the bits are transmitted to the wireless channel. In this chapter we will discuss how these bits travel or propagate through the wireless channel before reaching to the receiver.

1. Wireless Radio Channel

Wireless radio channel is different than a wired channel. The radio channel is 'open' in the sense that it does not have anything to protect or guide the signal as it travels from source to destination. As a result, the signal is subject to many issues, which we must be aware of to understand how the receiver will receive the signal. These issues will be discussed in this chapter.

2. Antenna

Transmitter converts electrical energy to electromagnetic waves and the receiver converts these electromagnetic waves back to electrical energy. It is important to note that the same antenna is used for both transmission and reception. Therefore, a device can use the same antenna for both transmitting bits and receiving bits.

Depending on how the antennas radiate or receive power, there can be three types of antennas as illustrated in Fig. 1. An antenna is called *omni-directional* if the power from it radiates in (or it receives power from) all directions. A *directional* antenna, on the other hand, can focus most of its power in the desired direction. Finally, an *isotropic* antenna refers to a theoretical antenna that radiates or receives *uniformly* in each direction in space, without reflections and losses. Note that due to reflections and losses in practical environments, the omni-directional antenna does not radiate or receive in all directions *uniformly.*

An isotropic transmitting antenna cannot produce much power at the receiver because the power is dissipated to all directions and gets wasted.

| Omni-Directional | Directional | Isotropic |

Fig. 1. Different types of antennas.

Given that the receivers are likely to be contained in some space, for example, in a horizontal plane rather than in a sphere, antennas are designed to control the power in a way so that the receivers receive more power compared to a theoretical isotropic antenna. Antenna *gain* refers to the ratio of the power at a particular point to the power with isotropic antenna, which gives a measure of power for the antenna. Antenna gain is expressed in dBi, which means 'decibel relative to isotropic'. For example, if an antenna is advertised as 3 dBi, it means that it will produce twice as much power than an isotropic antenna. Note that an isotropic antenna will have a gain of 0 dBi.

Example 1

How much stronger a 17 dBi antenna receives (transmits) the signal compared to the isotropic antenna?

Solution

Let

Power of isotropic antenna = P_{iso}

Power of 17 dBi antenna = P

We have

$17 = 10\log_{10}(P/P_{iso})$

Thus $P/P_{iso} = 10^{1.7} = 50.12$, i.e., the 17 dBi antenna will receive (transmit) the signal 50.12 times stronger than the isotropic antenna albeit using the same transmit power.

Antennas are designed to transmit or receive a specific frequency band. For example, antennas used in wireless routers operating with 2.5/5 GHz are too small to receive TV signals operating with 700 MHz. Fundamentally, end-to-end antenna length must be half the wavelength so that electrons on the antenna can travel back and forth in one cycle. Small consumer devices, such as mobile phones, may hide their antennas within the device, but the fundamental relationship between antenna size and frequency exists, i.e., we would need larger antennas for lower frequencies, and vice versa.

3. Reflection, Diffraction, Scattering

When the transmitting antenna transmits a signal, the signal can reach the receiver antenna directly in a straight path if there is a line-of-sight (LoS) between the transmitter and the receiver. However, the signal also *bounces* from many other objects around us and the bounced signals reach the receiver by traveling different paths.

Figure 2 shows that there are three types of bouncing that can happen for the signal transmitted by a car antenna on the street. *Reflection* happens when the signal hits a large solid object, such as a wall. *Diffraction* happens when the signal bounces off a sharp edge, such as a corner of a block. Finally, a signal may hit very small objects, such as a thin light post or even dust particles in the air, which cause *scattering*. Note that reflection and diffraction are more directional, but scattering is more omni-directional. There are complex mathematical formulae to capture the effect of reflection, diffraction, and scattering on the received signal at the receiving antenna, but those are outside the scope of this book. Our main objective here is to be aware of the fact that the transmitted signal reaches the receiver in many different ways, which may cause certain issues when designing the communication protocols.

Now let us try to understand the effect of these signal-bouncing phenomena on wireless communication. Reflection happens when the surface is large, relative to the wavelength of the signal. When the reflected signal reaches the receiver, it may have a phase shift. Depending on the phase shift,

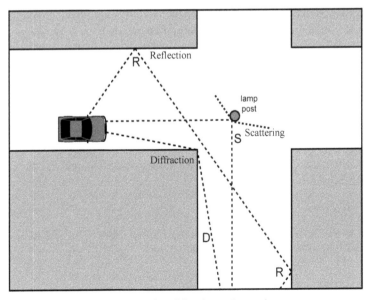

Fig. 2. Reflection, diffraction, and scattering.

the reflected signal may actually cancel out the original signal (destructive), or strengthen it (constructive).

Similarly, diffraction happens when the edge of an impenetrable body is large, relative to signal wavelength, but the phase shift is calculated differently than a reflection.

Finally, scattering happens when the size of the object is in the order of the wavelength. This means a light post can cause scattering for low frequency signals (large wavelength), but would cause reflection for very high frequency signals, such as 60 GHz. However, for 60 GHz, very tiny objects, such as snowflakes, hailstones, can cause scattering.

An interesting outcome of reflection, diffraction, and scattering is that the receiver can still receive the signal even if there is no LoS between the transmitter and the receiver. This is a great advantage for wireless communications. For example, it is not possible to have a LoS to the Wi-Fi access point or router located in the garage or in a central location from every room in the house. We, however, can still receive signals from the AP. It is because of this bouncing property of wireless signals. On the other hand, when we have LoS, we do not have to depend on signal bouncing, but the reflection, diffraction and scattering then actually cause some form of interference with the LoS signal.

4. Channel Model

Now that we have some appreciation of the signal propagation through the radio channel and how it can get affected by different physical phenomena, we need to find a way to predict or estimate the signal that may be received at a given location under certain transmissions. This is called *channel modeling*.

Figure 3 shows that there is a transmitter mounted on a tower to transmit signals to subscriber devices, which may be located anywhere around the tower. Power profile of the received signal at the subscriber station can be obtained by *convolving* the power profile of the transmitted signal with the impulse response of the channel. Note that *convolution* in time is *multiplication* in frequency.

Mathematically, after propagating through the channel H, transmitted signal x becomes y, i.e.,

$$y(f) = H(f).x(f) + n(f) \tag{1}$$

where $H(f)$ is *channel response*, and $n(f)$ is the noise. Note that x, y, H, and n are all functions of the signal frequency f.

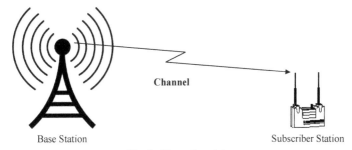

Fig. 3. Channel model.

5. Path Loss

When a signal travels through space, it loses power. This is called 'path loss' or signal attenuation. As a result of path loss, the power of a signal at the receiver (received power) is usually only a fraction of the original or input power used at the transmitter to generate the signal.

Path loss depends on the length of the path travelled by the signal. The larger the distance between the transmitter and receiver, the higher the path loss, and vice versa. Clearly, the path loss must be estimated and factored in properly when a wireless link is designed. Different path loss models are used for estimating path loss in different scenarios. Two popular path loss models are the Frii's model designed for free space with no reflections, and the 2-ray model that takes reflections from the ground into consideration. Frii's model is used as a guide for ideal scenarios whereas 2-ray is a more practical model used widely in wireless communications. We will examine 2-ray later in the chapter after discussing multipath reflections.

In free space without any absorbing or reflecting objects, the path loss depends on the distance as well as on the frequency (or wavelength) according to the following Frii's law:

$$P_R = P_T G_T G_R \left(\frac{\lambda}{4\pi d} \right)^2 = P_T G_T G_R \left(\frac{c}{4\pi f d} \right)^2 \tag{2}$$

where P_R and P_T are the received and transmitted powers (in Watts), respectively, while G_T and G_R are transmitter and receiver antenna gains in linear scale, respectively. We see that, for a given frequency, path loss increases as *inverse square of distance*, which is sometimes referred to as the d^{-2} law (path loss exponent = 2). It is also observed that path loss increases as inverse square of the frequency, which means that the signal power attenuates more rapidly for higher frequency signals, and vice versa.

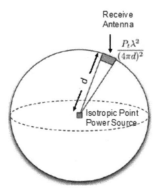

Fig. 4. Power spreading in space and received power calculation for Frii's law.

Equation (2) shows path loss in linear scale. For the convenience of calculating the link budget, however, path loss is actually measured in dB. By converting Equation (2) in dB, we obtain:

$$P_R^{dB} = P_T^{dB} + G_T^{dB} + G_R^{dB} + 10log_{10}\left(\frac{\lambda}{4\pi d}\right)^2 \qquad (3)$$

where P_R^{dB} and P_T^{dB} refer to receive and transmit powers, respectively, in dBm, while G_T^{dB} and G_R^{dB} are the antenna gains in dBi. Thus, the path loss is obtained as:

$$Path\ Loss = P_T^{dB} - P_R^{dB} = -G_T^{dB} - G_R^{dB} - 10log_{10}\left(\frac{\lambda}{4\pi d}\right)^2 \qquad (4)$$

For isotropic antennas (G_T^{dB} and G_R^{dB} are both 0 dB), path loss is reduced to the following simple formula:

$$\begin{aligned}
Path\ loss(dB) &= -10log_{10}\left(\frac{\lambda}{4\pi d}\right)^2 = 20log_{10}\left(\frac{4\pi d}{\lambda}\right) = 20log_{10}\left(\frac{4\pi fd}{c}\right) \\
&= 20log_{10}(d) + 20log_{10}(f) + 20log_{10}\left(\frac{4\pi}{c}\right) \\
&= 20log_{10}(d) + 20log_{10}(f) - 147.55
\end{aligned} \qquad (5)$$

where d is in meter, f in Hz, and $c = 3 \times 10^8$ m/s. Equation (5) implies that for free-space propagation, the received power decays with distance (transmitter-receiver separation) or frequency at a rate of 20 dB/decade, i.e., the signal loses 20 dB for every decade (tenfold) increase in distance or frequency.

A simple explanation for Frii's path loss formula in Equation (2) can be given, using a sphere around an isotropic point power source at the center radiating a power of P_T as shown in Fig. 4. Basically, the power from the source spreads in space in all directions equally. As such, the power density on the surface of the sphere decreases with increasing sphere radius, d. With $4\pi d^2$ being the area of the sphere, we have a power density of $P_T/4\pi d^2$. Therefore, the total power received at an antenna located at the sphere surface becomes equal to the power density times the antenna area. We have learned that antenna size is dependent on the frequency or the wavelength. Given that the ideal antenna has an area of $\lambda^2/4\pi$, the received power at the antenna is equal to $P_T\left(\dfrac{\lambda}{4\pi d}\right)^2$, which is given by the Frii's law in Equation (2) for isotropic antennas with unit gains.

Example 2
If 50 W power is applied to a 900 MHz frequency at a transmitter, find the receive power at a distance of 100 meter from the transmitter (assume free space path loss with unit antenna gains).

Solution
Unit antenna gain means: $G_T = G_R = 1$.
We have $d = 100$ m, $f = 900 \times 10^6$ Hz, $P_T = 50$ W, c $= 3 \times 10^8$ m/sec, and $\pi = 3.14$

$$P_R = P_T \left(\frac{c}{4\pi fd}\right)^2 = 3.5\,\mu W$$

Example 3
What is the received power in dBm at 10 meters from a 2.4 GHz Wi-Fi router transmitting with 100 mW of power (assume free space path loss with unit antenna gains)?

Solution
Unit antenna gain means: $G_T = G_R = 0$ dBm.
We have $d = 10$ m, $f = 2.4 \times 10^9$ Hz, $P_T = 100$ mW $= 20$ dBm, c $= 3 \times 10^8$ m/sec, and $\pi = 3.14$

$$Pathloss = 20 log_{10}\left(\frac{4\pi fd}{c}\right) dB = 60\,dB$$

$$P_R = P_T - pathloss = 20 - 60 = -40\ dBm$$

---

6. Receiver Sensitivity

If the path loss is too much, the SNR at the receiver could be too low for decoding the data. The noise at the receiver is a function of the channel bandwidth, i.e., larger the bandwidth, the higher the total noise power, and vice versa. The noise is also sensitive to the circuits and hardware of the receiver and the operating temperature, which is called the 'noise figure' of the receiver. Receiver sensitivity refers to the minimum received signal strength (RSS) required for that receiver to be able to decode information. Noise, bandwidth, and modulation affect the receiver sensitivity. For example, Bluetooth specifies that, at room temperature, devices must be able to achieve a minimum receiver sensitivity of –70 dBm to –82 dBm [BTBLOG].

Example 4
To increase the coverage with low transmit power, a manufacturer produced Bluetooth chipsets with a receiver sensitivity of –80 dBm. What is the maximum communication range that can be achieved for this chipset for a transmit power of 1 mW? Assume Free Space Path Loss with unit antenna gains.

Solution
Bluetooth frequency f = 2.4 GHz, P_T = 1 mW, P_R = –80 dBm = 10^{-8} mW
We have

$$P_R = P_T \left(\frac{c}{4\pi df} \right)^2$$

$$d = \frac{c}{4\pi f} \sqrt{P_T / P_R}$$

= 99.5 meter

---

7. Multipath Propagation

As wireless signals reflect from typical objects and surfaces around us, they can reach the receiver through multiple paths. Figure 5 illustrates the multipath phenomenon and explains its effect at the receiver. Here we have a cellular tower transmitting radio signals omni-directionally. A mobile phone antenna is receiving not just one copy of the signal (the LoS), but another copy of the same signal that is reflected from a nearby high-rise building (NLoS). We make two observations:

- The LoS signal reaches the receiver first followed by the NLoS copy. This is due to the longer path length of the NLoS signal compared to the LoS path.
- The signal strength for LoS is higher compared to that of NLoS. This is because the NLoS signal travels further distance and hence attenuates more compared to the LoS.

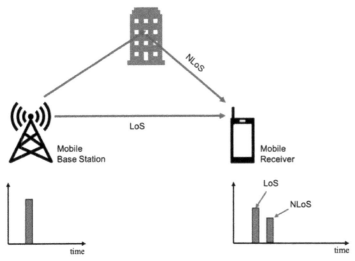

Fig. 5. Effect of multipath.

Figure 5 considers only a single NLoS path. In reality, there are many NLoS paths due to many reflecting surfaces. For multipath, there are also phase differences among the received signals copies due to the differences in their travelling time (different paths have different lengths). Such phase differences, however, are not shown in Fig. 5 as it illustrates the signals only as simple impulses.

8. Inter-symbol Interference

One problem with multipath is that the receiver continues to receive the signal well after the transmitter has finished transmitting the signal. This increases the time the receiver has to dedicate to decode one symbol or one bit, i.e., the symbol interval has to be longer than the ideal case when no NLoS paths exist. If we do not adjust the symbol interval adequately, then the signals from the previous symbol will enter into the next symbol interval and interfere with the new symbol. As a result, even if there were no other transmitters, the same transmitter would interfere with its *own* signal at the receiver. This phenomenon is called *inter-symbol interference*.

The process of inter-symbol interference is illustrated in Fig. 6 with two short pulses, dark and light at the transmitter, which become much wider at the receiver due to multipath. We can see that the dark symbol, which was transmitted before the light, is interfering with the light symbol. To reduce this interference at the receiver, the transmitter has to use much wider symbol intervals. As a result of having to widen the bit intervals at the receiver, we

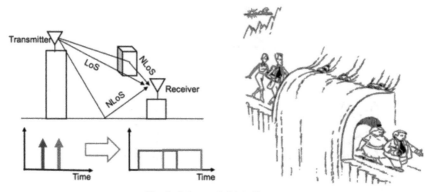

Fig. 6. Inter-symbol interference.

have to reduce the data rate or bits per second as the data rate is inverse of the symbol length.

9. Delay Spread

Now let us examine the effect of multipath more closely. Recall that when a single pulse is transmitted, multiple pulses arrive at the receiver. As a result, the transmitter cannot transmit two pulses quickly, one after the other. Otherwise the late arrivals will collide with the new transmission.

One good thing, however, is that the subsequent arrival of the signal copies are attenuated further and further. So we really do not have to wait too long, but just enough so that the next arrivals are below some threshold power.

The time between the first and the last versions of the signal above the power threshold is called the *delay spread*. The concept of delay spread is illustrated in Fig. 7. One thing to notice here is that the amplitude of the late

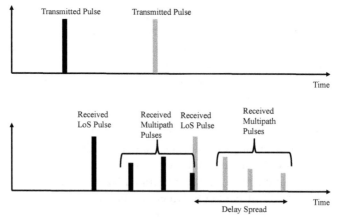

Fig. 7. Multipath propagation and delay spread.

arrivals can actually fluctuate, although they, on an average, consistently diminish with time.

10. 2-ray Propagation Model and d^{-4} Power Law

Earlier we learned that in the absence of any multipath (no reflector), Frii's formula can be used to estimate the received power at the receiver where the power decreases as square of distance, which is the d^{-2} law. Later, significant measurements were done in real environments, revealing that the attenuation follows a d^{-n} law where n is called the path loss exponent and varies from 1.5 to 5 [Munoz, 2009].

It was also found that the antenna heights significantly affect the received power when multipaths are present. Based on this observation, a new propagation law was derived, which is called the 2-ray model or d^{-4} Power Law, which is illustrated in Fig. 8. This model, which considers 1 LoS and 1 reflection from the ground, considers a transmitter at height h_t and a receiver at height h_r separated by distance d. The received power is then described as:

$$P_R = P_T G_T G_R \left(\frac{h_t h_r}{d^2} \right)^2 \tag{6}$$

And, the path loss in decibel,

$$pathloss(dB) = 40log_{10}(d) - 20log_{10}(h_t h_r) \tag{7}$$

From Equation (7), we see that with the 2-ray model, the received power decays with distance (transmitter-receiver separation) at a rate of 40 dB/decade. It is interesting to note that the 2-ray model is independent of the

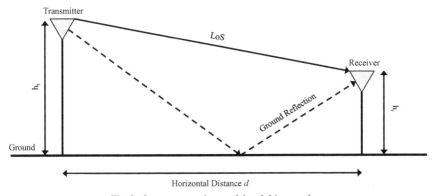

Fig. 8. 2-ray propagation model and d^{-4} power law.

frequency. However, the 2-ray pathloss of Equation (7) is valid only when the distance is greater than a threshold (cross-over distance), i.e., when $d \geq d_{break}$:

$$d_{break} = 4\left(\frac{h_t h_r}{\lambda}\right) = 4\left(\frac{h_t h_r f}{c}\right) \tag{8}$$

The 2-ray model shows that the higher the base station antenna, the higher the received power at the mobile device on the ground. This explains why the radio base stations are mounted on high towers, on the rooftop, and so on.

Example 5

A 2 m tall user is holding his smartphone at half of his height while standing 800 m from a 10 m-high base station. The base station is transmitting a 1.8 GHz signal using a transmission power of 30 dBm. What is the received power (in dBm) at the smartphone? Assume *unit gain* antennas.

Solution

We have h_t = 10 m, h_r = 1 m, d = 500 m, f = 1.8×10⁹ Hz, P_T = 30 dBm, c = 3×10⁸ m/sec

$$d_{break} = 4\left(\frac{h_t h_r f}{c}\right) = 240m$$

This means that the 2-ray model can be applied to estimate the pathloss at 800 m.

$$pathloss = 20log_{10}\left(\frac{d^2}{h_t h_r}\right) = 87.96\,dB$$

The received power = 30 – 87.96 = –57.96 dBm (approx.)

---

11. Fading

One interesting aspect of multipath we discussed earlier is that the multipath signals can be either constructive or destructive. It depends on how the phase changes happen due to reflection. As Fig. 9 shows, if the phases are aligned, multipath can increase the signal amplitude. On the other hand, the multipath can cancel out the signal if totally out of phase.

Sometimes by moving the receiver only a few centimetres, big differences in signal amplitude can be brought about due to changes in multipath. This is called *small-scale fading*.

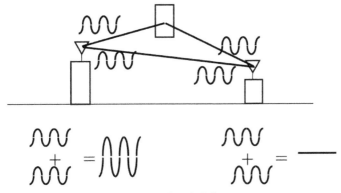

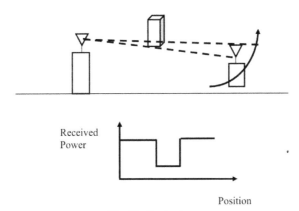

Fig. 9. Small-scale fading.

12. Shadowing

If there is an object blocking the LoS, then the power received will be much lower due to the blockage. Figure 10 shows how the power suddenly decreases due to the shadowing effect when the receiver is moved.

Received Power

Position

Fig. 10. Shadowing.

13. Total Path Loss

Now we see that there are many phenomena that affect the path loss. Multipath, shadowing, etc., can cause path loss in some way. Figure 11 shows the total effect of all these phenomena on path loss. The y-axis shows the attenuation in dB and the x-axis the distance in log. If there is no multipath, shadow, etc., then the path loss is a straight line. However, due to fading, actual path loss fluctuates, but does consistently decrease with increasing distance.

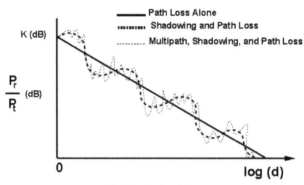

Fig. 11. Total path loss.

14. MIMO

Traditionally, single antennas were used for all types of wireless communications. In recent years, multiple antennas are increasingly being used to increase the quality, reliability, and capacity of wireless communication systems. Multiple Input Multiple Output (MIMO) is a framework used to describe such systems where 'multiple input' refers to multiple antennas at the transmitter while 'multiple output' refers to multiple antennas at the receiver. Under this framework, the transmitter or receiver could have single antennas, leading to four possible MIMO configurations as explained in Table 1.

These configurations are typically enumerated using two numbers. For example, a 2×2 MIMO refers to a system with 2 Tx antennas and 2 Rx antennas while a 4×2 MIMO refers to 4 Tx antennas and 2 Rx antennas.

A fundamental benefit of MIMO comes from the fact that, if the antennas are spaced $\lambda/2$ or more apart, then the signals from different antennas can be uncorrelated, creating multiple independent *spatial channels* over the same frequency as illustrated in Fig. 12. These spatial channels can be exploited to either improve the reliability of the communication using a technique called *spatial diversity* or increase the data rate by exploiting *spatial multiplexing*. Finally, it is also possible to increase the coverage range and signal strength by exploiting multiple Tx antennas to focus the beam at a narrow angle, which is known as *beam forming*.

Table 1. MIMO configurations.

Configuration	Explanation
SISO	single input (1 Tx antenna) single output (1 Rx antenna)
SIMO	single input (1 Tx antenna) multiple output (> 1 Rx antenna)
MISO	multiple input (> 1 Tx antenna) single output (1 Rx antenna)
MIMO	multiple input (> 1 Tx antenna) multiple output (> 1 Rx antenna)

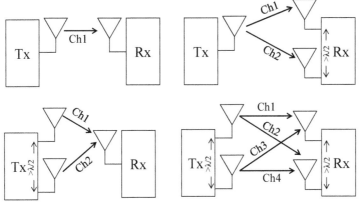

Fig. 12. Examples of spatial channels.

14.1 Spatial Diversity

As we can see from Fig. 12, there are a total of $N_T \times N_R$ independent spatial channels where N_T represents the number of transmit antennas and N_R the number of receive antennas. Spatial diversity refers to the technique that transmits every data bit over all of the $N_T \times N_R$ channels. Such redundant transmissions do not increase the data rate but improve the reliability of communication because of the probability that all channels will experience severe fading simultaneously is low. The improved SNR at the receiver is called the *diversity gain*.

14.2 Spatial Multiplexing

The goal of spatial multiplexing is to send different bits in the data stream over different spatial channels to increase the effective data rate of the communication link. The difference between diversity and multiplexing is illustrated in Fig. 13. The increase in data rate due to multiplexing is referred to as *multiplexing gain*, which is limited by the degrees of freedom defined as the $\min(N_T, N_R)$.

Example 6
What is the degrees of freedom for an 802.11ac WiFi system with the access point having 8 antennas and communicating to a laptop equipped with 2 antennas?

Solution
Degrees of freedom = $\min(8,2) = 2$

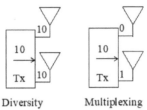

Diversity   Multiplexing

Fig. 13. Diversity vs. multiplexing.

14.3 Beamforming

The idea of beamforming is to direct the wireless signal towards a specific receiver, thus creating a strong signal at the intended receiver but no or weak signal elsewhere. Figure 14 shows an example of beamforming used by a Wi-Fi router to create strong beams towards intended receivers. Beamforming is also used by cellular towers to direct beams to specific houses or mobile users. The primary advantage of beamforming is to concentrate the transmit power in narrow beams instead of radiating it in all directions. This in turn improves the signal quality and eventually the data rate and reliability of the communication links between the transmitter and the intended receivers.

Single-antenna transmitters cannot realize beamforming. To create beams, a transmitter would need to transmit the signal via multiple closely spaced antennas. A typical way to achieve beamforming is to exploit an array of antennas where each antenna sends the same signal at slightly different times (phase shifted) to create constructive signal combinations at the target receiver (within the beam) and destructive interference elsewhere (outside the beam). We have already seen examples of such constructive and destructive signal combinations in the context of small-scale fading due to multipath reflections (Fig. 9). For beamforming, however, only line-of-sight signals transmitted by multiple antennas located at the transmitter are involved.

In practical wireless communication systems, the beam needs to be steered dynamically as the location of the receiver changes, either because a new receiver is targeted, or the target receiver has moved to a new location. Even for a fixed beam, changes in the wireless propagation environment require adjustment in antenna phase shifts and amplitudes to maintain the beam properties. The phase shifts and amplitudes for all individual antennas of the antenna array will thus have to be recomputed continuously, which is computationally complex. Special digital signal processing (DSP) chips are used to achieve this, which however lead to increased cost and power consumption for beamforming systems. Fortunately, with advancements in DSP and low-power electronics, beamforming is becoming widely available in consumer electronics, such as in WiFi routers.

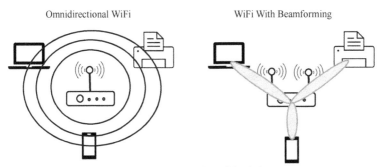

Omnidirectional WiFi   WiFi With Beamforming

Fig. 14. Beamforming with WiFi.

15. OFDM

It turns out that instead of using a big fat pipe or a wide band/channel on its entirety for modulation and coding, it is much more effective to divide the band into many narrower orthogonal subbands/subcarriers or subchannels and then modulate each subchannel independently with a BPSK, QPSK, 16-QAM, 64-QAM, etc., depending on the fading in the channel. The frequency selective modulation helps address the frequency selective fading experienced in typical environments, leading to many advantages, such as better protection against frequency selective burst errors and narrowband interference which affects only a small fraction of subchannels. This process is called Orthogonal Frequency Division Multiplexing (OFDM). Figure 15 illustrates the OFDM process highlighting the fact that the symbol durations in OFDM get extended due to the lower data rates caused by narrower channels. Less inter-symbol interference due to longer symbols is therefore another added advantage of OFDM.

So how many subdivisions are good? The higher the number of subdivisions the better it can address the frequency selective fading and interference, but they have to be orthogonal to avoid inter-channel interference. Two channels are orthogonal if the peak power of a channel is at the bottom of the neighbouring channel, as shown in Fig. 16.

Due to its many benefits, both WiFi and cellular systems employ OFDM. Having many subcarriers allows OFDM to use some of them as *pilots* to

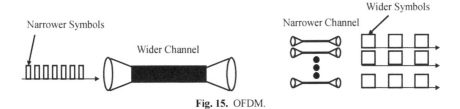

Narrower Symbols   Narrower Channel   Wider Symbols

Wider Channel

Fig. 15. OFDM.

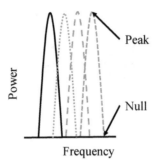

Fig. 16. Orthogonal subcarriers in OFDM.

help estimate the channel in real-time while data is being sent over the other subcarriers. For example, the basic 802.11a WiFi has a total of 64 OFDM subcarriers for each of its 20 MHz channels where 4 of them are used as pilots. We will examine the details of WiFi OFDM in later chapters.

Example 7

With a subcarrier spacing of 10 kHz, how many subcarriers will be available in an OFDM system with 20 MHz channel bandwidth?

Solution

#of subcarriers = channel bandwidth/subcarrier spacing = 20 MHz/10 kHz = 2000

---

16. OFDMA

OFDM, which is a multiplexing technology, can also be used as a multiple access technology. Orthogonal Frequency Division Multiple Access (OFDMA), is based on OFDM. Note that the 'M' in OFDM stands for *multiplexing*, but the 'M' in OFDMA stands for *multiple*.

In OFDM, the spectrum is divided into many subcarriers for multiplexing efficiency, such as longer symbol durations, etc. Now we can do multiple access over OFDM by allocating different subsets of subcarriers to different users. We can even change the subcarrier subset over time to make more efficient allocation over time. Such dynamic allocation of subcarrier subsets of OFDM is called OFDMA.

Figure 17 illustrates the difference between OFDM and OFDMA. In OFDM, all subcarriers are given to the same user. Then using TDMA, OFDM subcarriers can be shared between different users, but that would be TDMA, not OFDMA. In OFDMA, we see a 2D scheduling framework, where different users are allocated a different 'block', i.e., a subset of subcarriers over certain

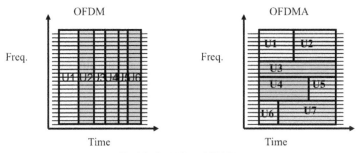

Fig. 17. OFDM vs. OFDMA.

time slots. OFDMA has been used in cellular systems for many years and is currently being considered for the latest WiFi standard.

17. Effect of Frequency

The choice of frequency has major impacts on wireless communications. Using a cartoon, Fig. 18 illustrates the wavelength differences between low and high frequency communications. The other effects of frequency are discussed below:

- Higher frequencies have higher attenuation, e.g., 18 GHz has 20 dB/m more than 1.8 GHz.
- Higher frequencies need smaller antennas. Note that antenna length has to be greater than half of the wavelength; for example, we need a 17 cm antenna to transmit data over 900 MHz.
- Higher frequencies are affected more by the weather. Higher than 10 GHz is affected by rainfall and 60 GHz is affected by oxygen absorption.
- Higher frequencies have more bandwidth and higher data rate.
- Higher frequencies allow more spatial frequency reuse because they attenuate close to cell boundaries. Low frequencies propagate far and wide, spilling over the cell boundaries and creating interference with other cells.
- Lower frequencies have longer reach.
- Lower frequencies require larger antenna and antenna spacing. This means that realizing MIMO is very difficult, particularly on mobile devices.
- Lower frequencies mean smaller channel width, which in turn needs more aggressive MCS, e.g., 256-QAM to achieve good data rates.

Fig. 18. Effects of frequency.

- Doppler shift = vf/c = Velocity × Frequency/(speed of light). This means that we have lower Doppler spread at lower frequencies. This allows supporting higher speed mobility more easily with lower frequencies.
- Mobility can be easily supported below 10 GHz, but becomes very difficult at higher frequencies.

18. Summary

1. An omnidirectional antenna radiates power in all directions, whereas a directional antenna focusses its power in a specific direction; isotropic antenna refers to a theoretical antenna that radiates *uniformly* in each direction in space, without reflections and losses.

2. In Frii's model, path loss increases at a power of 2 with distance as well as frequency.

3. In 2-ray model, path loss increases at a power of 4 with distance but is not dependent on the frequency; it rather depends on the antenna heights.

4. Fading = Changes in received signal power with changes in position or environment.

5. Multipath effect can cause inter-symbol interference if symbol intervals are not adequately designed.

6. Multiple antennas can help create multiple independent spatial channels over the same frequency.

7. An array of omnidirectional antennas can help realize directional transmissions by creating the so-called beams.

8. OFDM is a multiplexing technique which splits a wide channel into many narrow orthogonal subcarriers, where each subcarrier is modulated independently.

9. OFDMA is a multiple access technology which shares blocks of OFDM subcarriers between users dynamically over time.

True/False and MCQ

Q1. With a subcarrier spacing of 10 kHz, how many subcarriers will be used in an OFDM system with 8 MHz channel bandwidth?
(a) 8,   (b) 80,   (c) 800,   (d) 8000

Q2. Let us consider an OFDM system that uses the same carrier spacing irrespective of the channel bandwidth used. It employs 1024 subcarriers for 10 MHz channel. How many subcarriers will be used if the channel was 1.25 MHz wide?
(a) 1000,   (b) 1024,   (c) 1280,   (d) 128

Q3. You have bought a 2.4 GHz WiFi router with two dipole antennas claiming effective antenna gain of 6 dB. Your laptop has a single dipole with 0 dB gain and it claims a receiver sensitivity of –64 dBm. What is the maximum distance from the router your laptop can receive data if the router always use a transmit power of 20 dB?
(a) 10 m,   (b) 20 m,   (c) 215 m,   (d) 315 m

Q4. You have bought a 2.4 GHz WiFi router with antenna gain of 6 dB and default transmission power of 100 mW. Your laptop has a 0 dB antenna gain and claims a receiver sensitivity of –60 dBm. Can you connect your laptop to the router from a distance of 150 m?
(a) YES,   (b) NO

Q5. An omni-directional antenna radiates power in ALL directions equally.
(a) True   (b) False

Q6. A lamp post would cause scattering for a 300 GHz transmission.
(a) True   (b) False

Q7. In the presence of multipath, symbols get wider at the receiver.
(a)True   (b) False

Q8. Symbols must be wider than the delay spread to avoid inter-symbol interference.
(a) True   (b) False

Q9. MIMO is only useful with the presence of multipath and scattering.
(a) True   (b) False

Q10. In OFDM, all subcarriers carry data.
(a) True   (b) False

Review Exercises

You want to set up an over-water link to provide data service to a ferry. The maximum distance from the terminal to the ferry is 10 km. The antenna heights are 20 m at the terminal and 10 m at the ferry. You can use 20 dBi antennas at each end and 1 W transmit power. What will be the received power in Watts and dBm?

References

[BTBLOG] Bluetooth Special Interest Group Blog; accessed 18 October, 2021. https://www.bluetooth.com/blog/.

[Munoz, 2009] Munoz, David, Frantz Bouchereau, Cesar Vargas and Rogerio Enriquez. (2009). *Position Location Techniques and Applications*, Academic Press, 2009.

Part III
WiFi and Wireless Local Area Networks

4

WiFi Basics

◇◇◇

WiFi, which stands for 'Wireless Fidelity', is one of the most widely used wireless networking technologies today, with millions of them deployed in our homes and workplaces. WiFi is also increasingly available in many indoor and outdoor public places, such as airports, shopping malls, parks, and university campuses. All personal mobile devices, such as smartphones, tablets, and laptops are fitted with WiFi interfaces, making them very easy to be connected to such networks wherever they are available. In most cases, WiFi is available for free to use or at least there is no limit imposed on the volume of data for paid subscriptions, making it the most desired option to get connected to the Internet. WiFi has gone through many years of developments and upgrades over the last decade, resulting in increased level of complexity adopted in its recent standards. This chapter will explain the basic features and functions of the WiFi technology, while the more advanced versions will be examined at later chapters.

1. WiFi vs IEEE 802.11

Both IEEE 802.11 and WiFi basically refer to wireless LANs. There is, however, a subtle difference between them. 802.11 is an IEEE standard for wireless LANs. Unfortunately, to satisfy a large number of different vendors contributing to the standardization process, 802.11 specification comes with many different options to implement. This raises a practical interoperability issue if different vendors choose to implement different options of the same 802.11 standard.

To overcome the potential interoperability problem of 802.11, an industry alliance was formed, called Wireless Fidelity or WiFi Alliance. This alliance is committed to a selected set of options which all members will implement, essentially guaranteeing the ultimate interoperability that was envisaged by IEEE 802.11. Now, any product displaying the WiFi logo is guaranteed to work with any other product displaying the same, irrespective of who manufactures

Fig. 1. WiFi logo (*left*) vs WiFi icon (*right*).

them. With WiFi, wireless LAN now has its 'fidelity', i.e., its ability to work with others. Note that the display of the WiFi icon, i.e., a small radar symbol, when trying to connect a device to a WiFi network is not about certifying the WiFi product, but to basically indicate that the device is connected to WiFi. Figure 1 shows the difference between WiFi logo and WiFi icon. Details of WiFi can be found from wi-fi.org, while IEEE 802.11 details are available from ieee.org.

2. IEEE Standards Numbering System

IEEE has a peculiar numbering system for all its standards. Anyone trying to follow the IEEE standards for wireless LANs must be familiar with this numbering system.

In the early 1980's, a group was formed, called 802, which defined logical link control (802.2), bridging and management (802.1) and security (802.10) functionalities for communication networks. Later, many different types of wired and wireless networks were formed and numbered, starting from 802.3, such as Ethernet (802.3), WiFi (802.11), and so on. All these networks, starting from 802.3 onwards, are defined by the same link control, bridging, management, and security standards. Consequently, IEEE 802.11 follows 802.1 and 802.2. The hierarchy of the numbering system is shown in Fig. 2.

802 Overview and Architecture		
802.2 Logical Link Control		
802.1 Bridging		
802.1 Management		
802.10 Security		
802.3 Ethernet ...	802.11 WiFi ...	802.17 Resilient Packet Ring (RPR) ...

Fig. 2. Hierarchy of IEEE 802 numbering system.

Standards with letters appended after an 802 standard applies only to that particular 802 network, but not to others, for example, 802.11i will apply to WiFi devices, but not Ethernet (802.3) devices.

When letters are appended, they can be either in lower case or upper case. Lower case letters represent temporary or interim revisions (also called 'amendments'), which will eventually disappear before merging with a standard with an uppercase letter. Standards with upper case letters are permanent and are called 'base standards'. For example, IEEE 802.1w-2001 was merged with IEEE 802.1D-2004. Standards were originally numbered sequentially, such as 802.1a,...802.1z, 802.1aa, 802.1ab, and so on. Now base standard letters are being shown during the amendments, such as IEEE 802.1Qau-2010, where Q is the base standard and au is the amendment.

It is interesting to note that while IEEE uses letters to refer to different versions of the technology, WiFi Alliance has recently opted to use numbers to name the WiFi versions. For example, WiFi 4 refers to IEEE 802.11n, 5 refers to 802.11ac and so on. Table 1 shows the WiFi Alliance numbers and their corresponding IEEE standards.

Table 1. WiFi Alliance numbers and their corresponding IEEE standards.

WiFi Alliance Number	IEEE Standard
WiFi 4	802.11n
WiFi 5	802.11ac
WiFi 6	802.11ax
WiFi 7	802.11be

3. IEEE 802.11 Features

The original 802.11 standard in 1997 specified only 1 and 2 Mbps. Newer versions offered successively higher speeds at 11 Mbps, 54 Mbps, 108 Mbps, 200 Mbps, and so on. All these versions were specified for 'license-exempt' or 'license-free' spectrum, i.e., spectrum which we are not required to be licensed by law.

When the spectrum is license-exempt, a technology is required to prevent spectrum hogging. 802.11 employs spread spectrum techniques at the physical layer to solve the hogging problem. More specifically, for the Industrial, Scientific, and Medical (ISM) bands, it uses either Direct Sequence (DS) spread spectrum or Frequency Hopping spread spectrum. 802.11 specifies a third physical layer, called Diffused Infrared, to be used with the infrared band in 850–900 nm.

802.11 supports multiple priorities to deliver both time-critical, such as voice, and data traffic over the same LAN infrastructure. It also supports power management, which enables nodes to go to sleep mode when there is no traffic to conserve power.

4. ISM Bands

The license-exempt spectrum to be used by wireless LANs is called the Industrial, Scientific, and Medical (ISM) band. As shown in Table 2, there are many different available ISM bands of varying bandwidth [ITU2018]. The bands available in the lower frequency have understandably smaller bandwidths whereas increasing bandwidth is available at higher frequency ISM bands. For example, the 6.765 MHz band has only 30 kHz bandwidth whereas a massive 150 MHz bandwidth is available at 5.725 GHz.

The original WiFi started with the 2.4 GHz band. However, 2.4 GHz was already in use by a large variety of products, such as medical equipment, microwave, garage-door openers, and so on. When the WiFi usage started to grow, 2.4 GHz became saturated, prompting the opening of a new WiFi band at 5.725 GHz, which is simply referred to as 5 GHz band. Most recent WiFi routers can operate over both bands, hence they are marketed as 'dual band' routers. In recent years, many more bands have been released to support new types of WiFi, which are listed in Table 3.

Table 2. ISM bands.

Frequency Range	Bandwidth
6.765 MHz–6.795 MHz	30 kHz
13.553 MHz–13.567 MHz	14 kHz
26.957 MHz–27.283 MHz	326 kHz
40.660 MHz–40.700 MHz	40 kHz
433.050 MHz–434.790 MHz	1.74 MHz
902 MHz–928 MHz	26 MHz
2.4 GHz–2.5 GHz	100 MHz
5.725 GHz–5.875 GHz	150 MHz
24.000 GHz–24.250 GHz	250 MHz
61 GHz–61.5 GHz	500 MHz
122 GHz–123 GHz	1 GHz
244 GHz–246 GHz	2 GHz

Table 3. WiFi bands.

WiFi Standard	Frequency Band
802.11b/g/n	2.4 GHz
802.11a/n/ac/ax	5 GHz
802.11be	6 GHz (not confirmed yet)
802.11p (car-to-car)	5.9 GHz (licensed band)
802.11ah (IoT)	900 MHz
802.11af (Rural)	700 MHz (unused TV channels)
802.11ad/ay (Multi Gbps wireless applications: e.g., cable replacement, VR, …)	60 GHz

5. IEEE 802.11 Channels

The WiFi bands are divided into separate channels to facilitate better management of congestion when multiple wireless LANs operate in close proximity. Two different LANs then can simply choose to operate in two different channels of the same band and yet avoid collisions and interference from each other. It should be noted that an AP and any WiFi device connected to it operate over a single channel, the channel that is selected by the AP at any given time.

Each channel is usually 20 or 22 MHz wide. WiFi operating in the 2.4 GHz band uses 22 MHz channels, while 5 GHz band uses 20 MHz channels. With newer WiFi versions, it is possible to combine two or more channels to get a wider channel for higher data rates.

2.4 GHz WiFi has a total of 14 channels although not all channels are available in all countries. Table 4 lists the lower, center, and upper frequencies for these 14 channels. As can be seen, each channel is 22 MHz wide while their center frequencies are 5 MHz apart from each other with the exception of channel 14. Table 4 also shows that with 22-MHz, only a small number of non-overlapping channels are possible. Specifically, for 2.4 GHz WiFi, we can choose from three available non-overlapping channels numbered as 1, 6, and 11. Most WiFi routers select channel 6 as default.

In contrast to 2.4 GHz, 5 GHz WiFi has 20 MHz non-overlapping channels. 5 GHz uses two types of channels. One type of channels is always available, while the others are actually shared with radars using a Dynamic Frequency Selection (DFS) algorithm. With DFS, 5 GHz WiFi APs monitor radar channels and immediately vacate them, i.e., switch to another channel, if radar is detected in the operating channel. User devices connected to such radar channels then will also need to switch to the new channel, which may cause momentary connection drop.

Table 4. Channel frequencies for 2.4 GHz WiFi.

Channel Number	Lower Frequency (MHz)	Center Frequency (MHz)	Upper Frequency (MHz)
1	2401	2412	2423
2	2406	2417	2428
3	2411	2422	2433
4	2416	2427	2438
5	2421	2432	2443
6	2426	2437	2448
7	2431	2442	2453
8	2436	2447	2458
9	2441	2452	2463
10	2446	2457	2468
11	2451	2462	2473
12	2456	2467	2478
13	2461	2472	2483
14	2473	2484	2495

6. Physical Layers

The physical layer technology directly affects the data rate achievable with WiFi. In the first version defined in 1997, spread spectrum was used to achieve only 1 and 2 Mbps, which was soon proved to be too slow for the emerging LAN applications. Two years later, in 1999, an advanced version of spread spectrum was introduced for 2.4 GHz, while OFDM was introduced for the 5-GHz band to increase the data rate to 54 Mbps. In 2003, OFDM was also successfully used in 2.4 GHz to achieve 54 Mbps channels, which was named 802.11g. OFDM has proved so successful that it still defines the physical layer standard for today's WiFi.

7. Hidden Node Problem

Unlike wired LAN (Ethernet), Wireless LAN suffers from a specific collision detection problem called *hidden node problem*. Let's consider the three wireless nodes, A, B, and C, as shown in Fig. 3. Let us assume that A can hear B, B can hear C, but C cannot hear A. Now, C may start transmitting to B while A is also transmitting to B. Clearly, collisions will be experienced at B, making it difficult for B to understand either of the communications. Unfortunately, the transmitters A and C cannot detect the collision. Only the receiver, B, can detect it. Therefore, unlike Ethernet, where transmitters can detect collision and back off, wireless LAN must implement some other

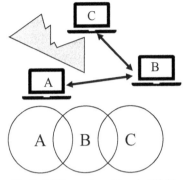

Fig. 3. Hidden node problem in 802.11.

techniques that can avoid such collisions in the first place. Wireless LANs therefore use collision avoidance (CA) in contrast to collision detection (CD) used in Ethernet.

8. Collision Avoidance with 4-way Handshake

In wireless LAN, CA is achieved by a 4-way handshake process as shown in Fig. 4. Essentially, four packets are transmitted for each data packet, i.e., three control packets are needed to avoid collision for each data packet transmitted.

The 4-way handshake begins with the transmitter first transmitting a ready-to-send (RTS) packet. If the receiver receives it and wishes to allow the transmitter to go ahead, then it will transmit a clear-to-send (CTS) packet. The transmitter sends the data packet only if and when it receives the CTS, which avoids collision with other potential transmitters as they defer their

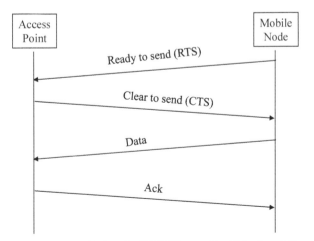

Fig. 4. 4-way handshake using RTS/CTS to avoid collision in 802.11.

transmissions upon hearing the CTS. Finally, the receiver transmits an acknowledgment to confirm the correct reception of the data packet from the transmitter. This procedure needs to be repeated for each data packet.

Although it may sound like too much overhead to avoid collision, the actual overhead of the 4-way handshake has to be analyzed more carefully. The RTS and CTS packets are very short, lasting only a few microseconds. The data packets, on the other hand, are long lasting with tens to hundreds of milliseconds depending on the speed of the network. Thus, avoiding collision of a long data packet with tiny RTS/CTS packets is worth the effort in many cases.

9. IEEE 802.11 Medium Access Control (MAC)

To completely realize the medium access control (MAC), the 4-way handshake must work in conjunction with the carrier sense multiple access (CSMA) function. CSMA basically says that a wireless node must first listen to the channel before even attempting the 4-way handshake and backoff for a random period if it finds the channel busy. The 4-way handshake is launched only if the channel is found idle.

The RTS and CTS packets contain the duration of the data packet, which allows other nodes who hear the CTS to stay away from attempting channel sensing. Finally, to achieve reliability, the transmitter must retransmit the data packet if it does not receive the ACK from the receiver.

9.1 IEEE 802.11 Priorities

Wireless LAN has different priorities for control and data packets. These priorities are achieved by enforcing different amounts of inter-frame space (IFS) as shown in Fig. 5. After the channel busy period ends, the RTS, CTS, and ACK packets can be transmitted by waiting only a short IFS (SIFS), but medium priority time-critical frames, such as those used for periodic channel reservation in Point Coordination Function (PCF) mode, will have to wait slightly longer than SIFS. Finally, the data frames, which use Distributed Coordination Function (DCF), will wait a bit more before attempting transmission.

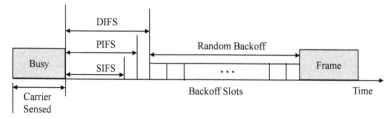

Fig. 5. Inter-frame spacing and priorities in 802.11.

9.2 Time Critical Services

The wireless LAN base station uses PCF to achieve a contention-free period (CFP) to allow transmission of data from time-critical services. The base station periodically transmits a beacon and then, using a polling frame, grants one node to access the channel without any contention. During the CFP, no other nodes will attempt accessing the channel. The duration of CFP will vary with the load of the time critical data. The channel will be opened for contention as soon as the PCF ends. Thus, the channel access alternates between PCF and DCF as shown in Fig. 6.

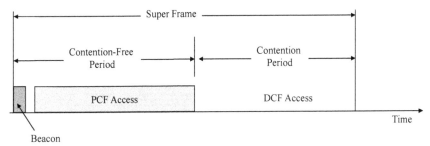

Fig. 6. Time critical services using the PCF function. DCF follows PCF.

9.3 IEEE 802.11 DCF Backoff

For effective sharing of the channel with many users, DCF uses a sophisticated backoff mechanism to prevent a node from hogging the channel. Each node maintains a FIFO (first in first out) queue to store the data packets to be transmitted. For transmitting the head of the queue, the node implements the DCF backoff mechanism, which requires three variables—Contention Window (CW), Backoff Count (BO), and Network Allocation Vector (NAV), to be maintained.

If a frame (RTS, CTS, Data, Ack) is heard, NAV is set to the duration in that frame. Nodes are allowed to sense the media only after NAV expires. NAV therefore is basically a timer that prevents a node from even sensing the channel if the node has explicit knowledge about the future busy time of the channel.

If the medium is idle for DIFS, and backoff (BO) is not already active, the node draws a random BO in [0, CW] and sets the backoff timer. The node can only start transmission if the channel continues to be idle during this backoff time. If the medium becomes busy during backoff, the timer is paused and a new NAV is set. After NAV, i.e., when the channel becomes idle again, the backoff continues from the previous BO value.

Because collisions can still occur after transmission, each transmitted packet is acknowledged by the receiver. DCF backoff time increases exponentially with successive failed (unsuccessful) transmission attempts, i.e., when no ACK is received, to make it more effective during heavy load. Initially and after each successful transmission (ACK is received), it sets $CW = CW_{min}$. Then after each unsuccessful attempt: $CW = min\{2CW + 1, CW_{max}\}$. It should be noted that CW is in units of slot time varying with 802.11 standards, as shown in Table 5. We also have PIFS = SIFS + 1 slot time and DIFS = SIFS + 2 slot time.

Table 5. Slot time and MAC parameters for WiFi standards.

WLAN	Slot-time (μs)	SIFS (μs)	CWmin	CWmax
11a	9	16	15	1023
11b	20	10	31	1023
11g	9 or 20	10	15 or 31	1023
11n (2.4 GHz)	9 or 20	10	15	1023
11n (5 GHz)	9	16	15	1023
11ac	9	16	15	1023

Example 1

Assume that we have $CW_{min} = 3$ and $CW_{max} = 127$ configured for a given WLAN. What would be the values of CW if there were eight successive unsuccessful attempts after initalizing the network?

Solution

After initialization, CW = CWmin = 3
After 1st unsuccessful attempt, CW = min(7,127) = 7
After 2nd unsuccessful attempt, CW = min(15,127) = 15
Then on, 31, 63, 127, 127, 127, ...

Example 2

What is the duration of PIFS and DIFS for IEEE 802.11b?

Solution

Slot time = 20 μs
SIFS = 10 μs
PIFS = SIFS + slot time = 10 + 20 = 30 μs
DIFS = SIFS + 2 x slot time = 10 + 40 = 50 μs

9.4 Virtual Carrier Sense

Continuous carrier sensing for a prolonged period of time can drain the batteries of wireless nodes. To avoid unnecessary carrier sensing, WiFi uses virtual carrier sensing using the NAV parameter. This is possible because every frame has a Duration ID field which indicates how long the medium will be busy for transmitting this frame. Table 6 shows how this duration is calculated for different types of frames.

Table 6. Durations for different types of frames.

Frame Type	Duration
RTS	RTS + SIF + CTS + SIF + Frame + SIF + Ack
CTS	CTS + SIF + Frame + SIF + Ack
Frame	Frame + SIF + Ack
Ack	Ack

Once a node hears a frame, it sets a NAV timer for the Duration ID of the frame and can go to sleep for conserving its battery. No physical carrier sensing is done during this period. The node wakes up after the NAV period, to start sensing again.

Example 3
Consider an 802.11b WLAN. A station estimates the transmission times of RTS, CTS, and ACK as 10 µs, 10 µs, and 25 µs, respectively. What would be the value of the duration field in the RTS header if the station wants to send a 250 µs long data frame?

Solution
802.11b has a SIFS duration of 10 µs.
Duration field in RTS = RTS_time + CTS_time + ACK_time + data_time +
$\qquad$ 3×SIFS
$\qquad\qquad$ = 10+10+25+250+3x10 = 325 µs

9.5 DCF Example

Figure 7 shows an example of how DCF works, where A, D, C, and R, represent ACK, Data, CTS, and RTS, respectively, and Table 7 traces the events at different points in time.

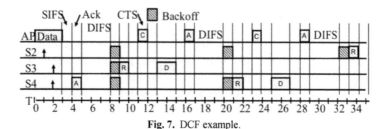

Fig. 7. DCF example.

Table 7. Event trace for DCF example.

Time	Event
T1	Station 2 wants to transmit but the media is busy.
T2	Stations 3 and 4 want to transmit but the media is busy.
T3	Station 1 finishes transmission.
T4	Station 1 receives ack for its transmission (SIFS = 1); Stations 2, 3, and 4 set their NAVs to 1.
T5	Medium becomes free.
T8	DIFS expires. Stations 2, 3, 4 draw backoff count between 0 and 5. The counts are 3, 1, 2.
T9	Station 3 starts transmitting and announces a duration of 8 (RTS + SIFS + CTS + SIFS + DATA + SIFS + ACK). Station 2 and 4 pause their backoff counters at 2 and 1, respectively.
T15	Station 3 finishes data transmission.
T16	Station 3 receives Ack.
T17	Medium becomes free.
T20	DIFS expires. Stations 2 and 4 notice that there was no transmission for DIFS. Stations 2 and 4 start their backoff counters from 2 and 1, respectively.
T21	Station 4 starts transmitting RTS.

10. IEEE 802.11 Architecture

Figure 8 shows how the various elements of WiFi networks are connected to each other. The architecture has the following elements:

Basic Service Set (BSS): Set of all nodes associated with one AP. Like the 'cell ID' in cellular networks, each BSS is identified with a unique Service Set ID (SSID), which is usually the 48-bit MAC address of the AP.

Distribution System (DS): A system of multiple APs connected together via a wired backbone. Usually the wired backbone is made from Ethernet and is hidden against ceiling or other infrastructure, so it is not visible to public.

Independent Basic Service Set (IBSS): Set of nodes connecting independently in *ad-hoc mode* without being connected to the WiFi infrastructure. Ad-hoc networks coexist and interoperate with infrastructure-based networks.

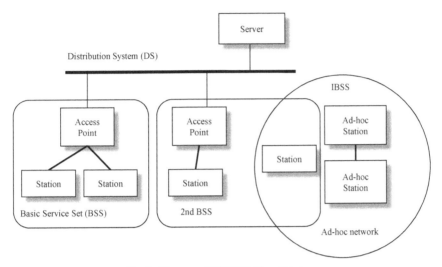

Fig. 8. Elements of IEEE 802.11 architecture.

11. IEEE 802.11 Frame Format

Figure 9 shows the WiFi frame format, all fields and their relative positions in the frame. There are a total of nine main fields in the frame as explained below:

Frame Control: A 16-bit field that defines many control functions for the frame, which will be described later.

Duration/ID: A 16-bit field that follows the Frame Control field. If used as duration field, it indicates the time in micro seconds the channel will be allocated for successful transmission of MAC frame, which includes time until the end of Ack. In some control frames, it contains association or connection identifier.

Adr 1/2/3/4: These are 48-bit address fields. It is interesting to see that WiFi uses four address fields, while most other networks, such as Ethernet, use only two. Use of four address fields will be explained later.

Seq Control: It is a 16-bit field. Its main function is to number frames between a pair of transmitter and receiver, using 12 bits and manage fragmentation and reassembly, using a 4-bit fragment sub-field.

Info: The field that carried user data or payload.

CRC: 32-bit cyclic redundancy check to detect frame errors.

The Frame Control field has 11 sub-fields:

Protocol Version: It provides the version number.

Type: Control, management, or data.

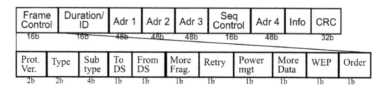

Fig. 9. Frame format of IEEE 802.11.

Sub-Type: Association, disassociation, re-association, probe, authentication, de-authentication, CTS, RTS, Ack,...

To DS: Going to Distribution System.

From DS: Coming from Distribution System.

More Fragment: Used to indicate whether this is the last fragment or more fragments are following. This helps with fragment reassembly at the receiver.

Retry: Whether it is a retransmission or original transmission.

Power mgt: Node indicating whether it is going to sleep (Power Save mode).

More Data: Whether there is more buffered data at AP for a station in Power Save mode.

Wireless Equivalent Privacy (WEP): Security info in this frame.

Order: Strict ordering.

12. Use of 802.11 Address Fields

There are four address fields to provide greater control of how packets can be 'routed' from source to destination. Figure 10 illustrates the various use contexts of these four addresses, where Source/Destination refers to the ultimate network devices that prepare and decode the frame for network layer, Tx/Rx could be the source/destination, or intermediate radio devices, e.g., access point (AP). The four address fields are defined by the 2 DS bits, as shown in Table 8 [GAST2005]. Uses of the four address fields in wireless client-server communications are further illustrated in Figs. 11 and 12.

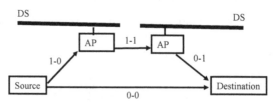

Fig. 10. 802.11 address fields and their use.

Table 8. Meaning of WiFi address fields.

Purpose	To DS	From DS	ADR1 (Rx)	ADR2 (Tx)	ADR3	ADR4
IBSS	0	0	DA	SA	IBSSID	N/A
From AP (from infra.)	0	1	DA	BSSID	SA	N/A
To AP (to infra.)	1	0	BSSID	SA	DA	N/A
AP-to-AP (W'lessBrdg)	1	1	RxA	TxA	DA	SA

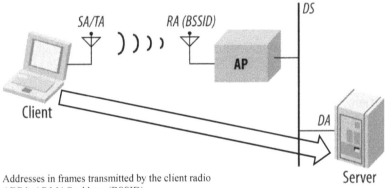

Addresses in frames transmitted by the client radio
ADR1: AP MAC address (BSSID)
ADR2: Client MAC address (source address)
ADR3: Server MAC address (destination address)
ADR4: Not applicable

Fig. 11. Wireless client transmitting to a wired server.

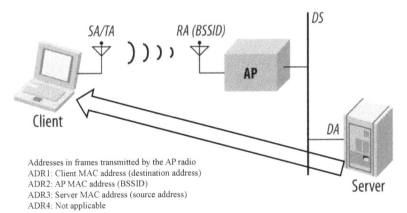

Addresses in frames transmitted by the AP radio
ADR1: Client MAC address (destination address)
ADR2: AP MAC address (BSSID)
ADR3: Server MAC address (source address)
ADR4: Not applicable

Fig. 12. Wired server transmitting to a wireless client.

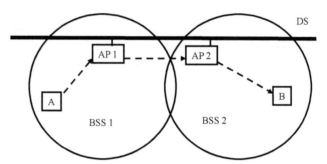

Fig. 13. Example of two BSSs interconnected via a DS.

Example 4

Consider the example WLAN in Fig. 13 where two BSSs are connected via a distribution system. What is the content of the Address 3 field when Station A wants to send a packet to Station B via AP 1?

Solution

In this case (To DS = 1, From DS = 0), Address 3 field should contain the address of the destination station. Therefore, it should be the address of B.

---

13. 802.11 Power Management

Extending the battery life of portable devices is one of the main challenges of wireless networks. As the battery technology itself is not advancing fast, mechanisms must be devised to let the device sleep as much as possible and wake up only when it needs to transmit or receive. If there are no packets to be received, a receiver could go to sleep and save battery power. To facilitate this kind of power saving, WiFi has a power management function.

To invoke the power management function, the node uses the Power Management bit in the frame control header to indicate to the AP that it is going to sleep. Upon receiving this information, the AP buffers all packets for this node. When the node wakes up, it waits for the beacon packet periodically sent by the AP. In the beacon packet, Traffic Indication Map (TIM) is a structure used by the AP to indicate which nodes has packets buffered.

If a node sees its bit turned on in the TIM, it does not go back to sleep. Instead, it sends a PS-Poll message to the AP and waits for the packet from the AP. The AP then sends one frame with buffered data and sets the More Data bit in the header if more data is waiting in the buffer. The client does not go back to sleep after receiving one frame if 'More' is set.

14. Summary

1. 802.11 PHYs: Spread spectrum in earlier versions, but OFDM in new versions.
2. 2.4 GHz channels (22 MHz) are mostly overlapped, while 5 GHz channels (20 MHz) are non-overlapped, but some are shared with the radar service.
3. 802.11 uses SIFS, PIFS, DIFS for priority.
4. WLAN frames have four address fields.
5. 802.11 supports power saving mode.

Multiple Choice Questions

Q1. Which of the following protocol mechanisms help achieve collision avoidance in WLAN?
  (a) Carrier Sensing
  (b) RTS/CTS
  (c) MIMO
  (d) Virtual Carrier Sensing
  (e) DCF

Q2. What is the slot-time for 5 GHz WLANs?
  (a) 9 ms
  (b) 9 μs
  (c) 12 ms
  (d) 12 μs
  (e) 12 ns

Q3. Although a total of fourteen 22-MHz channels is defined for 2.4 GHz DSSS WLANs, the 14th channel is not always available. The first 13 channels follow the 5 MHz channel spacing for the center frequency (starting from 2412) with 11 MHz assigned on both sides of the center frequency. If we consider the first 13 channels, a maximum of three non-overlapping channels exist. (1, 6, 11) is an example of a set of three non-overlapping channels. Can you identify another set of three non-overlapping channels among the first 13 channels?
  (a) (2, 7, 12)
  (b) (1, 5, 12)
  (c) (1, 11, 13)
  (d) (3, 8, 11)
  (e) (5, 10, 13)

Q4. How many successive unsuccessful transmission attempts are required for the Congestion Window (CW) variable to reach its maximum value in an 802.11n WLAN operating in the 5 GHz band?
(a) 3
(b) 4
(c) 5
(d) 6
(e) 7

Q5. Consider an 802.11a WLAN. A station estimates the transmission times of RTS, CTS, and ACK as 16 µs, 16 µs, and 25 µs, respectively. After receiving the RTS, the AP generates a CTS. What would be the value of the Duration field in the CTS header if the station wanted to send a 250 µs long data frame?
(a) 339 µs
(b) 355 µs
(c) 400 µs
(d) 323 ms
(e) 323 µs

Q6. A WiFi frame has the following contents in its first three address fields, ADR1 to ADR3: Destination Address, BSSID, and Source Address. Which of the following is a likely transmission event for this frame?
(a) Server to mobile client
(b) Client to mobile server
(c) Mobile to Mobile direct communication without any access point (adhoc WiFi)
(d) Mobile from one Distribution System to a mobile in another Distribution System connected via two WiFi access points (wireless bridge)
(e) None of these

Q7. Which of the following bits are used for power saving in WiFi?
(a) Power management and Retry bits
(b) Power management and Order bits
(c) Power management and To DS bits
(d) Power management and From DS bits
(e) Power management and More Data bits

Q8. Dynamic Frequency Selection (DFS) is required for 5 GHz WiFi irrespective of the choice of channel.
(a) True
(b) False

Q9. It is always wise to combine two channels into a wider channel of larger bandwidth.
(a) True
(b) False

Q10. What would be the channel width if two adjacent channels in a 5 GHz band WiFi are combined into a single one?
(a) 44 MHz
(b) 40 MHz
(c) 44 GHz
(d) 40 GHz
(e) None of these

References

[GAST 2005] Matthew S. Gast. (2005). *802.11 Wireless Networks: The Definitive Guide*, 2nd ed., O'Reilly.
[ITU 2018] *Recommendation ITU-R SM.1896-1*, International Telecommunication Union, Sept. 2018.

5
Mainstream WiFi Standards

Since the introduction of the basic 802.11 wireless LAN in 1997, there have been many amendments and advancements to date to address the requirements of new applications and demands. While some of these amendments sought to improve the capacity and efficiency of the mainstream WiFi used by billions of people to access the Internet, others targeted some niche applications to further enhance the utility of the technology. In this chapter, we will focus on the mainstream WiFi standards while the niche standards will be examined in the following chapter.

1. 802.11 Amendments and WiFi Evolution

Since its first appearance in 1997, WiFi has gone through significant evolutions, increasing its efficiency and data rates to meet the growing demand for wireless connectivity. Table 1 provides a chronological list of the major amendments along with the key enhancements and the maximum data rates they can support. As we can see, WiFi data rate has increased from a mere 2 Mbps in 1997 to a whopping 9.6 Gbps in 2020, approximately a five-fold increase in 23 years. Interestingly, the next version of WiFi is striving to achieve another three-fold increase to 30 Gbps in just four years, possibly beating the speed of wired LANs for the first time in history.

While it is easy to see the benefits of higher data rates, the details that contribute to data rate increase are less trivial to understand. In the rest of this chapter, we shall examine the factors that contribute to data rate enhancements for each of these amendments.

Table 1. Chronological list of mainstream IEEE 802.11 amendments.

802.11 Amendment	Key Enhancements	Max. Data Rate
802.11-1997	Legacy WiFi in 2.4 GHz (now extinct!)	2 Mbps
802.11b-1999	Higher speed modulation in 2.4 GHz	11 Mbps
802.11a-1999	Higher speed PHY (OFDM) in 5 GHz	54 Mbps
802.11g-2003	Higher speed PHY (OFDM) in 2.4 GHz	54 Mbps
802.11n-2009	Higher throughput in 2.4/5 GHz	600 Mbps
802.11ac-2013	Very high throughput in 5 GHz	~ 7 Gbps
802.11ax-2020	High efficiency in 2.4/5 GHz	~ 9.6 Gbps
802.11be-2024 (expected)	Extremely high throughput in 2.4/5/6 GHz	~ 30 Gbps

2. Basics of WiFi Data Rates

Each WiFi version supports a range of specific data rates. For example, 802.11a [802-11a] supports eight different data rates: 6, 9, 12, 18, 24, 36, 48, and 54 Mbps. Fundamentally, data rate of WiFi or for any other communications technology is derived as:

Data rate = symbol rate × data bits per symbol

While the symbol rate is defined by the PHY, the number of data bits carried in a symbol depends on the choice of modulation and coding. It should be noted that only 802.11b used DSSS, while all subsequent WiFi amendments used OFDM as their PHY. Usually, many different combinations of modulation and coding are available for a given PHY, which leads to a range of specific available data rates for a given WiFi. When MIMO is employed, data rates can be further increased linearly with the number of independent spatial streams supported by the MIMO system. Next, we are going to examine each of the mainstream WiFi amendments, discuss the main enhancements they introduced compared to their predecessor, and how these enhancements increase their achievable data rates.

3. Data Rate in DSSS-based WiFi: IEEE 802.11-1997 and 802.11b-1999

Recall that the original 802.11 released in 1997 supported only 2 Mbps for 22 MHz channels, using the Direct Sequence Spread Spectrum (DSSS) technique at the physical layer. In this section, we will examine how the data rate for DSSS is computed and how 802.11b was able to increase the DSSS rate to 11 Mbps for the same 22 MHz channel.

First, let us look at the use of chips in a DSSS system as illustrated in Fig. 1, where a binary coded symbol (single bit per symbol) is spread with

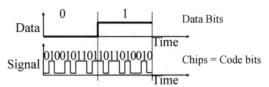

Fig. 1. An example of DSSS with binary modulated symbols spread with a chip rate of 10 chips per symbol.

10 chips. Both the original 802.11 and 802.11b [802-11b] operate at 1/2 chip per Hz, which gives a chip rate of 11 Mchips/s for the 22 MHz channel. Second, we note that 802.11 uses a Barker code, which uses 11 chips per symbol. On the other hand, to increase the data rate, 802.11b employs Complementary Code Keying (CCK), which employs only eight chips to code a symbol. This means we have a symbol rate of 1 Msps (Mega symbol per second) for the 2 Mbps rate and 1.375 Msps for the 11 Mbps data rate. The third factor that determines the final data rate is the symbol coding, which determines how many data bits are conveyed per symbol. For 2-Mbps rate, 802.11 uses 2 bits per symbol, whereas for the 11 Mbps, it uses 8 bits per symbol.

Now we can verify the final data rates by multiplying the symbol rates with the bits per symbol for each data rates. Specifically, for the 2 Mbps, we have 1 Msps × 2 bits/symbol = 2 Mbps. For the 11 Mbps, we have 1.375 Msps × 8 bits/symbol = 11 Mbps.

Example 1
A WLAN standard is employing a spread spectrum coding with only ½ rate, which produces chips at a rate of ½ chips per Hz. It uses eight chips to code a symbol and 16 QAM modulation to modulate the symbol stream. What would be the data rate for 22 MHz channels?

Solution
Chip rate = ½ × 22 = 11 Mcps (cps = chips per second)
Symbol rate = 11/8 = 1.375 Msps (sps = symbols per second)
Bits per symbol = $\log_2(16)$ = 4 [16 QAM produces 4 bits per symbol]
Data rate = symbol rate × bits per symbol = 1.375 × 4 = 5.5 Mbps

---

4. Data Rate in OFDM-based WiFi

OFDM, which was adopted in WiFi from 802.11a onwards, has a completely different structure than its predecessor, DSSS. The symbol rate in OFDM is obtained as the inverse of the symbol interval (a.k.a. symbol length or duration), which includes a data interval followed by a guard interval. The actual symbol is contained within the data interval, whereas the guard interval is used to avoid inter-symbol interference. The longer the delay spread, the longer the guard interval and the lower the symbol rate.

The number of bits carried in an OFDM symbol depends on the subcarrier structure and the modulation order of the symbol. OFDM divides a WiFi channel into many subcarriers. All these subcarriers are divided into three categories: data subcarriers, pilot subcarriers, and guard subcarriers. Only the data subcarriers carry the OFDM symbols. Pilots estimate the wireless channel, while the guards protect the symbol against interference from the adjacent channels. The guard subcarriers are thus equally distributed to the front and rear of the middle subcarriers.

Although the allocation of subcarriers to pilot and guard reduces the total number of data subcarriers, it is interesting to note that each OFDM symbol is carried over all the data subcarriers in parallel, which significantly boosts the effective bits per symbol. For example, an OFDM with N data subcarriers, each applying M-ary modulation, then the effective number of bits sent per symbol is obtained as $N \times \log_2 M$.

Finally, the actual number of data bits per symbol is affected by the choice of error correcting codes and their coding rates. For example, with a coding rate of ¾, 4 bits are actually transmitted for every 3 data bits. Similarly, a coding rate of 2/3 implies 2 data bits for every 3 bits transmitted, and so on. The number of data bits per OFDM symbol therefore is obtained as:

Data bits per OFDM symbol = coding rate $\times$ $\log_2 M$ $\times$ #-of-data-subcarriers

---

Example 2
What is the data rate of an OFDM WiFi applying 64-QAM and a coding rate of ¾ to its 48 data subcarriers? Assume a symbol interval of 4 μs.

Solution
$\log_2 M = \log_2 64 = 6$
Coded bits per symbol = $\log_2 M$ $\times$ #-of-data-subcarriers = 6 × 48 = 288
Data bits per symbol = coding rate × 288 = ¾ × 288 = 216
Symbol rate = 1/symbol-interval = ¼ Msps (0.25 million symbols per sec)
Data rate = symbol rate × data bits per symbol = 216 × ¼ Mbps = 54 Mbps

---

Table 2 summarizes the five key parameters that affect data rates in OFDM-based WiFi. In the rest of this chapter, we will examine how the successive amendments exploited these parameters to enhance the data rates from their predecessors.

Table 2. Five key parameters affecting WiFi data rates.

Parameter	Description
Modulation	Affects the number of bits per symbol; Log_2M bits per symbol for M-ary modulation; usually multiple modulation option are available.
Coding	Error correcting coding affects the actual number of data bits per symbol; usually multiple coding options are available; an integer number, called MCS (modulation and coding system), defines a particular combination of modulation and coding.
Guard interval	Affects symbol rate; the longer the interval, the lower the symbol rate and vice versa.
Channel Width	Affects the number of achievable OFDM subcarriers and hence ultimately the data rate; channel width can be increased by combining multiple channels into a single one (a.k.a. channel bonding), an option available from 802.11n onwards.
MIMO streams	Number of independent data streams that can be sent in parallel; more streams means higher achievable data rates, and vice versa; MIMO available from 802.11n onwards; newer amendments have increased number of MIMO streams compared to their predecessor.

5. IEEE 802.11a-1999

802.11a is the first amendment to use OFDM, which allowed it to push the date rates to 54 Mbps. Actually, 802.11a supports eight different data rates, from a mere 6 Mbps up to 54 Mbps, by selecting a combination of modulation and coding to dynamically adjust for the noise and interference.

802.11a divides the 20 MHz channel bandwidth into 64 subcarriers. Out of these 64 subcarriers, six at each side are used as guards (a total of 12 guards) and four as pilot, which leaves 48 of them to be used to carry data.

802.11a OFDM has a symbol length of 4 microseconds, which gives a symbol rate of 0.25 M symbols/s. Therefore, with a modulation of BPSK, for example, there will be 1 coded bit per subcarrier for each OFDM symbol, or 48 coded bits per OFDM symbol in total as the symbol is transmitted over all of the 48 subcarriers in parallel. The actual data bits transmitted per symbol will, however, depend on the coding used. 802.11a supports three coding rates, 1/2, 2/3, and 3/4.

The modulation schemes are fixed and cannot be changed, i.e., to operate at a particular data rate, the corresponding combination of modulation and coding scheme (MCS) has to be selected. Table 3 shows the MCS combinations of each data rate in 802.11a. Note that the *data bits per symbol* has to be multiplied by the *symbol rate* of 0.25 M symbols/s to obtain the final net data rate shown in the last column.

Table 3. Modulation, coding, and data rates for 802.11a.

Modulation	Coding Rate	Coded Bits per Subcarrier	Coded Bits per Symbol	Data Bits per Symbol	Data Rate (Mbps)
BPSK	½	1	48	24	6
BPSK	¾	1	48	36	9
QPSK	½	2	96	48	12
QPSK	¾	2	96	72	18
16-QAM	½	4	192	96	24
16-QAM	¾	4	192	144	36
64-QAM	2/3	6	288	192	48
64-QAM	¾	6	288	216	54

6. IEEE 802.11g-2003

Although 802.11a was able to push the date rates to 54 Mbps, it used the 5 MHz band and was not compatible with the previous version (802.11b), which was operating in the 2.4 GHz and at 11 Mbps. 802.11g [802-11g] achieved 54 Mbps at 2.4 GHz using OFDM, but it could fall back to 802.11b data rates using CCK modulation. More specifically, 802.11g OFDM data rates are identical with 802.11a, i.e., it supports 6, 9, 12, 18, 24, 36, 48, 54 Mbps as per Table 3, while CCK supports data rates of 1, 2, 5.5, and 11 Mbps. This seamless backward compatibility made 802.11g very popular because previous hardware designed to operate in the 2.4 GHz band can now benefit from the higher data rates without having to switch to a new spectrum.

7. IEEE 802.11e-2005 (Enhanced QoS)

While amendments 802.11a and 802.11g were racing to increase the data rates through enhancements in the PHY layer, 802.11e [802-11e] was released in 2005 to enhance the WiFi medium access control (MAC) for supporting quality of service (QoS). To achieve QoS, delay sensitive traffic, such as voice and video, must be given priority over delay-tolerant traffic, such as web browsing and file transfer. 802.11e provided the necessary protocol support is available at the MAC layer to achieve that.

802.11e achieves QoS by introducing a Hybrid Coordination Function (HCF) for MAC. HCF allows both contention-free access, using a Point Cordination Function (PCF), where the stations are polled by the access point. When PCF is used, stations cannot attempt to access the channel unless the AP provides access to it, which eliminates contentions. On the other hand, the stations can also use a contention-based access, called Enhanced Distributed Control Function (EDCF), where they can contend for the medium access, but with priority assigned to each packet based on the type of service.

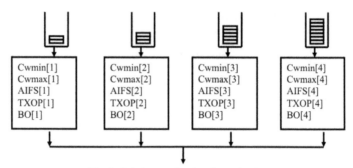

Fig. 2. Priority queuing in enhanced DCF.

Basically, EDCF achieves priority by implementing four separate priority queues within the station (*see* Fig. 2). When a packet is delivered to the MAC from the upper layer, it is queued in the appropriate queue, based on the priority required for the service. Each queue has separate values for the transmission parameters, such as the minimum and maximum congestion window values.

7.1 Frame Bursting

802.11e also introduces batch transmission of multiple frames, which is called frame bursting. Instead of sending one frame at a time, a station can request, in an RTS packet for example, for a maximum transmission opportunity (TXOP) duration and send multiple frames back-to-back within that time. The receiver can then acknowledge all the frames together instead of acknowledging them one by one. Voice or gaming has high priority, but is allowed to use small TXOP. In contrast, data has low priority but can access long TXOP to send many frames in burst. Figure 3 shows how EDCF TXOP works.

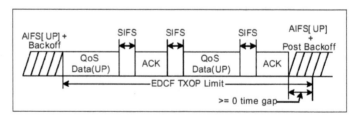

Fig. 3. Frame bursting with TXOP.

7.2 Direct Link

Another new feature of 802.11e is to allow stations to send packets directly to another station within the same BSS without going through the BS. Figure 4 illustrates this feature. This will further reduce the latency for some delay-sensitive communication.

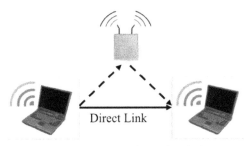

Fig. 4. The direct link feature in 802.11e.

8. IEEE 802.11n-2009

The data rate of 54 Mbps achieved in 1999 with 802.11b served the application demands well at that time. Since then, demand for more bandwidth continued to soar, fueled by more devices being connected to the LAN, growing popularity of on-demand video streaming, and so on. In late 2000, it became apparent that new amendments must come forth to boost the speed and capacity of wireless LANs. In fact, some vendors already started to release products with some proprietary enhancements to meet the market demand. It was time to standardize these developments.

In 2009, IEEE introduced 802.11n [802-11n] to significantly increase the data rates of wireless LAN from the previous versions of 802.11a/b/g. The target was to break the 100 Mbps mark and go well beyond that. To achieve this major WiFi data rate boost in history, 802.11n introduced five important techniques, which promised a massive maximum data rate of 600 Mbps.

First, it employed the MIMO technology in WiFi history for the first time to capitalize on the potential of multiple independent streams existing over the same frequency. Second, it reduced the *coding overhead* by employing a 5/6 coding rate which is much lower than the previous minimum allowed rate of ¾ used in 802.11a. Third, the *guard interval* and *inter-frame spacing* were reduced to increase the number of OFDM sub-carriers that can carry data. Fourth, it allowed a new physical layer mechanism, called *channel bonding*, to combine two consecutive 20-MHz channels into a single 40-MHz channel, without any guard intervals between them. Fifth, it promoted reduction of MAC layer overhead by packing multiple frames inside a single frame, called *frame aggregation*, thereby amortizing the frame header bits over many data bits.

8.1 MIMO: Number of Antennas and Number of Streams

Recall from our earlier discussion on MIMO that multiple antennas at the transmitter and the receiver help transmit data in multiple simultaneous *independent* streams. Clearly, the larger the number of these independent streams, the higher the effective data rates. However, the maximum number of independent streams are limited by the minimum number of antennas available at the transmitter or receiver. The individual implementations may further reduce the number of independent streams limiting the total capacity of the MIMO infrastructure.

The convention $n \times m{:}k$ is used to describe the number of antennas and streams in a given system, where n is the number of available antennas in the transmitter and m is the number of antennas in the receiver. The number of streams is represented by k, where k is less than or equal to $\min(n,m)$. For example, $4 \times 2{:}2$ means that the transmitter has four antennas, but the receiver has only two. Only two parallel streams are used to transmit the data in this configuration.

802.11n allows a maximum of $4 \times 4{:}4$ configurations. When there are more receive antennas than the number of streams, then the throughput can be maximized by selecting the best subset of antennas. For example, with a $4 \times 3{:}2$ configuration, the best two receive antennas should be selected for processing the received data.

8.2 Reduction of Coding Overhead

Recall that the coding rate directly affects the net data rates. Given the raw bit rate, C_raw, of a channel, which shows the number of coded bits transmitted per second, the net data rate, C_data, is derived as C_data = C_raw × C_rate, where C_rate is the fraction representing the coding rate.

Previously, ¾ was the minimum coding rate allowed in any 802.11 amendments. 802.11n allows a coding rate as low as 5/6, which directly increases net data rate by a factor of $(5/6)/(3/4) = 11\%$. Of course, this 11% increase in data rate is entirely due to the reduction of the coding rate. As we will see in the remaining section, the ultimate data rate boost will be much more than this, once all other techniques are employed simultaneously.

8.3 Reduction of Guard Interval and Increase of Data Sub-carriers

Guard intervals are time-domain guards used between every two consecutive data symbol transmissions to overcome the effect of multipath or inter-symbol interference at the receiver. A direct consequence of guard interval is the reduction of data rates, as no data can be transmitted during the guard interval. Clearly, data rate can be increased by using shorter guard intervals between two data symbols. Figure 5 illustrates how, by reducing the guard interval slightly, six data symbols can be transmitted instead of five during the same time interval. 802.11n therefore targets reduction of guard interval as another means for increasing the net data rate.

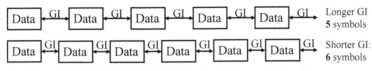

Fig. 5. Increasing data rate by decreasing guard interval.

The rule of thumb is to allow a guard interval four times the multi-path delay spread. Initial 802.11a design assumed 200 ns delay spread, which led to 800 ns guard interval. For 3200 ns data blocks, this incurs a overhead of 800/(800 + 3200) = 20%. Detailed experimental analysis revealed that most indoor environments have a delay spread in the range of 50–75 ns. 802.11n therefore selects a guard interval of 400 ns, which is more than four times this value. Now the guard interval-related overhead is reduced from 20% to only 11%.

With reduced guard intervals in time domain, the number of sub-carriers used for guard is reduced from six to four on either side of the data subcarrier block. This directly increases the data sub-carriers from 48 to 52 for the legacy 20-MHz channels, which will directly increase the number of data bits per OFDM symbol and hence the ultimate net data rates.

Finally, 802.11n supports power-saving option for MIMO, which allows putting antennas to sleep selectively. This way the power saving is extended beyond stations, i.e., the antenna power saving can be activated even when the station is awake.

8.4 Reduction of Inter-frame Spacing

At the MAC layer, frame spacing is needed to improve medium access control, but it directly reduces net data rates. It is therefore possible to improve data rates by reducing the inter-frame spacing. 802.11n reduces the inter-frame spacing (SIFS) from 10 microsecond to 2 microsecond.

8.5 Channel Bonding

The Channel Bonding option in 802.11n refers to the mechanism to combine two 20-MHz channels into a single 40-MHz channel. The bonding therefore directly doubles the bandwidth of the channel. This means that the data rate will be at least double the legacy 20-MHz channel. This will allow very high-speed links, which may be required to watch a very high-resolution video, such as 4K, over the wireless LAN. We will see shortly that the channel bonding actually increases data rate by more than a factor of two!

In the frequency-domain, guard bands are used between two consecutive channels to reduce interference. One way to reduce this guard overhead is to use wider channels, so that the guard overhead is amortized over a larger bandwidth. This bonded 40-MHz channel can be operated with 108 data subcarriers plus six pilots. Note that, without channel bonding, only 52 data subcarriers can be used with four pilots. Therefore, combining two channels with channel bonding actually provides more than double the performance (108 data subcarriers instead of 52 + 52 = 104 subcarriers)!

Example 3

Compared to 802.11a/g, 802.11n has higher coding rate, wider channel bandwidth, lower coding overhead, and reduced guard interval. On top of this, 802.11n uses MIMO multiplexing to further boost the data rate. Given that 802.11a/g has a maximum data rate of 54 Mbps, can you estimate the maximum data rate for 802.11n that uses 4 MIMO streams (assume 64 QAM for both of them, i.e., there is no improvement in modulation)?

Solution

Let us first estimate the maximum data rate of 802.11n by adding up the various factors that increase data rates compared to 802.11a/g.

54 Mbps is achieved with ¾ coding for 3200 Data + 800 GI for a/g, which basically uses a single stream (no MIMO).

802.11n has the following improvement factors:

      Streaming factor = 4

      Coding factor = (5/6)/(3/4) = ~ 1.11

      OFDM subcarrier (plus wider bandwidth) factor = (108/48) = 2.25

      Guard interval factor = (3200 + 800)/(3200 + 400) = ~ 1.11

      Total improvement factor = 4 × 1.11 × 2.25 × 1.11 = ~ **11.1**

Improved data rate for 802.11n = 4 × [(5/6)/(3/4)] × (108/48) × [(3200 + 800)/(3200 + 400)] × 54 = **600 Mbps**

We can also arrive at the 600 Mbps rate by directly calculating the data rate for 802.11n from its various parameters as follows: Minimum guard interval: 400 ns (data interval = 3200 ns) → 3.6 μs symbol interval

Maximum modulation: 64 QAM

Maximum coding: 5/6

Maximum # of MIMO streams: 4 (4 × 4 MIMO)

Maximum # of data carriers: 108 (for 40 MHz bonded channels)

Coded bits per symbol = $\log_2 64$ ✗ #-of-data-subcarriers = 6 × 108 = 648

Data bits per symbol = coding rate × 648 = 5/6 × 648 = 540

Symbol rate = 1/symbol-interval = 1/3.6 Msps

Data rate (single MIMO stream) = symbol rate × data bits per symbol = 1/3.6 × 540 Mbps = 150 Mbps

Data rate with 4 streams = 4 × **150 = 600 Mbps**

Available data rates for 802.11n for a single stream is shown in Table 4. These data rates will increase linearly with increasing number of streams. For

Table 4. Modulation, coding, and data rates for 802.11n: Single stream.

MCS index	Modulation type	Coding rate	Data rate (Mbit/s)			
			20 MHz channel		40 MHz channel	
			800 ns GI	400 ns GI	800 ns GI	400 ns GI
0	BPSK	1/2	6.5	7.2	13.5	15
1	QPSK	1/2	13	14.4	27	30
2	QPSK	3/4	19.5	21.7	40.5	45
3	16-QAM	1/2	26	28.9	54	60
4	16-QAM	3/4	39	43.3	81	90
5	64-QAM	2/3	52	57.8	108	120
6	64-QAM	3/4	58.5	65	121.5	135
7	64-QAM	5/6	65	72.2	135	150

example, with three streams, the data rate for MCS 3 would be $3 \times 26 = 78$ Mbps for 20 MHz channel with 800 ns symbol interval.

8.6 MAC Header Overhead Reduction using Frame Aggregation

Each layer receives a service data unit (SDU) as its input from the upper layer, and then packs it up into a protocol data unit (PDU) as its output to communicate with the corresponding layer at the other end. Each MAC PDU has a header and a payload. The header bits are considered overhead, which reduces the net data rate for the payload. This overhead can be large for small payloads. For example, when someone is typing, using a remote terminal, each typed character forms a TCP segment, which is transmitted in a single MAC PDU.

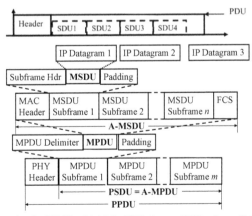

Fig. 6. Frame aggregation in 802.11n: Multiple SDUs in one PDU, where all SDUs must have the same transmitter and receiver address (*top*), and illustration from IP layer (*bottom*).

Frame aggregation is proposed in 802.11n to amortize the frame header overhead over a large payload by combining multiple short payloads into a single one. This process is shown in Fig. 6. Obviously, this is possible when many such small payloads are generated for the same destination within short intervals. For example, for someone typing fast, the consecutive characters are generated within milliseconds, which provides an opportunity to exercise the frame aggregation option without delaying the data noticeably.

8.7 802.11n Channel State Information

High Throughput Control (HTC) is a new field added to 802.11n frames (*see* Fig. 7). A key information carried in this field is the channel state information (CSI). In general, CSI refers to information regarding the channel properties of a communication link between the transmitter antenna and the receiver antenna. This information helps understand how scattering, fading, etc., may affect the channel. CSI can help both ends of the link to take actions which optimize the channel capacity.

For the receiver, it can usually derive the CSI from the pilots embedded in the transmission, but the transmitter cannot learn the CSI directly, unless the receiver communicates this information back to the transmitter. The CSI field can be used by the 802.11n client stations to send this information to the AP, and vice versa.

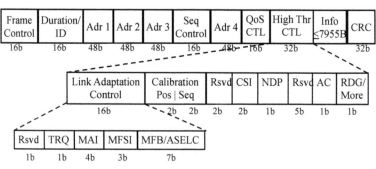

Fig. 7. 802.11n MAC frame and the CSI field.

9. IEEE 802.11ac

The race for higher data rates continues. While the goal with 802.11n was to break the 100 Mbps mark, 802.11ac aims to hit the Gbps mark. To achieve this incredible rate at the existing 5 GHz ISM band, 802.11ac basically continues to tighten the 802.11n parameters to squeeze more bits out of the same spectrum. These include more aggressive channel bonding, modulation, spatial streaming, and piloting. A further notable enhancement in 802.11ac [802-11ac] is to enable multi-user MIMO (MU-MIMO), which allows it to benefit from the MIMO technology introduced in 802.11n even when user equipment do not support multiple antennas. We will first examine the parameter updates for data rate increase followed by the discussion on MU-MIMO.

9.1 Data Rate Increase

Several parameters have been updated in 802.11ac to boost the data rate significantly. First, 802.11ac supports 80 MHz and 160 MHz channels, which is a significant jump from the 20 MHz and 40 MHz channels used in its predecessor 802.11n. Second, it allows 256-QAM modulation, which yields an $8/6 = 1.33x$ throughput increase over the previous maximum of 64-QAM. Third, it supports eight spatial streams for MIMO, which is a two-fold increase from 802.11n. Finally, it proposes to use a smaller number of pilots to increase the number of data subcarriers and ultimately boost the data rates. Table 5 shows the combination of data and pilot subcarriers for different channel bandwidths, while the available data rates for a single stream 802.11ac are summarized in Table 6. Note that 802.11ac continues to use the same subcarrier spacing of 312.5 kHz as used in 802.11a/g/n.

Table 5. Data and pilot subcarriers for in 802.11ac.

Bandwidth	# of Data Subcarriers	# of Pilot Subcarriers
20 MHz	52	4
40 MHz	108	6
80 MHz	234	8
160 MHz	468	16

Table 6. Modulation, coding, and data rates for 802.11ac: Single stream.

MCS index	Modulation type	Coding rate	20 MHz channel		40 MHz channel		80 MHz channels		160 MHz channels	
			800 ns GI	400 ns GI	800 ns GI	400 ns GI	800 ns GI	400 ns GI	800 ns GI	400 ns GI
0	BPSK	1/2	6.5	7.2	13.5	15	29.3	32.5	58.5	65
1	QPSK	1/2	13	14.4	27	30	58.5	65	117	130
2	QPSK	3/4	19.5	21.7	40.5	45	87.8	97.5	175.5	195
3	16-QAM	1/2	26	28.9	54	60	117	130	234	260
4	16-QAM	3/4	39	43.3	81	90	175.5	195	351	390
5	64-QAM	2/3	52	57.8	108	120	234	260	468	520
6	64-QAM	3/4	58.5	65	121.5	135	263.3	292.5	526.5	585
7	64-QAM	5/6	65	72.2	135	150	292.5	325	585	650
8	256-QAM	3/4	78	86.7	162	180	351	390	702	780
9	256-QAM	5/6	N/A	N/A	180	200	390	433.3	780	866.7

Example 4

Calculate the maximum achievable data rate for an 802.11ac mobile client with a *single antenna*.

Solution

Single antenna $\rightarrow$ only 1 stream possible (even if the AP has many antennas)

Minimum guard interval: 400 ns (data interval = 3200 ns) $\rightarrow$ 3.6 μs symbol interval

Maximum modulation: 256 QAM

Maximum coding: 5/6

Maximum # of data carriers: 468 (for 160 MHz bonded channels)

Coded bits per symbol = $\log_2 256$ ✗ #-of-data-subcarriers = $8 \times 468 = 3744$

Data bits per symbol = coding rate $\times 3744 = 5/6 \times 3744 = 3120$

Symbol rate = 1/symbol-interval = 1/3.6 Msps

Data rate (single MIMO stream) = symbol rate $\times$ data bits per symbol = 1/3.6 $\times$ 3120 Mbps = 866.67 Mbps

---

Example 5

An 802.11ac mobile client fitted with two antennas is connected to a wireless LAN via an 802.11ac access point equipped with four antennas. Calculate the maximum achievable data rate for the mobile client.

Solution

Max. # of streams = min(2,4) = 2

Max. data rate with single stream (from previous example) = 866.67 Mbps

Therefore, max. data rate with 2 streams = 2×866.67 Mbps = 1.733 Gbps

---

Example 6

What is the maximum achievable data rate in 802.11ac?

Solution

802.11ac allows a maximum of eight MIMO streams

Maximum achievable with single stream = **866.67** Mbps

Maximum achievable data rate of 802.11ac = $8 \times 866.67 =$ **6.9** Gbps

---

9.2 *MU-MIMO*

MU-MIMO extends the concept of MIMO over multiple users. In MU-MIMO, the user equipment does not have to have multiple antennas on it to benefit from MIMO. Antennas at different user equipment can be combined seamlessly and transparently to form a MIMO system as illustrated in Fig. 8. The users do not even have to know that their antennas are being used

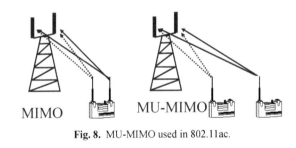

Fig. 8. MU-MIMO used in 802.11ac.

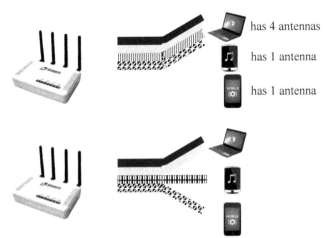

Fig. 9. The top figure illustrates the conventional case where all MIMO streams are consumed by a single multi-antenna device. The bottom figure shows that with MU MIMO, multiple client devices can share the MIMO streams generated by the transmitter, which enables even single-antenna devices to take part in the MIMO transmission.

in a MIMO system. Figure 9 further illustrates the utility of MU-MIMO with flexible sharing of streams among client devices with different antenna capabilities.

10. 802.11ax-2020

Up until now, 802.11 evolution was purely driven by pushing the data rates and throughput. From the humble 2 Mbps in 1997 with 802.11 legacy, we have reached to ~ 7 Gbps in 2013 with 802.1111ac, which is an amazing increase of 3500X in just 16 years!

Unfortunately, WiFi is being deployed so densely, especially in urban areas, that we cannot really use all that speed due to congestion, collisions, and interference from neighbouring installations. A new amendment was in order that could work efficiently in dense deployments and also support the new type of short message communications between IoT machines.

802.11ax [802-11ax, 802-11ax-TUT] is therefore more about efficiency for such new environments than pushing the data rates. As a matter of fact, 802.11ax provides only a modest data rate increase of 37% against its predecessor 802.11ac; whereas 1802.11ac increased data rate by 10X compared to 802.11n. The new developments and the ensuing data rates are explained in this chapter.

10.1 Parameters of 802.11ax

While some WiFi parameters remain unchanged, 802.11ax does introduce some changes for the others. These are discussed below.

Band: 802.11ax supports both 2.4 GHz and 5 GHz bands.

Coding Rate: There is no change for the coding rate; 5/6 remains the maximum allowed coding rate.

Channel Width: There is also no change for the allowed channel width, i.e., 40 MHz and 160 MHz remain the maximum for 2.4 GHz and 5 GHz bands, respectively.

MIMO Streams: Like its predecessor, 802.11ax maintains the maximum number of MIMO streams to eight only.

Modulation: 802.11ax supports an increased modulation rate of up to 1024 QAM.

Symbol Interval: 802.11ax uses increased symbol intervals to address longer delay spread in challenging outdoor environments. Symbol data interval is increased to 12.8 μs (vs. 3.2 μs in 11a/g/n/ac) while the guard interval is also increased to 0.8 μs, 1.6 μs, or 3.2 μs (3 options).

OFDM Subcarrier: Subcarrier spacing is reduced to 78.125 kHz (vs. 312.5 kHz in 11a/g/n/ac), which yields a total number of subcarriers as follows: 256 for 20 MHz, 512 for 40 MHz, 1024 for 80 MHz, and 2048 for 160 MHz, which includes two new types of subcarriers, DC and null subcarriers, in addition to the conventional data, pilot, and guard subcarriers used in previous WiFi versions. The number of data carriers available are as follows: 234 for 20 MHz, 468 for 40 MHz, 980 for 80 MHz, and 1960 for 160 MHz.

802.11ax OFDM parameters along with the allowed modulation and coding combinations are summarised in Table 7 and the data rates are shown in Table 8.

Table 7. IEEE 802.11ax OFDM parameters.

Modulation	Coding	# of Data Subcarriers				Symbol Data Interval	Guard Interval		
		20 MHz	40 MHz	80 MHz	160 MHz		Short	Med	Long
BPSK	½								
QPSK	½, 3/4								
16QAM	½, 3/4	234	468	980	1960	12.8 μs	0.8 μs	1.6 μs	3.2 μs
64QAM	½, 2/3, 3/4								
256QAM	2/3, 5/6								
1024QAM	¾, 5/6								

Example 7

Calculate the maximum achievable data rate for 802.11ax OFDM

Solution

Minimum guard interval: 0.8 μs (data interval = 12.8 μs) → 13.6 μs symbol interval

Maximum modulation: 1024 QAM

Maximum coding: 5/6

Maximum # of MIMO streams: 8

Maximum # of OFDM data subcarriers: 1960 (for 160 MHz channels)

Coded bits per symbol = $\log_2 1024$ ✗ #data-subcarriers = $10 \times 1960 = 19600$

Data bits per symbol = coding rate $\times 19600 = 5/6 \times 19600 = 16333.33$

Symbol rate = 1/symbol-interval = 1/13.6 Msps

Data rate (single MIMO stream) = symbol rate × data bits per symbol = 1/13.6 × 5/6 × 19600 Mbps = 1.2 Gbps

Data rate with 8 streams = 8 × 1.2 = 9.6 Gbps

10.2 OFDMA

OFDMA, which stands for Orthogonal Frequency Division Multiple Access, has been used in cellular networks for many years. In WiFi networks, it is introduced for the first time as an option in 802.11ax to centrally allocate channel resources to each competing station, using fine-grained time and frequency resource units (RUs) just like cellular networks. In OFDMA, subcarriers are also called *tones*; thus each tone consists of a single subcarrier of 78.125 kHz bandwidth. The tones are then grouped into 6 different sizes of resource units (RUs): 26, 52, 106, 242, 484, or 996 tones. The smallest resource,

Table 8. IEEE 802.11ax OFDM data rates in Mbps: Single stream.

MCS Index	Modulation	Coding rate	20 MHz			40 MHz			80 MHz			160 MHz		
			0.8 µs GI	1.6 µs GI	3.2 µs GI	0.8 µs GI	1.6 µs GI	3.2 µs GI	0.8 µs GI	1.6 µs GI	3.2 µs GI	0.8 µs GI	1.6 µs GI	3.2 µs GI
0	BPSQ	1/2	8.6	8.1	7.3	17.2	16.3	14.6	36.0	34.0	30.6	72.1	68.1	61.3
1	QPSK	1/2	17.2	16.3	14.6	34.4	32.5	29.3	72.1	68.1	61.3	144.1	136.1	122.5
2	QPSK	3/4	25.8	24.4	21.9	51.6	48.8	43.9	108.1	102.1	91.9	216.2	204.2	183.8
3	16-QAM	1/2	34.4	32.5	29.3	68.8	65.0	58.5	144.1	136.1	122.5	288.2	272.2	245.0
4	16-QAM	3/4	51.6	48.8	43.9	103.2	97.5	87.8	216.2	204.2	183.8	432.4	408.3	367.5
5	64-QAM	2/3	68.8	65.0	58.5	137.6	130.0	117.0	288.2	272.2	245.0	576.5	544.4	490.0
6	64-QAM	3/4	77.4	73.1	65.8	154.9	146.3	131.6	324.3	306.3	275.6	648.5	612.5	551.3
7	64-QAM	5/6	86.0	81.3	73.1	172.1	162.5	146.3	360.3	340.3	306.3	720.6	680.6	612.5
8	256-QAM	3/4	103.2	97.5	87.8	206.5	195.0	175.5	432.4	408.3	367.5	864.7	816.7	735.0
9	256-QAM	5/6	114.7	108.3	97.5	229.4	216.7	195.0	480.4	453.7	408.3	960.8	907.4	816.7
10	1024-QAM	3/4	129.0	121.9	109.7	258.1	243.8	219.4	540.4	510.4	459.4	1080.9	1020.8	918.8
11	1024-QAM	5/6	143.4	135.4	121.9	286.8	270.8	243.8	600.5	567.1	510.4	1201.0	1134.3	1020.8

i.e., 26 tones, allocated to an OFDMA communication is approximately 2 MHz (26 × 78.125 kHz = 2031.25 kHz), while the largest RU has ~ 80 MHz (996 × 78.125 kHz = 77812.5 kHz). A station can have a maximum of two 996 tones allocated, which would occupy ~ 160 MHz of bandwidth.

Different RUs can be mixed together to achieve enhanced flexibility required in many practical deployments. For example, to allocate ~ 20 MHz to a station, the AP can either allocate a single 242-tone RU (242 subcarriers), or it can allocate 4 52-tone RUs plus a single 26-tone RU (=234 subcarriers) to the station. Table 9 shows the RU allocations for typical channel bandwidths expected in WiFi networks, where $^{+n}$ means 'plus n 26-tone RUs'. For example, to allocate ~ 20 MHz, the access point would allocate four 52-tone RUs plus one 26-tone, which results in a total of 4 × 52 + 26 = 234 subcarriers allocated to the station.

Example 8

A single antenna 802.11ax client receives a 26-tone RU allocation from the AP when trying to transmit a 147-byte data frame. What could be the minimum possible time required to transmit the frame?

Solution

Single antenna means single stream

Maximum data rate for single-stream 26-tone (1024-QAM@5/6, 0.8 µs GI) = 14.7 Mbps

Data frame length in bits: 147 × 8 bits

Minimum frame transmission time: (147 × 8)/14.7 µs = 80 µs

Table 9. IEEE 802.11ax resource units.

RU	20 MHz	40 MHz	80 MHz	160(80+80) MHz
26-tone	9	18	37	74
52-tone	4^{+1}	8^{+2}	16^{+5}	32^{+10}
106-tone	2^{+1}	4^{+2}	8^{+5}	16^{+10}
242-tone	1	2	4^{+1}	8^{+2}
484-tone	NA	1	2^{+1}	4^{+2}
996-tone	NA	NA	1	2

11. The Upcoming Amendment: 802.11be-2024

While the latest release, 802.11ax, is perfectly capable to meet the data rates and networking needs of current applications, IEEE continues to work on further advancing the technology to ensure that WiFi remains future-proof and scalable. The work for the next amendment therefore has already begun at IEEE under the task group, called 802.11be [802-11be, 802-11be-LOPEZ] Extremely High Throughput. 802.11be is expected to be released in 2024 supporting data rates in tens of Gbps along with several advanced features to make WiFi even more scalable.

11.1 Parameters and Data Rates

Data rates for 802.1be will be increased by enhancing several parameters in parallel. The most significant enhancement will be the doubling of the maximum allowable channel bandwidth from 160 MHz to 320 MHz. This will be achieved by allowing WiFi to access the unlicensed spectrum in the 6 GHz band for the first time. To increase the number of bits per symbol, 802.11be will further use 4096 QAM. Finally, it will take advantage of higher processor powers in future chips to allow for 16 MIMO streams, doubling the number of spatial streams from its predecessor. These planned improvements are summarized in Table 10.

Example 9
Calculate the maximum data rate of 802.11be.

Solution
Enhancements against 802.11ax:

Channel bandwidth factor: 320 MHz/160 MHz = 2

Modulation factor: 12 bits/symbol ($\log_2 1024 = 10$)/10 bits/symbol ($\log_2 4096 = 12$) = 1.2

MIMO factor = 16 streams/8 streams = 2

Therefore, 802.11be is expected to achieve a 4.8X ($2 \times 1.2 \times 2 = 4.8$) improvement against 802.11ax.

Given that 802.11ax has a maximum data rate of 9.6 Gbps, 802.11be is expected to achieve a maximum data rate of $4.8 \times 9.6 = 46.08$ Gbps.

Table 10. Comparison of 802.11be with previous amendments.

Parameter	802.11n	802.11ac	802.11ax	802.11be
Band	2.4/5 GHz	5 GHz	2.4/5 GHz	2.4/5/6 GHz
Max. Channel Bandwidth	40 MHz	160 MHz	160 MHz	320 MHz
Max Modulation	64QAM	256QAM	1024QAM	4096QAM
MIMO	4 streams	4 streams	8 streams	16 streams
Max. Data Rate	600 Mbps	6.9 Gbps	9.6 Gbps	46 Gbps

11.2 New Features

Besides directly increasing the data rate through enhancements in bandwidth, modulation, and MIMO, 802.11be plans to introduce several new features. Here we examine two interesting new features that have not been used in previous WiFi.

Multiband Communication: 802.11be will be standardized to operate over three distinct bands, 2.4 GHz, 5 GHz, and 6 GHz. The multiband communication refers to accessing all three bands simultaneously to increase the throughput or reliability as illustrated in Fig. 10.

Multi-AP Coordination: Two or more APs can coordinate to serve the local clients in a given area to improve the spectral efficiency and quality of experience for the users. Figure 11 illustrates one use case for such coordinated

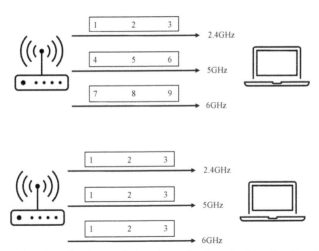

Fig. 10. Illustration of multiband transmissions: improving throughput by allocating data from one traffic stream to multiple bands (*top*); improving reliability by sending duplicate data from one traffic stream over multiple bands (*bottom*).

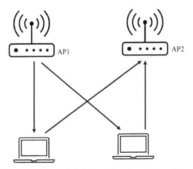

Fig. 11. Multi-AP coordination. Downlink is handled by AP1, while AP2 handles the uplink.

communications where AP1 serves the downlink traffic, while the uplink is handled by AP2.

12. Summary

1. 802.11a/g use OFDM with 64 subcarriers in 20 MHz, which includes 48 Data, 4 Pilot, 12 guard subcarriers.
2. 802.11e introduces four queues with different AIFS and TXOP durations and a QoS field in frames to provide enhanced support for QoS.
3. 802.11n adds MIMO, aggregation, dual band, and channel bonding.
4. IEEE 802.11ac supports multi-user MIMO with 80+80 MHz channels 256-QAM and eight streams to achieve 6.9 Gbps
5. IEEE 802.11ax supports 1024QAM, reduces OFDM carrier spacing to 78.125 kHz and increases data symbol interval to 12.8 μs. It introduced OFDMA.
6. 802.11be expects to increase data rates up to 46 Gbps by using 4096QAM, 320 MHz channel bandwidth, and 16 MIMO streams. It uses 6 GHz band along with 2.4 GHz and 5 GHz.

Multiple Choice Questions

Q1. A WLAN standard is employing a spread spectrum coding, which produces chips at a rate of 1 chip per two cycles (two Hz). It uses 8 chips to code a symbol. To achieve a data rate of 11 Mbps for a 22 MHz channel, what level/order of QAM is needed to modulate the signal?
(a) 16-QAM
(b) 32-QAM
(c) 64-QAM
(d) 128-QAM
(e) 256-QAM

Q2. The original OFDM for 802.11a-1999 has a 3200 ns data pulse, but the effective symbol interval is extended by another 800 ns guard interval (GI) to cater for multi-path delay spread. If a low-spread environment reduces the GI by half, what will be the increase in symbol rate?
(a) About 5%
(b) About 12%
(c) About 50%
(d) About 100%
(e) None of these

Q3. 802.11a-1999 supports 8 data rates, ranging from 6 Mbps to 54 Mbps. What data rate could be achieved if 256 QAM was used with a coding rate of 5/6?
(a) 80 Mbps
(b) 100 Mbps
(c) 125 Mbps
(d) 150 Mbps
(e) 175 Mbps

Q4. What could be the maximum achievable data rate for 802.11n if it were allowed to use a 128-QAM?
(a) 650 Mbps
(b) 700 Mbps
(c) 750 Mbps
(d) 1 Gbps
(e) 1.2 Gbps

Q5. Which of the following WiFi would allow multiple mobile clients to communicate with the access point simultaneously?
(a) 802.11a
(b) 802.11n
(c) 802.11ac
(d) 802.11ax
(e) None of these

Q6. With 8 antennas, it is possible for an 802.11ac access point to deliver eight times the throughput of a single-antenna access point irrespective of the number of antennas fitted to individual mobile clients associated with this access point.
(a) True
(b) False

Q7. Which WiFi has the lowest symbol rate?
(a) 802.11a
(b) 802.11b
(c) 802.11n
(d) 802.11ac
(e) 802.11ax

Q8. 802.11ax achieves higher data rates compared to its predecessor, 802.11ac, by further shortening the guard interval.
(a) True
(b) False

Q9. 802.11ax uses wider subcarriers compared to 802.11ac.
(a) True
(b) False

Q10. Which of the following WiFi flavors has more than two options for selecting its guard interval?
(a) 802.11a
(b) 802.11n
(c) 802.11ac
(d) 802.11ax
(e) None of these

References

[802-11a] (30 Dec. 1999). IEEE standard for telecommunications and information exchange between systems – LAN/MAN specific requirements – Part 11: Wireless medium access control (MAC) and physical layer (PHY) specifications: High speed physical layer in the 5 GHz band. pp. 1–102. *In: IEEE Std 802.11a-1999.* doi: 10.1109/IEEESTD.1999.90606.

[802-11b] (20 Jan. 2000). IEEE standard for information technology – telecommunications and information exchange between systems – local and metropolitan networks – specific requirements – Part 11: Wireless LAN medium access control (MAC) and physical layer (PHY) specifications: Higher speed physical layer (phy) extension in the 2.4 GHz band. pp. 1–96. *In: IEEE Std 802.11b-1999.* doi: 10.1109/IEEESTD.2000.90914.

[802-11g] (27 June 2003). IEEE standard for information technology – local and metropolitan area networks – specific requirements – Part 11: Wireless LAN medium access control (MAC) and physical layer (PHY) specifications: Further higher data rate extension in the 2.4 GHz band. pp. 1–104. *In: IEEE Std 802.11g-2003 (Amendment to IEEE Std 802.11, 1999 Edn. (Reaff 2003) as amended by IEEE Stds 802.11a-1999, 802.11b-1999, 802.11b-1999/Cor 1-2001, and 802.11d-2001).* doi: 10.1109/IEEESTD.2003.94282.

[802-11e] (11 Nov. 2005). IEEE standard for information technology – local and metropolitan area networks – Specific requirements – Part 11: Wireless LAN medium access control (MAC) and physical layer (PHY) specifications – amendment 8: Medium access control (MAC) quality of service enhancements. pp. 1–212. *In: IEEE Std 802.11e-2005 (Amendment to IEEE Std 802.11, 1999 Edition (Reaff 2003)).* doi: 10.1109/IEEESTD.2005.97890.

[802-11n] (29 Oct. 2009). IEEE standard for information technology – local and metropolitan area networks – specific requirements – Part 11: Wireless LAN medium access control (MAC) and physical layer (PHY) specifications amendment 5: Enhancements for higher throughput. pp. 1–565. *In: IEEE Std 802.11n-2009 (Amendment to IEEE Std 802.11-2007 as amended by IEEE Std 802.11k-2008, IEEE Std 802.11r-2008, IEEE Std 802.11y-2008, and IEEE Std 802.11w-2009).* doi: 10.1109/IEEESTD.2009.5307322.

[802-11ac] (18 Dec. 2013). IEEE standard for information technology – telecommunications and information exchange between systems. Local and metropolitan area networks – Specific requirements, Part 11: Wireless LAN medium access control (MAC) and physical layer (PHY) specifications – amendment 4: Enhancements for very high throughput for operation in bands below 6 GHz. pp. 1–425. *In: IEEE Std 802.11ac-2013 (Amendment to IEEE Std 802.11-2012, as amended by IEEE Std 802.11ae-2012, IEEE Std 802.11aa-2012, and IEEE Std 802.11ad-2012)*. doi: 10.1109/IEEESTD.2013.6687187

[802-11ax] (19 May 2021). IEEE standard for information technology – telecommunications and information exchange between systems local and metropolitan area networks – specific requirements Part 11: Wireless LAN medium access control (MAC) and physical layer (PHY) specifications amendment 1: Enhancements for high-efficiency WLAN. pp. 1–767. *In: IEEE Std 802.11ax-2021 (Amendment to IEEE Std 802.11-2020)*. doi:10.1109/IEEESTD.2021.9442429.

[802-11ax-TUT] (Firstquarter 2019). E. Khorov, A. Kiryanov, A. Lyakhov and G. Bianchi. A tutorial on IEEE 802.11ax high efficiency WLANs. pp. 197–216. *In: IEEE Communications Surveys & Tutorials*, vol. 21, no. 1. doi: 10.1109/COMST.2018.2871099.

[802-11be] (2020). E. Khorov, I. Levitsky and I. F. Akyildiz. Current status and directions of IEEE 802.11be, the Future Wi-Fi 7. pp. 88664–88688. *In: IEEE Access*, vol. 8. doi: 10.1109/ACCESS.2020.2993448.

[802-11be-LOPEZ] D. (September 2019). Lopez-Perez, A. Garcia-Rodriguez, L. Galati-Giordano, M. Kasslin and K. Doppler. IEEE 802.11be extremely high throughput: The next generation of Wi-Fi technology beyond 802.11ax. pp. 113–119. *In: IEEE Communications Magazine*, vol. 57, no. 9. doi:10.1109/MCOM.001.1900338.

6

Niche WiFi

WiFi has been primarily used as a networking technology for implementing wireless LAN in enterprise and residential domains, as well as connecting personal mobile devices, such as mobile phones, tablets, laptops, etc., to the Internet in homes, cafes, airports, and university campuses. The mainstream WiFi predominantly used the ISM bands 2.4 GHz and 5 GHz, with the new versions aiming to using the 6 GHz band. In addition to these mainstream WiFi, IEEE has also released several 802.11 amendments that target some niche applications. These niche WiFi standards operate outside the mainstream bands, both at the very low end of the spectrum, i.e., below 1 GHz, as well as at the very high end, i.e., 60 GHz (*see* Fig. 1). For example, 802.11af is targeting the exploitation of 700 MHz spectrum recently vacated by TV stations due to their digitization, 802.11ah using 900 MHz to connect emerging Internet of Things operating at low power, and 802.11ad/ay at 60 GHz to support multi-gigabit applications at short range. In this chapter, we shall examine the features and techniques used by these niche WiFi standards.

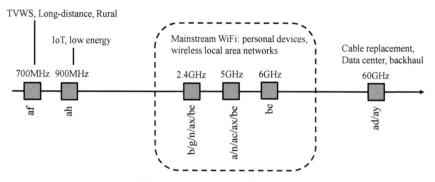

Fig. 1. Mainstream and niche WiFi.

1. 802.11af (a.k.a. White-Fi)

When TV transmissions switched from analog to digital, they vacated a lot of spectrum in the licensed TV bands. The vacated TV spectrum is called the White Space. IEEE 802.11af [802-11af], which is also referred to as White-Fi (or Super-Fi), was designed to effectively exploit the white space for data communications.

1.1 Over-the-Air Television Channels

When TV was invented, it was using analog signals for transmitting and distributing programs over the air. Analog television channels used the spectrum between 30 MHz to 30 GHz. The channels are called High Frequency (HF), Very High Frequency (VHF), Ultra High Frequency (UHF), and so on, as shown in Fig. 2. VHF is basically a *meter band* as the wave length is between 1 to 10 meters. UHF could be called *decimeter band* and so on.

Each channel uses 6 MHz in USA, 8 MHz in Europe, and 7 MHz in some other parts of the world. The numbering system for the VHF and UHF TV channels in USA is shown in Fig. 3. Channel 37 is used for radio astronomy, hence excluded from TV transmissions. Also, some channels between 88 and 174 are reserved for FM radio.

At least one channel is skipped between two analog stations in neighboring areas to avoid interference. For example, if a small town has channel 2, then it will not have channel 3. Basically, all channels cannot be allocated to all cities and towns.

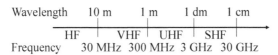

Fig. 2. TV spectrum and channels.

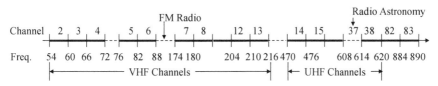

Fig. 3. TV VHF and UHF channel numbers in USA (Frequencies are in MHz).

1.2 Digital TV

Analog TV broadcast has been discontinued recently in most parts of the world. The world has switched to digital broadcast due to many advantages. The main mantra for digital TV is that all pictures are represented as pixels and each pixel is represented by some bits. Once the pictures are converted to bits, it becomes like computer communications. Encryption, multiplexing, mixing with different services and types of data, etc., all become very efficient, just like computer communication networks.

Another main advantage of going digital is that we no longer need to provide significant guard bands between occupied frequencies because interference from adjacent frequencies can be managed by sophisticated framing and error-control techniques. Digital transmission also uses compression at the transmitter and decompression at the receiver, which further reduces spectrum usage for digital TV. Consequently, multiple digital channels can be transmitted within 6 MHz, which was previously used to transmit only one analog TV program. This bandwidth efficiency has freed up a lot of TV spectrum, which is dubbed as Digital Dividend.

There was a particular demand for this 'new' spectrum in 700 MHz band for Cellular, Emergency Services, and ISM. Consequently, governments were able to raise significant revenue by auctioning a part of this spectrum to cellular companies while reserving the rest for unlicensed use. Similar practices were adopted in other countries.

Figure 4 illustrates the basic differences between 700 MHz and higher frequency. The wavelength in 700 MHz is much longer and hence it can travel far and penetrate many obstacles, such as buildings.

700 MHz has lower attenuation (1/7th to 1/9th of 1800/1900/2100 MHz), which means it requires lower transmission power and can provide longer mobile battery life for mobile devices. It can have larger cell radius, which means smaller number of towers. Such long-distance propagation is good for rural areas. It means providing cellular and wireless broadband services to rural areas becomes more cost effective and affordable. Because of these reasons, availability of new spectrum in 700 MHz is considered a very good opportunity for wireless networking.

Fig. 4. Differences between 700 MHz and higher frequency. A wave cycle in 700 MHz can travel much further than that in 2.4 GHz.

1.3 Spectral White Spaces

A lot of spectrum is allocated to certain services. However, the spectrum is not fully used at all locations and times. In general, white space is defined as any spectrum in a given area at a given time available for use on a non-interfering basis. The white space may be due to unallocated spectrum, allocated but underutilized, channels not used to avoid interferences in adjacent cells, or spectrum available in the TV band due to digital dividend.

Figure 5 shows that allocation does not mean it is always used. It is called 'white' because when spectrum usage is plotted in blue, the white gaps are the spectrum not used. Figure 6 shows a measurement conducted in Ottawa, Canada, for the UHF spectrum and we can see that most of it is white!

Well, it is clear that if we can use the white space, which appears to be in abundance, we can address some of the high demands for data. However, we must acknowledge that the white space that belongs to licensed spectrum poses interesting legal and policy issues, because the spectrum was already licensed for a massive amount of fee to certain companies. Under previous ruling, these companies actually had the right to say no to the use of their spectrum whether they used it or not. Effective use of white space therefore requires new rules to be in place first.

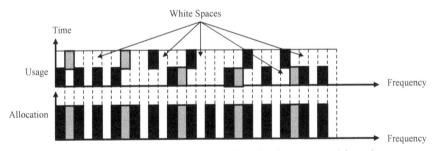

Fig. 5. Concept of spectral white space. Allocation does not mean it is used.

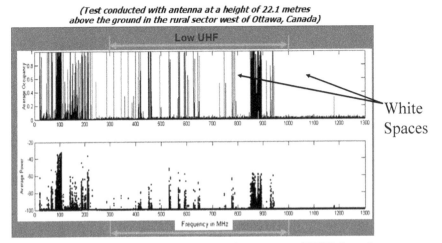

Fig. 6. Spectral usage example from real measurements [TVWS-Ottawa].

1.4 TVWS Databases

It has been agreed that the TVWS databases, a.k.a. geolocation database (GDB), which would hold information about which channel is free and when, would be operated by third parties. These databases do the following four things:

1. Get info from FCC database.
2. Register fixed TVWS devices and wireless microphones.
3. Synchronize databases with other companies.
4. Provide channel availability lists to TVWS devices.

Google was one of the third parties that acquired the license to operate such databases, but it does not provide this service anymore. Figure 7 shows an example of what was available in the city of St. Louis (zip code 63130) using the Google database. We can see that there were 17 channels available at the time of accessing the WS database.

1.5 802.11af Database Operation

Recall that in whitespace networking, the APs do not have a fixed set of channels, as the available spectrum is not known in advance, but rather must be found out dynamically. Therefore, to implement 802.11af, which uses white space, protocols and mechanism must be developed for the LAN to obtain the available channels from the white space databases, i.e., GDBs maintained by the third parties and distribute such channels within the 802.11af network.

To achieve these objectives, a local cache or database called Registered Location Secure Server (RLSS) is maintained which stores the channel availability information learned from the public GDBs. This provides faster access to channel information. The idea is that all large companies and ISPs will have their own RLSSs, just like DNS cache or local DNS server.

To facilitate communication with GDBs and RLSSs, two new protocols are defined. One is called PAWS [PAWS2015], defined by IETF, which is used by the GDBs and the APs. PAWS is a general protocol that can be used by 802.11, or any other network to query the spectrum in GDB. The other protocol is called Registered Location Query Protocol (RLQP), defined by IEEE, to be used *locally* between the AP and the stations. The use of these two protocols in accessing the white space databases is shown in Fig. 8. The APs are called Geolocation Database Dependent (GDD) *enabling*, as they can interface directly with GDB, while the stations are called GDD *dependent*, because they cannot talk to GDB directly.

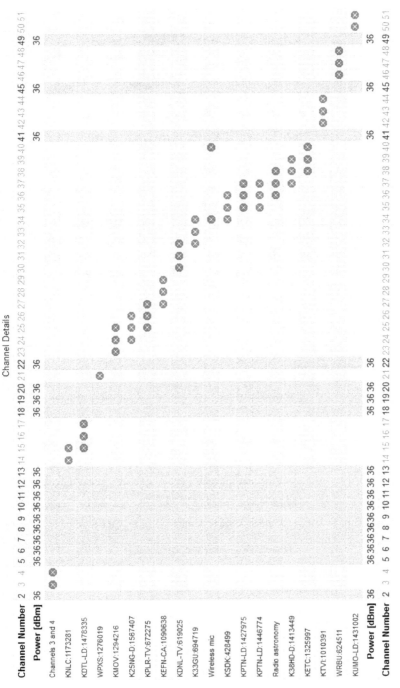

Fig. 7. White space available near University of Washington in St. Louis.

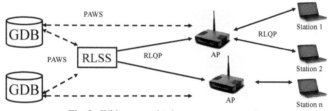

Fig. 8. White space database access protocols.

1.6 Registered Location Query Protocol (RLQP)

RLQP is a protocol for exchange of white space map (WSM), a.k.a. Channel Schedule Management (CSM), among RLSS, APs, and stations. An example of message exchanges for RLQP is shown in Fig. 9.

As we can see, AP uses CSM request and response to obtain the available channels first before these channels can be allocated internally within 802.11af network. Stations can be disassociated by the APs if necessary, such as if the channel becomes unavailable. Table 1 explains the meaning of all the other messages.

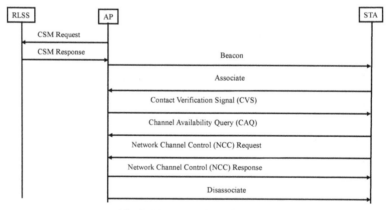

Fig. 9. Message exchange in RLQP.

Table 1. Description of RLQP messages.

Message	Description
CSM Request	APs asks other APs or RLSS about white space map
CSM Response	White space map is provided
CVS	APs supply white space map to their stations and confirm that stations are still associated
CAQ	Stations ask AP if they do not receive the map within a timeout interval
NCC Request	Sent by stations to AP requesting use of a channel. AP may forward to RLSS
NCC Response	Permission to transmit on requested channel

1.7 Protocol to Access White Space (PAWS)

There can be many different technologies, such as 802.11, 802.22, etc., that may work on white space and need access to WS databases. For a WS database provider, it would then be necessary to design interfaces for all these different networking technologies. Instead, IETF has decided to come up with a single protocol, called PAWS, which is independent of any network technologies as well as the underlying spectrums. All WS networks will have to implement PAWS to access the WS databases and all WS database providers will have to implement PAWS to support WS networking.

PAWS has the concept of master and slave. Master device is the one that can directly interface with the GDB using PAWS. A slave device is a WS networking device that cannot talk to a GDB directly, i.e., does not implement PAWS. Instead, the slave devices will need to communicate to a master device to find out spectrum availability. A device can act as both master as well as a slave. In Fig. 10, the RLSS is a master device. The AP and BS are acting as both masters, as they can talk directly with the GDB, as well as slaves, because they can get spectrum information from RLSS. Some 802.11af clients, not shown in the figure, that must get channel information from the AP are slaves only.

How does the WS networking devices find out the addresses or URLs of the GDBs in the first place? There are several ways that this can be implemented. One method could be to preconfigure devices with certificates to talk to some known database authority; another could be to use a listing server to list all national database servers.

Query is a pull-based method. In pull-based, the master sends a query to the database each time it needs to know the availability of white space. For a master device, it may also be possible to receive push notifications from the GDB. The master can register with the GDB for such push notifications

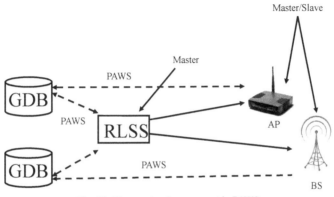

Fig. 10. The master-slave concept in PAWS.

using its certificate and the database can push channel availability information whenever some new spectrum is available or availability of an old channel changes. Finally, to ensure security, all PAWS messages are encrypted.

Some sample PAWS messages and how they are exchanged are shown in Fig. 11. As we can see, after the exchange of initialization messages, the registration messages are exchanged. It is only after the registration that the master device can send a query message to the database server and get a response. The master device can also send batch query to include requests for a set of slave devices located in different locations with different antenna heights, etc., and get a batch response.

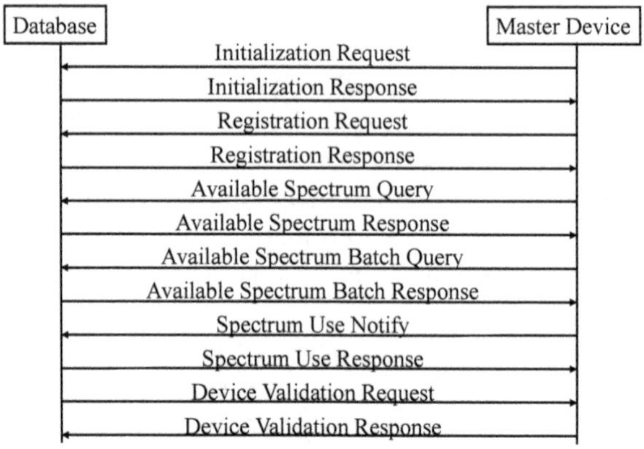

Fig. 11. Message exchange in PAWS.

1.8 802.11af Channels and Data Rates

In 802.11af, a Basic Channel Unit (BCU), a.k.a. W, is one TV channel. In the USA, this means that W = 6 MHz. While the use of single channel is default, channel bonding is optional. Two kinds of channel bonding are allowed. For contiguous channel bonding, 2W or 4W are allowed, i.e., 2 or 4 contiguous channels can be bonded together. This means that it is possible to have 12 MHz or 24 MHz contiguous spectrum as a single (bonded) channel.

802.11af uses a maximum of 256-QAM and 5/6 coding. It uses OFDM similar to 40 MHz in 802.11n, but down clocked by 7.5x. This gives a total of 144 subcarriers, of which 108 are data subcarriers. The down clocking increases the GI from 0.4 μs to 3 μs, and the data interval from 3.2 μs to 24 μs. As a result, the total symbol interval becomes 27 μs, which yields a maximum data rate of 26.67 Mbps for a single stream and single channel link. Note that 802.11af supports MIMO with up to 4 streams, which can further boost the data rate. Table 2 shows the various data rates supported by 802.11af for a 6 MHz channel.

Table 2. 802.11af data rates in Mbps: Single Stream, single unbonded (6 MHz) channel.

MCS	Modulation	Coding	Data Rate
0	BPSK	1/2	2
1	QPSK	1/2	4
2	QPSK	3/4	6
3	16-QAM	1/2	8
4	16-QAM	3/4	12
5	64-QAM	2/3	16
6	64-QAM	3/4	18
7	64-QAM	5/6	20
8	256-QAM	3/4	24
9	256-QAM	5/6	26.7

Example 1

What is the maximum possible data rate achievable with 802.11af?

Solution

Data rate with single stream and single 6 MHz channel = 26.67 Mbps

Data rate with 4 streams and 4 bonded channels = $4 \times 4 \times 426.7 = 426.7$ Mbps.

2. 802.11ah (a.k.a. HaLow)

IEEE 802.11ah [802-11ah] is also known as HaLow. The most interesting and historical change in 802.11ah compared to all previous versions is that this is the first time 802.11 is considering *wide area* networking, while all other versions were in the space of *local area* networking. Its ability to support *long range* is therefore the key difference.

To achieve the long range, spectrum is shifted from high frequency (above GHz, e.g., 2.4 GHz and 5 GHz) to sub-GHz. With the lower frequency come several key advantages for IOT. At sub-GHz, signals can travel longer distances with low power and penetrate buildings, roads, and other infrastructure, which will hide many future IOT devices. Also, there is less congestion at sub-GHz as all other WiFi devices work in either 2.4 GHz or 5 GHz. Also, the number of devices that use sub-GHz are not many.

With the lower frequency band, the achievable bit rate is low, but this is not an issue for IOT because the sensors do not need to stream high definition video, but only short messages. With low data rate, we can also reduce MAC overhead, which is important for short messages. In fact, with MIMO, the data rate can be from 150 kbps to 78 Mbps per spatial stream (up to 4 streams are allowed), which is sufficient for all types of IOT devices. Finally, the low data

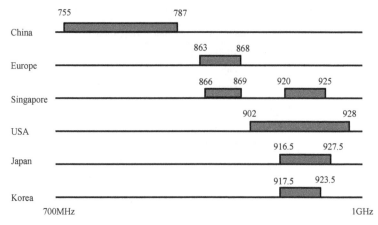

Fig. 12. Spectrum allocation for HaLow [802-11ah-bands].

rate allows APs to connect 4 times more devices than existing WiFi, which is very important for densely deployed IOT.

The spectrum allocation for HaLow is shown in Fig. 12. We can see that different countries have allocated slightly different spectrums, but they are close to 900 MHz, just below the GHz mark.

2.1 Sample Applications

As Fig. 13 shows, the main application of 802.11ah is the neighborhood area network (NAN). The NAN is used to read various meters from houses as well as some municipality-owned devices for monitoring smart cities, such as monitoring manholes, underground pipes, cables, etc. The 802.11ah APs, which could be deployed on the streetlight poles, are then connected via wire to the cloud, where all the data ends up for processing by the data analytic.

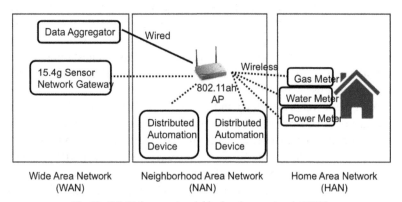

Fig. 13. 802.11ah supports neighborhood area network (NAN).

2.2 *802.11ah PHY*

802.11ah PHY is actually built on top of 802.11ac PHY, but down clocked by 10x. This means that each clock tick is now 10 times longer than 802.11ac, which will have a 10x effect on many aspects of the protocol.

First of all, 802.11ah will have 2/4/8/16 MHz channels in place of 20/40/80/160 MHz in 802.11ac, i.e., the channels are 10x smaller in MHz. However, the number of data subcarriers for 802.11ah channels are the same as the corresponding higher channel bandwidths in 802.11ac. For example, 20 MHz 11ac and 2 MHz 11ah, both have 52 data subcarriers plus 4 pilots, which means 1/10th inter-carrier spacing in 11ah. The shorter spacing may mean higher inter-carrier interference, but as we shall see shortly, this is well compensated by longer symbol lengths.

802.11ah has 10x longer symbols, which allow 10x delay spread. Therefore, longer multipath can be accommodated within the symbol, which avoid inter-symbol interference even in long-distance communication (longer distance means longer multipath).

In 802.11ah, all type of times, such as SIFS, are 10x longer. 802.11ah defines a new 1 MHz PHY with 24 data subcarriers. However, channel bonding is defined for two 1 MHz channels to form a single 2 MHz channel. All stations have to support both 1 MHz and 2 MHz channels.

With 1 MHz channel, 802.1ah defines a new modulation and coding scheme, MCS10, which is basically the previous MCS0, but after MCS0, every bit is transmitted twice. This allows 802.11ah to achieve long range as it can now sustain more errors. The rest of the MCS indices, i.e., the modulation and coding combinations remain the same, but the data rates are 10x lower from the corresponding MCS in 11ac. For example, for MCS 0 (BPSK with 1/2 coding), data rates for 11ac and 11ah, respectively are 6.5 Mbps and 0.65 Mbps for single stream 2/20 MHz channels using the longer GI option.

802.11ah supports 4 spatial streams instead of 8 in 802.11ac. 802.11ah supports beamforming to create sectors, which can be used by a single AP to read meters from houses in different sectors more efficiently.

Example 2

If we reduce the clock speed of 802.11ac by a factor of 10, what would be the new symbol rate (symbols/s)?

Solution

802.11ac has a symbol duration of 3.6 μs (for 400 ns GI).
New symbol duration with a 10x slower clock = 36 μs
New symbol rate = $1/(36 \times 10\text{-}6) = 27,777$ sym/s

Example 3

In USA, 902–928 MHz has been allocated for 802.11ah. How many different channels can be used if 16 MHz channel option is used?

Solution

902–928 MHz has a total bandwidth of 26 MHz. There is only one (non-overlapping) 16 MHz channel possible out of 26 MHz.

2.3 IEEE 802.11ah MAC

802.11ah MAC faces some new challenges due to IOT requirements and hence new features are introduced to address these challenges.

Large Number of Devices: IOT has to support many thousands of sensors in a very small area. For example, an 802.11ah AP in a NAN has to read many meters and city sensors. For this reason, it uses a Hierarchical Association Identifier (AID), which we will examine shortly.

Relays: Usually, in WiFi, we do not use relays, but 802.11ah allows 2-hop relays. This will allow reaching houses in the neighborhood which may be far from a light pole or obstructed by metal infrastructure, etc. The relays are installed by the network operators just like in cellular networks. These relays can be connected to the mains power supply for sustained operation.

Enhanced Power Savings: 802.11ah allows all devices, including the relays, to sleep for extended periods, even for days. For example, meters can sleep for days. Stations can negotiate target wake times (TWTs) to facilitate such sleeps, which will be explained later in more detail.

Speed Frame Exchange: When stations wake up, they will be allowed to transfer all backlogs at a high speed and then go back to sleep.

2.4 MAC Protocol Versions

Two MAC versions are allowed in 802.11ah. Protocol Version 0 (PV0) is the same as that for b/a/g/n/ac. It can be selected to operate in the old MAC, but many of the advantages of the new MAC cannot be achieved. However, there may be situations where long range, energy saving, etc., may not be very critical, such as connecting the entire indoor of an airport, which can be achieved using PV0. Protocol version 1 (PV1) is a totally new MAC not compatible with version 0. This version is optimized for IOT. There are four main advantages or new features for PV1 compared to PV0:

Short Headers: Headers have been shortened for short message transfers without incurring too much overhead.

Null Data Packets: It is possible to transmit directly over the PHY with zero-length packet.

Speed Frame Exchange: Many frames can be transmitted back-to-back when a station wakes up to reduce duty cycling.

Improved Channel Access: Time needed to access the channel is shortened. Therefore, sensors that have urgent data can quickly access the network and start transmitting their data.

Next, these features are explained in more detail.

2.5 Short MAC Header

Figure 14 compares 802.11ah headers with the legacy 802.11 header. We see that in 802.11ah, High Throughput Control, QoS, and Duration fields are removed. Then there is only one compulsory address field, instead of four and it is only 2-byte instead of 6-byte. The Seq. field indicates whether the 3rd or 4th address fields, which are both 6-byte, are used. In summary, it saves 12–26 bytes.

Example 4
A garbage bin sensor uses 802.11ah to upload 10 bytes of bin-fill-level data once every hour. Compared to legacy 802.11 (a/b/g/n/ac), the bin sensor has to upload how many less bytes per day?

Solution
Legacy 802.11 MAC header length = 36 bytes
Total bytes uploaded with legacy 802.11 = 24x(10 + 36) = 1104 bytes/day
Total bytes uploaded with 802.11ah = 24x(10 + 10) = 480 bytes/day (min)
1104–480 = 624 less bytes per day

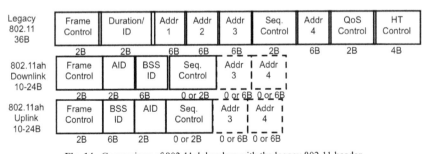

Fig. 14. Comparison of 802.11ah headers with the legacy 802.11 header.

2.6 Null Data Packet (NDP)

There are many 802.11 packet types, such as ACK, RTS, CTS, etc., which have no data. However, the MAC header consumes too much overhead for these packets. 802.11ah removes the entire MAC header for these packets and identifies these packets via the modulation and coding scheme at the PHY. That is, ACK, Block ACK, CTS, etc., all use different MCSs.

2.7 Speed Frame Exchange

Initiator sends a frame with response indicator set to 'long response'. Upon receiving this, the receiver can send data instead of ACK within a SIFS as shown in Fig. 15. Frames are sent until there are no more frames or the TXOP limit is reached. The ACK can be sent at the end of all frames as a block ACK. This can be done at both ends; hence, this scheme is also called 'Bidirectional Transmit (BDT)'.

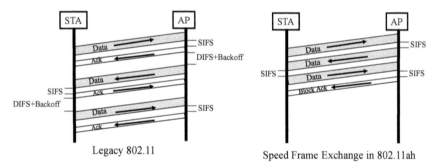

Legacy 802.11   Speed Frame Exchange in 802.11ah

Fig. 15. Speed frame exchange in 802.11ah.

2.8 Types of Stations

There are three types of stations in 802.11ah based on how they handle Traffic Indication Map (TIM) that is transmitted within the beacon.

The first of the three types of stations is high-traffic station, also known as TIM stations, which remains awake all the time to listen to all beacons and the TIMs therein to transmit accordingly within a restricted access window (RAW). The second type is a periodic low traffic station, also known as non-TIM station. This type of station does not listen to beacons but negotiates a transmission time allocated in a periodic RAW. The third type is very low-traffic station, also known as unscheduled station. It sends a poll to the AP and gets a transmission opportunity in response.

2.9 Page Segmentation

Announcing all buffered frames in each beacon would require a lot of bits in the TIM, especially for large 802.11ah networks connecting thousands of devices scattered in a neighborhood. To reduce the size of the beacon and better manage the contentions, AP divides the TIM stations in segments and announces only one segment at a time. Each station knows which segment it belongs to.

Every Delivery TIM (DTIM) interval, AP announces the TIM for the first segment as well as a *segment map* which indicates the segment that has pending data. All stations listen to the DTIM. Stations which belong to the first segment actually have to listen to the DTIMs only, because the rest of the beacons within the DTIM interval are for other segments. If a station is not in the first segment, then it will find out from the DTIM whether there is any data for its segment. If so, it will wake up for that beacon only and sleep for the rest of the time.

For example, if DTIM announces that there is data available only for the fourth segment, then a station which belongs to segment 2 will not wake up until the next DTIM beacon because it knows that there is no data available for it. Figure 16 illustrates the transmissions of DTIM and other beacons.

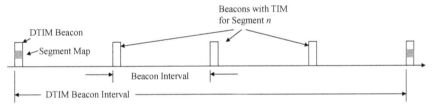

Fig. 16. Transmissions of DTIM and other beacons in 802.11ah.

2.10 Channel Access for TIM

Once a TIM station listens to the beacon for its segment, it can find out which slot it can use to contend for the channel. If the map indicates that the AP has buffered packets for a station, the station uses DCF (distributed coordination function) at that slot to send a PS-poll to get the packet. If a station has a packet to send, it listens to the map and uses DCF to send RTS at that slot.

Note that the TIM indicates which slots are allocated to which station, but the slots are not strictly reserved for individual stations; rather, a few stations are allocated the same slot. So, strictly speaking, there may be collision if two or more stations have data to send and they try to send at the same slot, which is allocated to all of them. However, a small number of stations per slot reduces the chances of collisions. Under low load, its performance approximates TDMA (time division multiple access).

2.11 Response Indication Deferral (RID)

Without any duration field in MAC header, 802.11ah can no longer use NAV (Network Allocation Vector). RID is a new virtual carrier sensing mechanism that replaces NAV. Like NAV, RID is also a time countdown mechanism, but it is different than NAV in many ways.

First, RID is done in PHY, while NAV was a MAC mechanism. As such, RID is set after the reception of PHY header, while NAV is set after the reception of a complete MAC frame. RID is set based on the 2-bit response indication field in the PHY header. With two bits, we have four combinations:

- Normal Response: RID ← SIFS + Ack or Block Ack time
- NDP Response: RID ← SIFS + NDP Frame time
- No Response (Broadcast frames): RID ← 0
- Long Response: RID ← SIFS + Longest transmission time (Used with Speed Frame Exchange)

Note that although ACK is a type of NDP, it is treated separately from the rest of the NDP packets.

2.12 Power Enhancements

Enhanced power savings in 802.11ah is achieved in three ways—page segmentation, RAW, and target wake time (TWT). As we have seen earlier, page segmentation allows the stations to sleep longer as they do not have to listen to every beacon to find out whether they have a packet buffered. Segmentation in 802.11ah is facilitated through a new hierarchical association identifier.

2.13 Hierarchical Association Identifier

As we have seen earlier, the whole network is divided into a few pages to better manage a large network. To appreciate the page segmentation procedure, we need to compare the TIM situation with that of legacy 802.11. 802.11 b/g/n/ac use 11-bit identifier, which allows 2007 stations to connect to the network. 2000+ bits are required in TIM to allocate slots to the stations.

802.11ah uses 16-bit identifier, which allows 8 times more stations to connect to the network. Therefore, the network is segmented into 8 pages of ~ 2^{11} stations each. Actually, 2007 stations are allowed per page to be strict. Currently only page 0 is allowed. Pages 1–7 are reserved.

Page 0 can serve a total of 2048 stations (a page has 11 bits). This is still too large. So, a page is divided into 32 blocks (a block has 5 bits), where each block can serve 64 stations. A block is then divided into 8 sub-blocks and each sub-block into 8 stations. This division is shown in Fig. 17.

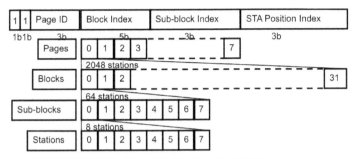

Fig. 17. Association identifier for 802.11ah.

2.14 Restricted Access Window

802.11ah has both contention period and contention-free period (CFP). However, due to large number stations possible under 802.11ah, it is not efficient or not possible to allocate one slot to one station. To make efficient use of the limited slots in CFP, the slots are allocated more intelligently, using a mechanism called Restricted Access Window (RAW) as follows:

RAW allows a set of slots to be restricted to a *group* of stations. Now this group of stations is not allowed to attempt to transmit in other slots, which reduces the probability of stations attempting to transmit in a given slot. In essence, RAW is using CFP for some level of contended access to the channel by allocating multiple stations to the same group of slots. However, by keeping the number of stations low, it can achieve good performance. Use of this mix, i.e., contention within contention-free period is a new concept brought forth in 802.11ah, but not seen in any legacy versions.

A TIM station can be allocated slots during RAW to transmit/receive packets. Access may be granted for transmission, reception, polling, etc., for one or a group of stations. A RAW schedule is transmitted at the beginning of RAW interval.

A station may have more data to transmit than possible in a given slot. Therefore, a station tells the AP that it has a frame to transmit using an Uplink Data Indication (UDI) bit in its frame. This helps the AP to find out which stations need access to slots in the next round, so it can calculate the slot allocations.

Dividing stations into groups and dividing time into slots for each group increases the efficiency under heavy load. At 100% load, RAW's utilization is close to 100%, whereas EDCF's performance drops to 0%—a classic phenomenon, known as *congestion collapse.*

In general, for heavy load, reservation is good and for light load, random access is better. This is similar to having traffic lights on the roads. If traffic is very light, no need to put a traffic light. Drivers can simply arrive at the intersection and use their judgment and resolve the priority (in some countries there are 4-way stops to help drivers sort out who should go first). However, in intersections where traffic is heavy, it is better to use some form of reservations and allocations, using traffic lights to restrict the movement of a group of cars at a time.

2.15 Other RAWs

We have seen how RAW works for allocating slots to TIM stations. The concept of RAW is extended to several other scenarios as follows:

Periodic RAW: Period and duration of PRAW are announced by AP for the periodic stations, i.e., stations that send data periodically.

Sounding RAW: This is used for sector sounding.

AP Power Management RAW: This is used by AP to announce the time when it will be sleeping.

Non-TIM RAW: Non-TIM stations do not have heavy traffic. If all slots are allocated to TIM stations, then non-TIM stations will starve. Therefore, this RAW is designed to protect transmission of non-TIM stations.

Triggering Frame RAW: This is used to allow stations to send power-save poll (PS-poll) frames, indicating their need to transmit.

2.16 Target Wake Time

For non-TIM stations, which may sleep for a very long time and send packets only once in a while, it is a waste for the AP to always include buffer information for this station in the beacon. Instead, such stations can specify a target wake up time (TWT), so that the AP does not bother about this station during the long sleep period.

Because the sleep period can be very long, it is difficult to exactly specify the duration in milliseconds or second accuracy. Instead the following three statistics are announced—the TWT, minimum wake duration, and the wake interval mantissa. AP sends an NDP to a station at its target wake up time containing buffering status. A station can then send a PS-poll and get its frames.

TWT also helps the AP to sleep. In the example shown in Fig. 18, the AP knows from the TWTs of the two stations that there will be no point in it to remain awake for the next long period when both of the stations will be sleeping. So, the AP goes to sleep and wakes up at the TWT of station 1 and starts sending beacons.

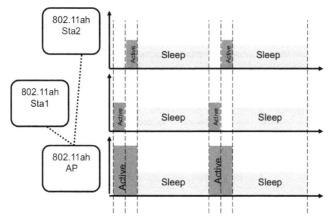

Fig. 18. Use of target wake time (TWT) in 802.11ah.

3. 802.11ad (a.k.a. WiGig)

IEEE 802.11ad [802-11ad] was released to make use of frequencies near 60 GHz.

3.1 60 GHz Frequency Allocation

To address the continuous demand for more spectrum, new spectrum in the higher frequency bands are being considered for release. The frequency band of 30–300 GHz, which corresponds to wavelengths 1–10 mm, is called millimeter wave band. This band is currently mostly unused and is a good candidate to explore for new spectrum allocation.

7–9 GHz in 57–66 GHz has been allocated worldwide as license-exempt ISM band, which is now called 60 GHz band. Since different countries have some incumbent allocations in this band, the exact allocations are slightly different as shown in Fig. 19. For example, the FCC in US as well as Korea have allocated 57–64 GHz, but Japan has allocated 59–64 GHz and EU 57–66 GHz. At least 59–64 appears to be globally available in this band. 2-GHz channels will be considered in this band.

There are many advantages for this band:

Large Bandwidth: It has a huge 7 GHz bandwidth. This means we can achieve 7 Gbps by using the very simple BPSK modulation. We can potentially reach hundreds of Gbps using more complex modulations, such as 256-QAM currently used in other bands.

Small Antenna Separation: 60 GHz has 5 mm wavelength. It means with lambda/4 separation rule, we can place antennas every 1.25 mm apart. This means large antenna arrays can be built in a single chip.

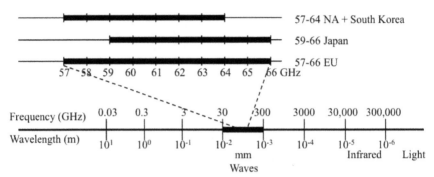

Fig. 19. Frequency allocation in 60 GHz band.

Easy Beamforming: With large antenna arrays, beams can be steered at any direction quickly and with high accuracy.

Low Interference: At 60 GHz, signals do not travel very far, cannot penetrate walls, and are very directional. This reduces interference with other 60 GHz communications happening nearby. This is particularly efficient in an urban environment where high density communications take place. For example, with existing 2.4 GHz and 5 GHz bands, WiFi signals from different apartments in the same building or even in adjacent buildings interfere with each other.

Directional Antennas: At 60 GHz, directional antennas and beamforming are used to focus the power to the receiver to achieve the communication range (power attenuates quickly at this high frequency). As a result, spatial reuse of the same spectrum is possible.

Inherent Security: Because the signal power attenuates very quickly, it is difficult to intercept 60 GHz communications from outside the room. This provides an inherent high-level of security.

Some of the advantages of 60 GHz band can also work as disadvantages:

High Attenuation: As explained earlier, 60 GHz has a very high attenuation. First, the attenuation increases with distance more rapidly than other bands due to the high frequency. Second, there is high oxygen absorption at this band. The combination causes significant loss of signal power at short distances. As a result, communication range is limited to only 10 meters and very high transmission power is needed. High antenna gain is required for omnidirectional communication.

Directional Deafness: Because all communication is highly directional, the conventional channel sensing-based MAC protocols, such as CSMA and RTS/CTS, do not work. Multicasting is also more challenging because two stations separated cannot receive the same beam at the same time; thus highly narrow beams are used.

Easily Blocked: 60 GHz signals are easily blocked by humans, dogs, or any moving object, making it necessary to deploy relays in dynamic environments.

3.2 60 GHz Applications

Despite some of the disadvantages, 60 GHz has received a lot of attention. We have almost run out of spectrum in the lower frequency bands and 60 GHz provides very high-speed connectivity in a license-exempt band. Some of the major applications envisaged for 60 GHz, mainly inspired by its extremely high-speed connectivity, are as follows:

Cable Replacement for TV: There are lots of cables behind a TV connecting the TV to the Blue-ray and DVD players, etc. These cables can be replaced with wireless if 60 GHz is used due to its multi-gigabit transmission capacity required for such high-resolution uncompressed video communication.

Interactive Gaming: Many interactive gaming uses uncompressed video, such as virtual reality-based games.

High Speed File Transfer: Very large files can be transmitted very quickly. For example, full-length movies can be copied to a mobile device within a few seconds.

Wireless Mesh Backhauls: A large number of small cells are expected to be deployed in the future to cope with the cellular traffic demand. These small cells require back-haul connectivity. 60 GHz can be used to provide highly directional wireless connectivity to provide back haul service to these cells.

3.3 802.11ad OFDM PHY and Data Rates

802.11ad was designed for single-stream SISO communications with ~ 2 GHz channels without any support for channel bonding. 802.11ad supports both single carrier and OFDM. With single carrier, data rates can vary between 385 Mbps up to 8.085 Gbps, depending on the modulation and coding. The OFDM, which is more complex to implement, is left as an optional feature for the vendors to implement.

For OFDM, 802.11ad uses a subcarrier spacing of 5.15626 MHz and a total channel bandwidth of 1830.47 MHz, which gives 355 subcarriers of which 336 are used as data subcarriers, 16 as pilots, and 3 as DC. The symbol interval is 336/1386 µs. The modulations supported include SQPSK (staggered QPSK), QPSK, 16-QAM, and 64-QAM. Note that SQPSK can transmit only 1 bit per symbol. 802.11ad supports 5 different coding rates as follows: 1/2, ¾, 5/8, and 13/16. OFDM data rates for 802.11ad are shown in Table 3.

Table 3. 802.11ad OFDM data rates in Mbps.

Modulation	Coding	Data Rate
SQPSK	1/2	693
SQPSK	5/8	866.25
QPSK	1/2	1386
QPSK	5/8	1732
QPSK	3/4	2079
16-QAM	1/2	2772
16-QAM	5/8	3465
16-QAM	3/4	4158
16-QAM	13/16	4504.5
64-QAM	5/8	5197.5
64-QAM	3/4	6237
64-QAM	13/16	6756.75

Example 5

What is the 802.11ad OFDM data rate for 64-QAM with 5/8 coding rate?

Solution

802.11ad symbol rate = 1386/336 Msym/s
# of data subcarriers = 336
Data rate = $\log_2(64) \times (5/8) \times 336 \times (1386/336) = 5197.5$ Mbps

3.4 MAC Challenges at 60 GHz

MAC for 60 GHz is a challenging problem for several reasons. The path loss at 60 GHz is significantly higher than conventional WiFi operating at much lower frequencies. For example, free space path loss is 28 dB higher than 2.4 GHz WLAN and 22 dB higher than 5 GHz WiFi. Therefore, 802.11ad stations must have high antenna gain to overcome the high path loss. This is achieved with directional antennas, which can focus the energy toward the receiver through beamforming. The narrower the beam, the higher the antenna gain.

Directional communication, however, complicates the MAC design. The AP can talk to a STA (station or client) only if their antenna beams point to each other. Similarly, two STAs must point their beams to each other before they can exchange data in the ad-hoc mode.

Therefore, the MAC has the responsibility to facilitate all stations to find the right beam directions at all times dynamically as they move and wish to communicate with different stations located at different locations. The problem becomes particularly challenging with many stations connecting to the network.

3.5 802.11ad MAC Topology

The MAC topology of an 802.11ad is shown in Fig. 20. In 802.11ad, BSS is called Personal BSS (PBSS), which defines the set of devices that wish to communicate with each other under the facilitation of a single control entity, called PBSS Central Point (PCP). Although PCP controls transmissions within the PBSS, much like the AP in previous 802.11 networks, we do not have a separate PCP device like we have an AP in other WiFi networks. Instead, PCP is a function that may be assumed by any of the member devices. For example, if the TV is the most powerful machine around, it could be configured as the PCP inside a room to control other devices working within the 802.11ad network.

Fig. 20. 802.11ad wireless local area network.

3.6 802.11ad Beacons

Beaconing is done slightly different than previous versions of 802.11. Beacons are transmitted every 'beacon interval' as shown in Fig. 21. All transmissions that happen within the beacon interval are called a 'super-frame'.

The super-frame starts with the beacon time (BT), within which only the PCP is allowed to transmit beacons. The rest of the beacon interval is divided into Association Beamforming Time (A-BFT), Announcement Time (AT), and Data Transfer Time (DTT).

As 802.11ad uses directional communication, the PCP needs to work out the direction for each of the member stations. This is figured out during A-BFT using antenna training.

During AT, the PCP polls every member to find out their requirements. For example, member A might request for a 5 ms time slot to communicate with member B. Members send these type of non-data responses to the PCP during AT.

All actual data exchanges happen during DTT. Data frames are transferred either in dedicated service period (SP), or by contention in a contention-based period (CBP). During AT, the SPs are finalized for different stations similar to CTS/RTS in previous 802.11 versions.

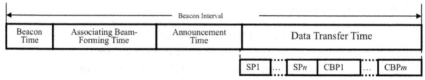

Fig. 21. IEEE 802.11ad beaconing.

Multiple transmissions may be scheduled on the same frequency at the same time if they do not interfere, which is called spatial frequency sharing (SFS). PCP asks stations to send results of 'Directional Channel Quality' during an overlapping SP. The stations measure the channel quality and send them to PCP. PCP then knows which station pairs can share the same slot. SFS will be examined in more detail later in the chapter.

When DT starts, a series of SPs are first completed followed by CBPs. During CBP, stations use the DCF function. All SP transmissions are controlled using the Hybrid Coordination Function (HCF), as defined in 802.11ac.

3.7 Beacon Transmission

Beacons transmitted by the PCP have to be received by all members. One way to achieve this would be to transmit a single beacon using an omnidirectional antenna, so it reaches all directions. However, the beacon signal in this case would be too weak, which may not be correctly received by all members. To ensure that beacons are received by everyone while still using directional transmission, the PCP must transmit the same beacon multiple times, one in every single direction.

Figure 22 shows that the PCP is transmitting the beacon in four directions (different colors represent different directions or antenna sectors), where the beam is 90 degree wide in each direction; so four antenna configurations cover 360 degree. Another PCP may decide to use narrower beams for beacon transmissions to achieve an extended range. In that case the beacon will have to be transmitted more than four times to cover 360 degrees.

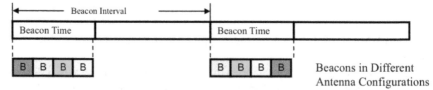

Fig. 22. Illustration of 802.11ad beacon transmission for a four sector antenna; the beam is repeated sequentially over the four sectors.

Example 6

An 802.11ad PCP has a multi-sector antenna with every sector covering 45 degrees. During a Beacon Time (BT), how many beacons the AP should transmit to ensure that stations located at any direction can receive the beacon successfully?

Solution

With 45-degree wide sectors, 360-degree coverage is achieved by 8 sectors. The AP therefore is required to send a total of 8 beacons (repeat the same beacons 8 times), one per sector.

3.8 Antenna Sector Search Options

As all communications in 802.11ad are directional, the communicating pair must work out their antenna configurations, i.e., they must align their sectors or select their best pair of sectors, before they send data packets to each other. There are two fundamental options available for selecting the best sector pairs—exhaustive search and semi-exhaustive search.

In the exhaustive search, every single pair is evaluated first to find the best performing pair. Exhaustive search is highly time and energy consuming as it has a complexity of $O(N1{\times}N2)$, where N1 and N2 represent the number of antenna sectors in the transmitter and receiver, respectively. For example, 1024 sector pairs will have to be evaluated if both stations have 32-sector antennas.

A more practical option, which is indeed adopted in 802.11ad, is semi-exhaustive. In semi-exhaustive approach, only the transmitter evaluates all of its antenna sectors while the receiver stays in the omni-directional mode. The pair of stations take turn to act as transmitter and receiver to complete the sector alignment procedure. This reduces the complexity to $O(N1{+}N2)$. For example, only a total of 64 sectors need to be evaluated if both stations have 32-sector antennas. Figure 23 illustrates the difference between exhaustive vs. semi-exhaustive approaches of antenna alignments.

Example 7

Two 802.11ad devices, STA1 and STA2, want to beamform. STA1 has 32 different antenna configurations (i.e., capable of steering the beam to 32 different directions). STA2 has only 4 beam directions. For exhaustive search, how many training frames are transmitted in total by these two devices before they discover the optimum beam pairs for communication?

Solution

Total combinations of antenna configurations between the two stations is $32{\times}4 = 128$. Therefore, 128 training frames are transmitted, one per specific pair of antenna configurations, before the best combination (pair) is finally selected.

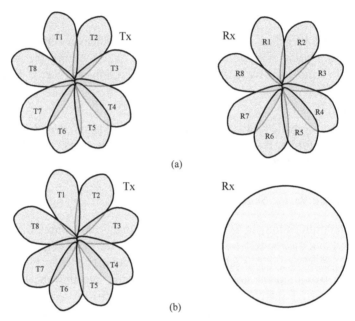

Fig. 23. Illustration of sector training approaches: (a) exhaustive search vs. (b) semi-exhaustive search.

Example 8
Two 802.11ad devices, STA1 and STA2, want to beamform. STA1 has 16 different antenna configurations (i.e., capable of steering the beam to 16 different directions). STA2 has only 4 beam directions. For Omni-direction Antenna approach, how many training frames are transmitted in total by these two devices before they discover the optimum beam pairs for communication?

Solution
STA1 first transmits 16 training frames while STA2 is listening in omnidirection. Then STA2 transmits 4 frames while STA2 is listening. Total frames transmitted: $16 + 4 = 20$.

3.9 802.11ad Beam Training

IEEE 802.11ad adopts the semi-exhaustive search approach in aligning the antenna beams between devices. The beam alignment is achieved in two stages. In the first stage, stations quickly figure out a rough direction and once the rough direction is established, they sweep that area more thoroughly for a more precise direction.

The first stage is called Sector Level Sweep (SLS), where the stations transmit in all sectors and identify the best sector for communication.

The purpose of SLS is to find a coarse beam quickly. Note that the entire 360 degree is divided into a few sectors, so this process can be quick. For example, if we have four sectors for devices, then the total number of sectors that need to be probed is only 8, given the semi-exhaustive search option.

Figure 24 illustrates the SLS process. First the initiator transmits a Sector Sweep (SS) frame over all sectors, sequentially identifying the sector ID in the frame. When the initiator is transmitting sector sweeping frames, the responder is receiving in the omni-directional mode. After the initiator completes frame transmissions over all of its sectors, the role of the two devices are reversed, i.e., the previous responder now becomes the initiator and vice versa. The initiator then acknowledges the sector number of the responder for which it received the highest signal strength. The responder acknowledges using an SS ACK frame and communicates the strongest sector number for the initiator. Now both devices know which sectors they need to use for communicating with each other.

After the SLS, the devices can choose to further refine the beam within the optimal sector by initiating an optional second stage, called Beam Refinement Procedure (BRP). Basically, in BRP, devices further search through their optimal sectors identified in SLS to find the optimal parameters in that sector to identify a narrower beam. Note that the narrower the beam, the stronger the signal strength is. Thus, BRP can be useful if devices need to achieve the highest possible data rates available in 802.11ad. SLS and BRP are illustrated in Fig. 25.

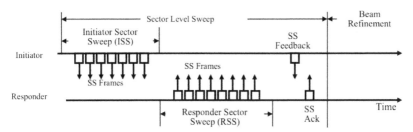

Fig. 24. Sector-level sweep for 802.11ad antenna alignment.

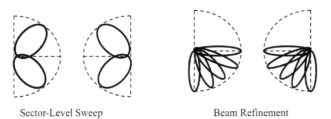

Sector-Level Sweep   Beam Refinement

Fig. 25. Beam refinement procedure during antenna alignment in 802.11ad.

3.10 PCP-STA Beam Training

Since wireless LAN clients or stations (STAs) mainly communicate with the access point (PCP in this case), let us first examine how the PCP-STA beams are formed.

The PCP-STA beamforming takes place during BT and A-BFT durations. During BT, the PCP transmits training frames on all its sectors while all STAs listen in omni-direction mode. Thus, during BT, the PCP acts as the initiator, while all stations serve as the responders. During A-BFT, roles of the PCP and the stations are reversed, the PCP becomes the responder listening in the omni-direction mode, while the stations assume the initiator role.

Given the existence of multiple stations in a wireless LAN, there has to be a protocol to ensure that only one station carries out its SLS at any given time while all other stations refrain from transmissions. This is achieved via slotting the entire A-BFT period into N finite time slots. Each STA selects a slot randomly and transmits its training frames on all its sectors during that slot. A consequence of random slot selection is that it may lead to collision if two or more stations select the same slot. In fact, the probability that a station will be able to randomly select one of the N slots without colliding is $(1-1/N)^{M-1}$, where M is total number of stations attempting SLS during the same beacon interval. Collisions would damage the frames and hence the stations involved in the collision will not receive any feedback from the PCP about the training outcome. The stations which do not receive any feedback, can try SLS again in the next beacon interval. Note that only SLS is completed during BT and A-BFT; BFP is optional and may only take place during DT.

Example 9
Table 4 shows the received signal strength (RSS) at the responder for each transmitted training frame from the beam training initiator during SLS. There are four sectors for both initiator and responder, and the number after the station letter denotes the sector number. For example, row 1 shows the frame transmitted by station A on its sector 1.
What is the optimum beam (sector) pair discovered after the SLS?

Solution
The sector that produces the strongest signal is selected as the best sector. For A, the strongest sector is 3 (–50 dBm). For B, sector 1 produces the strongest signal at A (–49 dBm). The optimum beam pair for (A,B) therefore is (3,1).

Table 4. SLS training details of Example 9.

Transmitted Sector	A.1	A.2	A.3	A.4	B.1	B.2	B.3	B.4
RSSS at Responder (dBm)	–70	–62	–50	–64	–49	–71	–75	–80

3.11 Spatial Frequency Sharing

An important advantage of highly directional beams is that 802.11ad can potentially schedule multiple transmissions on the same frequency at the same time if their paths do not intersect. This is achieved in 802.11ad as follows: First, the PCP asks every station to send their results of any STA-STA beamforming that they may have performed. PCP then has the complete knowledge of beam pairing among all the stations within its PBSS. PCP then can work out which station pairs can share the same time slot without interfering with each other.

Example 10

In a given PBSS, all stations have 12 antenna sectors with 30-degree transmission angle. Table 5 shows the beam pairs learned from beam training among 6 stations, A to F. For example, the first row of the Table shows that A would use its sector #1 to communicate with B while B would use its sector #7 to communicate with A. If a communication, SP1, between A and B has already been scheduled, can SP2, a new communication between E and F, be spatially shared with SP1, i.e., be allocated during the same time slots without interference?

Solution

No. During SP1, B will transmit on its beam #7, which is the same beam number found to be optimum to communicate with E (Row 3 in the Table). Therefore, B's transmissions to A during SP1 will affect E. SP2 therefore cannot be spatially shared with SP1 without interference.

Table 5. SLS training details of Example 10.

STA Pair	(A,B)	(A,E)	(B,E)	(B,F)	(C,D)	(A,F)	(E,F)
Sector Pair	(1,7)	(4,12)	(7,2)	(9,10)	(10,4)	(2,7)	(3,7)

4. 802.11ay

802.11ad only supports single stream and cannot bond channels (each channel is 2.16 GHz wide). As we have seen in Table 3, a maximum of ~ 7 Gbps can be achieved for a single channel and single stream with 802.11ad. To push the data rates in the 60 GHz band, IEEE is about to release an extension, named 802.11ay [802-11ay], which will support 4 streams and bond up to 4 channels, pushing the maximum achievable data rate in excess of 170 Gbps.

5. Summary

1. Mainstream WiFi operates in 2.4/5 GHz band: Hugely popular and used in many consumer products, e.g., mobile phones, tablets, laptops, and wireless LANs. The following WiFi standards are used for these mainstream applications: IEEE 802.11a/b/g/n/ac/ax (11n = WiFi4, 11ac = WiFi5, 11ax = WiFi6).

2. Niche WiFi introduced at both sub-GHz and 60 GHz.

3. Sub-GHz: 802.11af (700 MHz TV Whitespace: long-distance) and 802.11ah (900 MHz: IoT, sensors networks, home automation, large number of connections).

4. 60 GHz: 802.11ad (7 Gbps; already penetrated some niche products) and 802.11ay (upcoming; 270+Gbps cable replacement, backhaul, etc.).

5. Analog to digital conversion of TV channels has freed up spectrum in 700 MHz band, which is called white space.

6. 700 MHz allows long-distance communication, which is useful for rural areas.

7. IEEE 802.11af White-Fi can achieve up to 426.7 Mbps using OFDM, 4-stream MIMO, 256-QAM at a coding rate of 5/6.

8. PAWS is the protocol for accessing the white space databases.

9. 802.11ah uses 900 MHz band which can cover longer distances compared to other WiFi standards.

10. 802.11ah is 802.11ac down clocked by 10x. It uses OFDM with 1/2/4/8/16 MHz channels; symbols are longer which can handle longer multi-paths.

11. 802.11ah MAC achieves higher efficiency by reducing header, aggregating ACKs, using null data packets, and implementing speed frame exchange.

12. 802.11ah can achieve higher energy saving by allowing stations as well as the AP to sleep using Target Wakeup Time and Restricted Access Window mechanisms.

13. 60 GHz, a.k.a. mmWave, has large bandwidth, small antenna separation allows easy beamforming and gigabit speeds but short distance due to large attenuation.

14. In 60 GHz WiFi, multiple transmission can take place on the same frequency at the same time, which is known as Spatial Frequency Sharing.

Multiple Choice Questions

Q1. White-space networking refers to the use of
A. Very high frequency spectrum
B. Spectrum in the TV bands freed up due to digitization of TV broadcasts
C. Very high bandwidth channels
D. Spectrum currently used by radar

Q2. Compared to the mainstream WiFi, White-Fi can
A. Reach longer distances
B. Extend battery lifetime
C. Both A and B
D. None of the above

Q3. TVWS databases enables
A. Whitespace use without the radio having to sense and detect free TV channels
B. Checking the number of TV sets used in a given area
C. Checking the number of TV stations in a given area
D. Efficient implementation of cognitive radios that can sense spectrum

Q4. IEEE 802.11ay is expected to significantly increase data rate compared to 802.11ad by
A. Using only channel bonding
B. Using only MIMO
C. Using both MIMO and channel bonding
D. Using sharper beams

Q5. Which of the following is a standard for white space networking?
A. IEEE 802.11ad
B. IEEE 802.11ah
C. IEEE 802.11af
D. IEEE 802.11ac

Q6. PHY-A uses a guard interval (GI) of 400 ns to combat inter-symbol inter-reference. PHY-B is derived by down clocking PHY-A by a factor of 5. What is the length of GI used by PHY-B?
A. 2 millisecond
B. 2 nanosecond
C. 2 microsecond
D. 80 nanosecond

Q7. What is the maximum number of non-overlapping channels possible in an 82.11ah network deployed in the U.S.A.?

A. 13

B. 15

C. 20

D. 26

Q8. To cover all directions (360 degrees), an 802.11ad PCP employs two 10-sector antennas. Each antenna sector covers 18 degrees. During a Beacon Time (BT), how many beacons the AP should transmit?

A. 2

B. 10

C. 18

D. 20

Q9. If two 802.11ad devices have 64 antenna sectors each, searching the best sector pair using omnidirectional (semi-exhaustive) approach can reduce the total number of training frame transmissions, compared to the exhaustive search, by

A. 4096 transmissions

B. 64 transmissions

C. 3968 transmissions

D. 4032 transmissions

Q10. In IEEE 802.11ad, BRP precedes SLS.

A. True

B. False

References

[802-11af] (October 2013). A. B. Flores, R. E. Guerra, E. W. Knightly, P. Ecclesine and S. Pandey. IEEE 802.11af: A standard for TV white space spectrum sharing. pp. 92–100. *In: IEEE Communications Magazine*, vol. 51, no. 10. doi: 10.1109/MCOM.2013.6619571.

[802-11ah] (5 May 2017). IEEE standard for information technology – telecommunications and information exchange between systems – local and metropolitan area networks – specific requirements – Part 11: Wireless LAN medium access control (MAC) and physical layer (PHY) specifications amendment 2: Sub 1 GHz license exempt operation. pp. 1–594. *In: IEEE Std 802.11ah-2016 (Amendment to IEEE Std 802.11-2016, as amended by IEEE Std 802.11ai-2016)*. doi: 10.1109/IEEESTD.2017.792036.

[802-11ah-bands] (2013). Weiping Sun, Munhwan Choi and Sunghyun Choi. IEEE 802.11ah: A long range 802.11 WLAN at Sub 1 GHz. *Journal of ICT Standardization*, 1: 1–25. doi: 10.13052/jicts2245-800X.125.

[802-11ad] (28 Dec. 2012). IEEE standard for information technology – telecommunications and information exchange between systems – local and metropolitan area networks – specific requirements-Part 11: Wireless LAN medium access control (MAC) and physical layer (PHY) specifications amendment 3: Enhancements for very high throughput in the 60 GHz band. pp. 1–628. *In: IEEE Std 802.11ad-2012 (Amendment to IEEE Std 802.11-2012, as amended by IEEE Std 802.11ae-2012 and IEEE Std 802.11aa-2012)*. doi: 10.1109/IEEESTD.2012.6392842.

[802-11ay] (Dec. 2017). Y. Ghasempour, C. R. C. M. da Silva, C. Cordeiro and E. W. Knightly. IEEE 802.11ay: Next-Generation 60 GHz Communication for 100 Gb/s Wi-Fi. pp. 186–192. *In: IEEE Communications Magazine*, vol. 55, no. 12. doi: 10.1109/MCOM.2017.1700393.

[TVWS-Ottawa] (20 October 2021). C. Stevenson, *et al*. Tutorial on the P802.22.2 PAR for: Recommended Practice for the Installation and Deployment of IEEE 802.22 Systems. https://grouper.ieee.org/groups/802/802_tutorials/06-July/Rec-Practice_802.22_Tutorial.ppt.

[PAWS2015] V. Chen et al. Protocol to Access White Space (PAWS) Databases. *IETF RFC* 7545.

Part IV
Cellular Networks

7
Cellular Networks

WiFi can provide high speed connectivity at low cost, but its coverage is limited to the home or office building. In contrast, cellular networks are designed to provide wide area coverage to both static and mobile users. Cellular network is the oldest communications network technology, which has now gone through several generations of evolution. In this chapter, we shall first learn the fundamental concepts of cellular networks before examining the advancements brought forth by each generation.

1. Beginning of Cellular Networks

Back in 1968, AT&T Bell Labs submitted a plan [Rappaport 2002] to FCC (Federal Communications Commission) that they could provide radio communication services to the entire nation with limited spectrum by dividing the spectrum into several frequency bands and then allocating them in hexagonal cells, as illustrated in Fig. 1. Using this pattern, no two adjacent cells would be using the same frequency band, making it possible to cover the entire nation with the limited frequency bands and still avoid interference.

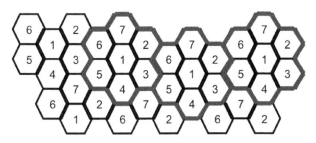

Fig. 1. Reusing 7 frequencies to cover a large area with hexagonal cells. No two adjacent cells use the same frequency.

2. Initial Deployments of Cellular Systems in the US

In 1981, FCC set aside a total of 40 MHz in 800 MHz spectrum for cellular licensing [FCC 800 MHz]. For the initial deployment of cellular systems in US, the whole country was divided into 734 areas, called Cellular Market Areas (CMAs). To avoid monopoly, it was decided that every CMA would be covered by two competing carriers, A and B (B stands for Bell, and A represents the *alternate*).

In the initial cellular deployments, uplink and downlink frequencies were different to avoid interference between transmit and receive antennas on the same device, i.e., Frequency Division Duplexing (FDD) was used. With FDD, a pair of frequencies therefore was needed to support a call. Each uplink/downlink channel was allocated 30 kHz for a total of 60 kHz for the duplex voice call [Rappaport 2002].

3. Cell Sites

Cellular systems need to install radio towers (base stations) to transmit and receive calls. Where should they put the tower? In the beginning, they were building towers from scratch in some places, which was very costly. Then the carriers wanted to use existing infrastructure, but due to wireless radiation as well as pollution of scenery, no one wanted cell towers near their house (There is this acronym NIMBY which means 'not in my backyard'). Finally, mobile operators started to install towers on rooftops of schools, churches, hotels, etc., as well on traffic lights, street lamps and so on for a fee to the owners. For non-profit organizations, such as schools and churches, that was a great way of making money. Even some fake trees were planted to hide base stations as shown in Fig. 2.

Fixed tower sites are good most of the time, but they cannot handle sudden increase in demand in a given area. To serve a sudden surge of people in a given area, such as a big circus or a fair, the operators brought in CoWs or Cell on Wheels. The whole base station is fitted on top of a van, so the van can go anywhere where there is a demand, as shown in Fig. 3.

Fig. 2. Base stations are erected on top of many different objects.

Fig. 3. Cell on Wheels.

4. Macro, Micro, Pico, Femto Cells

As the population started to grow, a single cell tower could not connect all users. So they started to deploy different sizes of cells to meet the demand. There are four different sizes of cell, Macro, Micro, Pico, and Femto, as shown in Fig. 4.

Macros are the normal original cells with roughly 1 km radius. Micro covers a neighborhood of less than 1 km. Pico cells are deployed in busy public areas, such as malls, airports, etc., covering an area of about 200 m. Finally, femto cells are installed inside a home or office, covering 10 m to

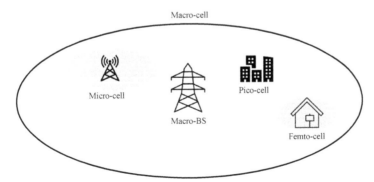

Fig. 4. Macro, Micro, Pico, and Femto cells.

provide good coverage (strong signals). Some operators provide femto cells for free to attract and retain customers.

5. Cell Geometry

Although there is no regular cell geometry in practice due to natural obstacles to radio propagations, a model is required for planning and evaluation purposes. A simple model would be for all cells to have identical geometry and tessellate perfectly to avoid any coverage gaps in the service area. Radio propagation models lead to circular cells, but unfortunately circles do not tessellate!

As shown in Fig. 5, three options for tessellation are considered: equilateral triangle, square, and regular hexagon. Hexagon has the largest area among the three; hence it is typically used for modeling cellular networks.

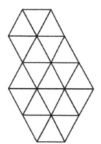 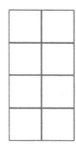 

Fig. 5. Tessellating cell shapes.

6. Frequency Reuse and Clustering

Earlier we discussed how AT&T proposed to cover the entire nation by simply reusing only 7 frequencies. Frequency reuse is possible because the signal from the cell tower gets weak at the cell border and hence loses its capacity to interfere with other communications happening far away from the current cell.

To keep the interference to a minimum, it's a common practice to avoid using the same frequency in adjacent cells. To achieve this, all cells in the service area are grouped into many clusters. The total spectrum is then divided into sub-bands that are distributed among the cells within a cluster in such a way that two adjacent cells do not share the same sub-band. Figure 6 shows examples of cluster sizes of 4, 7 and 19 where N represents the cluster size and the cluster borders are shown with solid black lines.

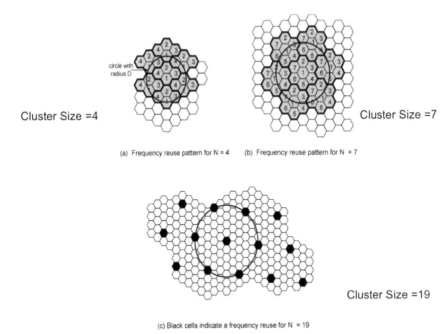

(a) Frequency reuse pattern for N = 4   (b) Frequency reuse pattern for N = 7

Cluster Size =4

Cluster Size =7

Cluster Size =19

(c) Black cells indicate a frequency reuse for N = 19

Fig. 6. Frequency reuse with different cluster sizes.

7. Characterizing Frequency Reuse

The next question we want to answer is: How much reuse, or what is the extent of frequency reuse, can we achieve for a given cluster size? Let us do the mathematics and find out. Let us assume the following notations, which are also illustrated in Fig. 7:

D = minimum distance between centers of cells that use the same band of frequencies (a.k.a. co-channel cells)

R = radius of a cell

d = distance between centers of adjacent cells. Note that d < 2R due to the overlapping of cells, which enables seamless handover from cell to cell for a mobile user. The exact value is $d = R\sqrt{3}$.

N = number of cells in repetitious pattern (**Cluster**), also called the *reuse factor*;[1] note that each cell in the cluster uses unique band of frequencies

For hexagonal cell pattern, N cannot assume arbitrary numbers. It is rather given by the following formula [Rappaport 2002]:

$N = I^2 + J^2 + (I \times J)$, where I, J = 0, 1, 2, 3, …

---
[1] Sometimes, the reuse factor is represented by the fraction 1/N.

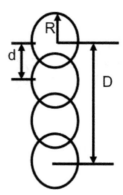

Fig. 7. Illustration of frequency reuse notations.

Therefore, the possible values of N are 1, 3, 4, 7, 9, 12, 13, 16, 19, 21, and so on. Note that some values are not possible. For example, we cannot have a cluster size of 5, because there are no combinations of integers, or I and J, that will provide 5.

Finally, D/R is called the **reuse ratio**. From hexagonal geometry, it can be shown that $D/R = \sqrt{3N}$, which means $D/d = \sqrt{N}$.

Example 1
What would be the minimum distance between the centers of two cells with the same band of frequencies if cell radius is 1 km and the reuse factor is 1/12?

Solution
R = 1 km, N = 12
$D/R = \sqrt{3N}$
D = $(3 \times 12)^{1/2}$ 1 km
= 6 km

---

8. Locating Co-channel Cells

Given a tessellated hexagonal cellular pattern of cluster size N, can we identify the co-channel cells? Yes, we can do this using the following simple rule.

First, obtain the I and J values that make up N. For example, for N = 4, we could have I = 0 and J = 2, or I = 2 and J = 0. Now, to identify the co-channel cell of a particular cell A, move I cells in any direction from the centre of A, turn 60° counter-clockwise and then move J cells. Note that there are 6 possible directions in a hexagonal cell, each separated by 60 degrees from their neighbors, as illustrated in Fig. 8. For N = 19, Fig. 9 illustrates the rule for finding the co-channel cells in a hexagonal cellular network.

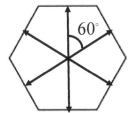

Fig. 8. Six directions of a hexagon.

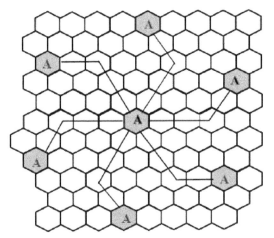

Fig. 9. Locating co-channel cells in hexagonal cellular network: N = 19 (I = 3, J = 2).

9. Spectrum Distribution within Cell Cluster

We have learned that the spectrum available to a cellular operator can only be reused outside the cluster. Next, we are going to examine how the spectrum is distributed among the cells within the cluster.

For simplicity, it is assumed that the total spectrum is divided equally among all cells in the cluster. Let T denote the total number of available channels, N the cluster size, and K the number of channels per cell. Then we have K = T/N.

Cells are usually divided into sectors where a frequency received in one sector may not be received in another. Channels allocated to a cell are then further sub-allocated to different sectors according to the load or demand in each sector. Sectorized allocation of channels can also help minimize inter-cell interference, which is a major issue arising from spatial reuse of spectrum in cellular networks. For example, the cellular network in Fig. 10 can reuse its spectrum with a cluster size of only 1, as two adjacent cell sectors do not use the same frequency.

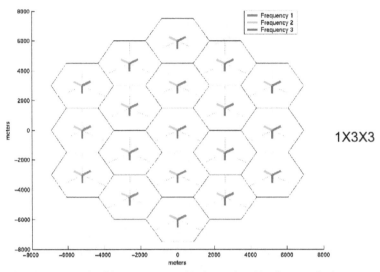

Fig. 10. An example of frequency reuse with cluster size of 1 using sectorized antenna.

10. Frequency Reuse Notation

To describe a given frequency reuse pattern for sectorized cells, we can use a notation like N×S×K, where N is the number of cells per cluster (cluster size), S is the number of sectors in a cell, and K is the number of frequency allocations per cell.

Figure 10 is an example of a 1×3×3 frequency reuse pattern where different colors represent different frequencies. Note that in this example, the same frequencies are used in every cell (N = 1). There are three sectors (S = 3) in each cell, as shown by the dotted line dividing each cell into three equal geographical regions. Three frequencies have been allocated per cell (K = 3).

In Fig. 10, each sector uses one frequency, but in real life, multiple frequencies may be allocated to a given sector (heavily populated), while other sectors may have just one or even no frequency allocated. Here K = 3 only means that three frequencies are allocated per cell, but how the frequencies are distributed between the sectors is not captured by the N×S×K notation.

Figure 11 shows 6 more examples of frequency reuse notations. In this figure, frequencies are shown as numbers within the sector. Again, frequencies are evenly distributed among the sectors. For example, if a cell is allocated 3 frequencies, each sector is allocated a different frequency.

Figure 11 also shows the location of a subscriber station (SS) within the cell and which tower it is likely to get the signal from, using an arrow from tower to the SS. There is an arrow from a tower if it is towards the sector with the same frequency. Let us examine how the SS receives signal from different towers by following the arrows in the figure for different patterns.

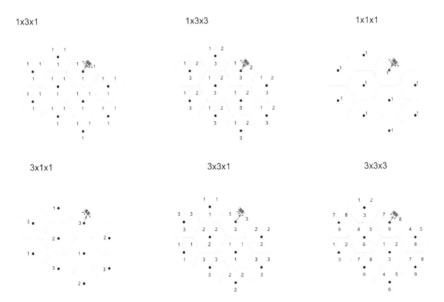

Fig. 11. Examples of 6 different frequency reuse patterns.

For the first pattern (1×3×1), there is only one frequency. Given the current location of the SS as shown in the figure, it can receive the same frequency signal from five other cells besides the current cell. Similarly, for 3×3×1, the SS is receiving frequency 2, so it will receive frequency 2 signal from 4 other cells. Fortunately, if the SS is located in the center of the cell, then the signal from the current cell tower will be the strongest, which will help it to connect to this tower without any confusion.

A problem arises when the SS is located close to the edge. If it receives the same frequency signals from both the cells, then the signal strengths may be close to each other, creating confusion. This leads to a so-called *ping-pong effect*, where the SS may switch between towers as it moves.

11. Fractional Frequency Reuse

The cell-edge problem can be addressed by a concept called *fractional frequency reuse,* which controls the signal strengths of the frequencies in a way such that some frequencies can only be heard in the center (not heard in the edge), while only one of them can be heard in the edge. This is shown in Fig. 12. We can see that with fractional frequency reuse concept, stations in the edge no more have the confusion because no border uses the same frequency.

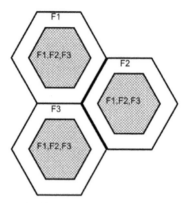

Fig. 12. Fractional frequency reuse.

12. Handoff

User mobility poses challenges for cellular networks. As the user starts to leave the coverage of a cell, the RSS becomes too weak. The user then must connect to a new BS with a stronger RSS to keep the connection to the network. Disconnecting from one and connecting to a new BS during an on-going session is called 'handoff', which is illustrated in Fig. 13.

To handoff successfully, the new BS must have available channels to support the on-going call; otherwise the call will be dropped. Dropping an ongoing call is worse than rejecting a new call. BSs therefore usually reserve some channels, called 'guard channels', exclusively for supporting handoff calls. Unfortunately, guard channels increase the blocking probability of new calls. The number of guard channels is left to the operators to optimize, i.e., it is not part of the standard.

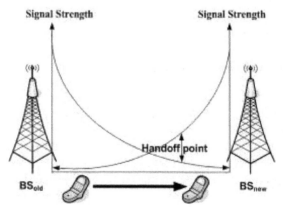

Fig. 13. The handoff process in cellular networks.

Example 2

A particular cellular system has the following characteristics: cluster size = 7, uniform cell size, user density = 100 users/sq. km, allocated frequency spectrum = 900–949 MHz, bit rate required per user = 10 kbps uplink and 10 kbps downlink, and modulation code rate = 1 bps/Hz. How many users per cell can be supported and what cell sizes are required?

Solution

49 MHz/7 = 7 MHz/cell; for symmetric bandwidth requirement in uplink/downlink, we have 3.5 MHz/uplink or downlink
10 kbps/user = 10 kHz/user (1 bps/Hz); users/cell = 3.5 MHz/10 kHz = 350
100 users/km²; to connect 350 users, the cell area has to be 350/100 = 3.5 km²
$\pi r^2 = 3.5$; r = 1.056 km

Example 3

A particular cellular system has the following characteristics: cluster size = 7, uniform cell size, user density = 100 users/sq. km, allocated frequency spectrum = 900–949 MHz, bit rate required per user = 10 kbps uplink and 10 kbps downlink, and modulation code rate = 1 bps/Hz. If the available spectrum for uplink/downlink is divided into 35 channels and TDMA is employed within each channel:

1. What is the bandwidth and data rate per channel?
2. How many time slots are needed in a TDMA frame to support the required number of users?
3. If the TDMA frame is 10 ms, how long is each user slot in the frame?
4. How many bits are transmitted in each time slot?

Solution

1. 49 MHz/7 = 7 MHz/cell; for symmetric bandwidth requirement in uplink/downlink, we have 3.5 MHz/uplink or downlink
   3.5 MHz/35 = 100 kHz/channel = 100 kbps per channel
2. With 10 kbps/user, we have 10 users/channel
3. 10 ms/10 = 1ms
4. 1 ms × 100 kbps = 100 b/slot

13. Cellular Telephony Generations

As we have discussed, cellular telephony started back in the 1980s. That was called the first generation of cellular networks. Since then, the technology continued to evolve to meet the demand in terms of number of people and devices that want to connect as well as the nature of traffic they want to send, such as voice vs. data.

In cellular word, the major changes are marked as a generation (G), which roughly lasts for 10 years. Any major change in between the 10 years is then marked as fraction of 10, such as 2.5G. Figure 14 shows the evolution of these generations. The figure shows how the evolution in terms of standardization happens in the US (or North America) and in Europe in the core technology, such as analog vs. digital, and in traffic types, such as voice vs. data.

The following are some of the key points to note:

Technology and Traffic: The first generation (1G) was analog and using FDMA to transmit only voice. It started digital transmission starting from 2G, but it was voice. Data could only be transmitted by converting it into voice signals using modems. Actual data transmission started from 2.5G and by now it is mostly data. Voice is now transmitted over data services.

Standardization in North America and Europe: North America and Europe continued using different standards until the end of 3G, when they converged to LTE (Long Term Evolution).

Table 1 shows more details of each generation. Most of the standards, such as GPRS, EDGE, WCDMA and so on are now almost extinct. One standard that survived and very much in use worldwide, including in North America, is GSM.

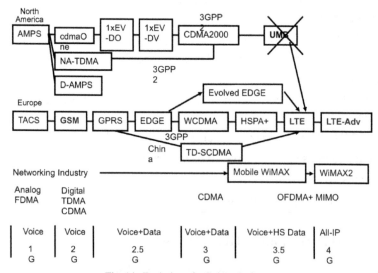

Fig. 14. Evolution of cellular telephony.

Table 1. Cellular generations.

Generation	Traffic	Standards
1G – 1980s	Analog Voice. FDMA	• AMPS: Advanced Mobile Phone System • TACS: Total Access Communications System
2G - 1990	Digital Voice. TDMA	• cdmaOne: Qualcomm. International Standard IS-95. • NA-TDMA • Digital AMPS (D-AMPS) • **GSM**: Global System for Mobile Communications
2.5G - 1995	Voice+data	• 1xEV-DO: Evolution Data Optimized • 1xEV-DV: Evolution Data and Voice • General Packet Radio Service (GPRS) • Enhanced Data Rate for GSM Evolution (EDGE)
3G - 2000	Voice+High-speed data. All CDMA	• CDMA2000: Qualcomm. International Standard IS-2000. • W-CDMA: Wideband CDMA • TD-SCDMA: Time Division Synchronous Code Division Multiple Access (Chinese 3G) • 384 kbps to 2 Mbps
3.5G	Voice+Higher-speed Data	• EDGE Evolution • High-Speed Packet Access (HSPA) • Evolved HSPA (HSPA+) • Ultra Mobile Broadband (UMB)
3.9G	High-speed data+VOIP. OFDMA	• WiMAX 16e (Worldwide Interoperability for Microwave Access) • Long Term Evolution (LTE)
4G - 2013	Very High-speed Data	• WiMAX 16m or WiMAX2 • LTE-Advanced • 100 Mbps – 1 Gbps
5G - 2020	Ultra High-speed data + Ultra Low Latency + Massive connectivity	IP-based

14. GSM

GSM stands for Global System for Mobile Communications. It is now implemented in most cell phones world-wide and most countries are using GSM. A phone without GSM support therefore would not do much.

The interesting thing is that GSM was designed back in 1990. Three decades on, it is still a very popular technology. GSM uses Time-Division Multiple Access (TDMA) instead of Frequency Division Multiple Access (FDMA) used in 1G. Figure 15 shows the difference between FDMA and TDMA. In FDMA, once a frequency was allocated to a user, no one else was allowed to use that frequency. This wasted a lot of system capacity. With TDMA, the same frequency could be used by multiple users shared

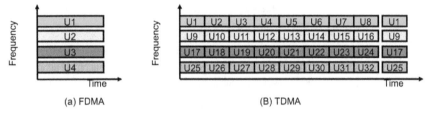

Fig. 15. Difference between FDMA and TDMA.

in time. This is possible because there are many silence periods in voice communication, which can used for other users.

GSM is defined for all major frequency bands used throughout the world. Specifically, it supports the four bands, 850/900/1800/1900 MHz; hence, called quad-band. Handsets, not supporting quad-band, may not operate in some countries.

The biggest invention of GSM was to separate the user from the handset. Prior to GSM, user subscription information was tied to the handset hardware. It made it difficult for people to change operators and share handsets. GSM introduced the concept of **Subscriber Identity Module (SIM)** card, which is a tiny plastic that contains user subscription information. Once inserted into a handset, that handset then is used by that user. With this concept, users can use the handset even when they switch subscriber.

15. GSM Cellular Architecture

GSM system has many components. The architecture of GSM is shown in Fig. 16. The phone handset is called a Mobile Equipment (ME), which has a SIM inside it. The SIM contains a micro-controller and storage. It contains authentication, encryption, and accounting info.

Using radio or wireless links, the ME connects to a radio tower, which is called a Base Transceiver Station (BTS). There is one BTS per cell.

A Base Station Controller (BSC) controls several BTSs via wired backbone. It allocates radio channels among BTSs, manages call handoff between BTSs, as well as controls handset power levels. MEs that are far from the tower will be asked to increase their power level, while the MEs closer to the tower will be instructed to use lower powers.

Many BSCs in turn are then connected to a Mobile Switching Center (MSC). Inside the switching center, which is usually a building housing many equipment, the MSC is connected to a range of other entities and functions, such as Home Location Register (HLR) and Visitor Location Register (VLR), Equipment Identify Register (EIR), Authentication Center (AuC), and so on.

The AuC stores the secret keys of all SIM cards. The EIR stores the unique hardware numbers for each handset. Each handset has an International

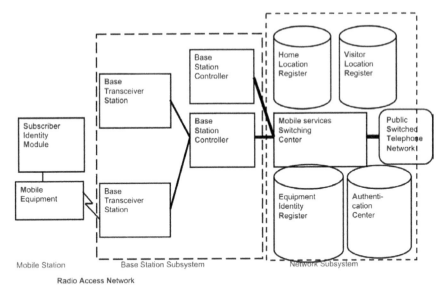

Fig. 16. GSM cellular architecture.

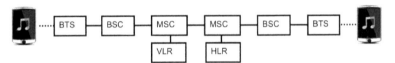

Fig. 17. End-to-end call in GSM.

Mobile Equipment Identity (IMEI) number. If a phone is stolen and reported as stolen, then that information, i.e., the IMEI of that phone, is stored there. So, if a call is made from that phone, the MSC can detect that it is originated from a stolen phone (the hardware number is transmitted along with the SIM) and take some action.

The MSC is also connected to the wired telephony network, which is called the Public Switched Telephone Network (PSTN), via a very high speed wired connection.

Figure 17 shows how the different functions that are invoked when an end-to-end call is established between a 'caller' and a 'callee'. The functions invoked at both ends are symmetric.

16. GSM Radio Link

GSM supports 24 traffic channels over each frequency. The number 24 is for historical reasons. In the beginning, 24 voice calls were carried over a T1 link. GSM therefore also started with combining 24 traffic channels into one multiframe.

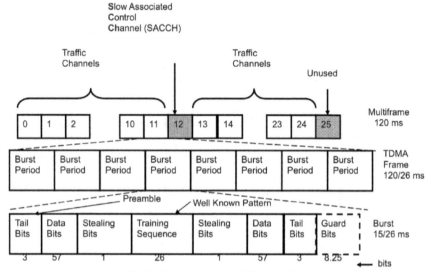

Fig. 18. Frame structure of GSM radio link.

This is achieved by dividing a frequency into a total of 26 equal-length time slots. The frame structure is shown in Fig. 18. The frame is called a 'superframe' because it supports many users. Basically, a superframe repeats every 120 ms. Therefore, each slot is 120/26 ms long. There are 24 slots used for carrying user traffic. Two out of 26 are not used for user traffic. One is used for control, and the other is unused.

Each 120/26 ms traffic slot is divided into 8 Burst Period. Therefore, each Burst Period is one-eighth of 120/26 or 15/26 ms long. One user is allocated to each burst period.

GSM has separate frequencies for uplink and downlink. 25 MHz between 890–915 MHz is used for uplink and 25 MHz between 935–960 MHz for downlink. The 25 MHz bandwidth is divided in frequency domain into 125 channels, each 200 kHz wide. Each of these 200 kHz channels is then divided in time domain into 24 traffic slots.

The control channel is usually called Slow Associated Control Channel (SACCH). It uses one traffic slot of 120/26 ms. If the control traffic requires more bandwidth than this, then it can steal some bandwidth from user slots as follows:

Note in Fig. 18, that each user burst has two bits reserved as 'stealing bits'. The control channel can set these bits to indicate to the receiving end that half of the user burst has been stolen and now carrier controls information instead of user data. Because voice is error-tolerant, occasional loss of bits can still be tolerated within limit.

Interestingly, the reverse use is also possible with control channels. If the control channel has no control information to carry, then some user traffic could be sent over it. But it has to be very short. This is how the short message service (SMS) concept was developed. Now SMS is so popular that carriers probably are dimensioning more control channels to make profit from it.

Each 200 kHz channel is ultimately used by 8 user slots. Each 200 kHz channel is modulated to 270.8 kbps data rate; that gives 270.8/8 = 33.85 kbps per user. After encryption and FEC, only 9.6 kbps per slot is given, i.e., if we send data over GSM, we can get 9.6 kbps data rate!

Voice, on the other hand, does not need high FEC. Therefore, voice can use a higher bit rate. It turns out that voice uses 16 kbps, which is a compressed version of the 64-kbps original voice. Note that original voice is 64 kbps because it is sampled at 8,000 samples per second and each sample is coded with 8 bits. The telephone system (PSTN) has a cutoff frequency at 4 kHz because human voice does not carry a very high frequency. Nyquist sampling theory says that we need sample at twice the frequency of the original analog signal to avoid loss of information. That's why voice signals are sampled at 8000 samples per second, which is twice the 4 kHz bandwidth.

This means that if you play music from a CD player over the phone, the quality of the music will be very poor at the other end as music contains some very high frequency components which will be filtered out by the telephone system.

17. LTE

LTE stands for Long Term Evolution. The whole world, Europe as well as North America, converges to the same cellular telephony technology starting with LTE. This is also the kick start for the fourth generation of telephony. 3GPP is now the single body that coordinates all standards for cellular telephony. Every year it releases new documents. LTE was released as 3GPP Release 8 in 2009.

LTE is the precursor for 4G. Technically, for a technology to be called 4G, it has to meet all the requirements specified in International Mobile Telecommunication (IMT) Advanced Requirements in ITU M.2134-2008. LTE did not meet every criterion in that document, so it is sometimes called pre-4G or 3.9G cellular technology. LTE was then later revised to LTE Advanced or LTE-A to meet all the 4G specifications.

LTE supports all different bands – 700/1500/1700/2100/2600 MHz, to satisfy spectrum allocations in different regions in the world as well as flexible bandwidth – 1.4/3/5/10/15/20 MHz, depending on the country [ASTELY 2009]. The bandwidth can be allocated very flexibly. It can be divided into many users during peak hours, or the whole network bandwidth can be allocated to a single user at off-peak time, if there are no other users competing. The maximum data rate possible in LTE can be very high.

LTE supports both Frequency Division Duplexing (FDD) and Time Division Duplexing (TDD). For FDD, *paired* spectrum allocation is required, which means that an equal amount of spectrum or frequencies have to be allocated for uplinks and downlinks. This suits well when both uplink and downlink have equal usage voice. In voice calls, a person speaks 50% of the time and listens 50% of the time. However, for data, downlink is used more heavily than uplink, as we tend to download more data than upload, although upload traffic is increasing rapidly due to pervasive availability of cameras and videos in mobile phones and use of social networks. TDD does not require paired allocation. It can be *unpaired* and can use the spectrum more flexibly for up and down use, which suits data very well.

LTE supports 4×4 MIMO as well as multi-user collaborative MIMO. It supports beamforming only in the downlink. When using 4×4 MIMO with 20 MHz, i.e., the full capacity, LTE can achieve 326 Mbps for downlink and 86 Mbps for uplink. For modulation, it supports OFDM with QPSK, 16 QAM, and 64 QAM. LTE supports OFDMA for the downlink.

18. LTE Frame Structure

LTE superframes are 10 ms long. This means superframes just repeat every 10 ms. Each superframe contains 10 1-ms subframes, as shown in Fig. 19. Each subframe has two 0.5 ms slots – one for downlink and the other for uplink. This allows a very quick turnaround time because a mobile handset can get an answer from the base station or vice versa within 0.5 ms.

How many OFDM symbols can be sent per 0.5 ms? This depends on the length of the cyclic prefix used for each symbol to address the multipath effect. Two types of cyclic prefixes are allowed. For small networks, cyclic prefix of 5.2 μs for the first symbol and 4.7 μs for others are used, which allows 7 symbols to be transmitted in a 0.5 ms slot. On the other hand, for larger networks, which have longer multipath, extended cyclic prefix of 16.7 μs is used, which allows only 6 symbols to be carried in a slot. These two types of cyclic prefixes are shown in Fig. 20.

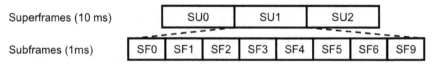

Fig. 19. LTE Superframe structure. Each superframe contains 10 1-ms subframes.

Normal Cyclic Prefix:5.2 us for 1st symbol, 4.7 us for others

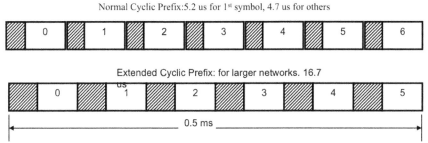

Extended Cyclic Prefix: for larger networks. 16.7 us

0.5 ms

Fig. 20. Two types of cyclic prefix.

19. LTE Resource Allocation

To transmit in the uplink or receive in the downlink, mobile handsets need to be allocated resources. Resources are defined by OFDM subcarriers (frequency) and slots (time). Each slot is 0.5 ms (equivalent to 6 or 7 symbols) and each subcarrier is 15 kHz.

With this definition of slots and subcarriers, a Physical Resource Block (PRB) is defined as a rectangle block of 12 subcarriers (180 kHz) over one time slot (0.5 ms) in the resource map, as shown in Fig. 21.

Given that each user has a downlink slot and an uplink slot in each subframe, the minimum allocation per subframe is 2 PRBs. However, these two PRBs do not have to be contiguous in the resource map but could be from anywhere. An example of two PRB allocations to a subframe, or a single user equipment (UE) is shown in Fig. 22.

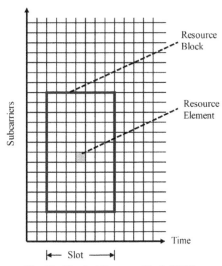

Fig. 21. Physical Resource Block (PRB).

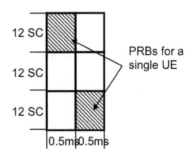

Fig. 22. An example of two PRB allocations to a subframe (single UE).

The allocation of the blocks changes every superframe, i.e., every 10 ms, unless for some persist scheduling, where the same resource blocks may be allocated over a long time (over several superframes).

Example 4

For *normal* cyclic prefix (CP), how many resource elements (REs) are there in 2 RBs?

Solution

With normal CP, we have 7 symbols per slot

Number of REs per RB = $12 \times 7 = 84$

Number of REs in 2 RB = $2 \times 84 = 168$

Example 5

What is the *peak data rate* of downlink LTE?

Solution

For peak data rate, we assume best conditions, i.e., 64 QAM (6 bits per symbol), short CP (7 symbols per 0.5 ms slot), and 20 MHz channel

Each symbol duration = 0.5 ms/7 = 71.4 μs

Number of RB for 20 MHz = 100

Number of subcarriers per RB = 12

Number of subcarriers for 20 MHz channel = $100 \times 12 = 1200$

Number of bits transmitted per symbol time = 6×1200 bits

Data rate = $(6 \times 1200$ bits)$/(71.4$ μs$) = 100.8$ Mbps (without MIMO)

---

20. Summary

1. In a cellular cluster of size N, the minimum distance between co-channel cells is $D = R\sqrt{3N}$, where R represents the cell radius.
2. With sectorized antenna, it is possible to have a cluster size of just 1, i.e., two adjacent cells can reuse the same spectrum.
3. 1G was analog voice with FDMA.
4. 2G was digital voice with TDMA. Most widely implemented 2G is GSM.
5. 3G was voice+data with CDMA.
6. LTE is the precursor of 4G. LTE uses a **super-frame** of 10 subframes of 1ms each. Each **subframe** has one 0.5 ms **slot** for uplink and downlink each. Each subcarrier in LTE is 15 kHz. 12 subcarriers (180 kHz) over 1 ms slot is used as a unit of resource in LTE.

Multiple Choice Questions

Q1. In a cellular deployment, assume that the distance between co-channel cells is required to be at least 6 km. What is the minimum cell radius allowed for the cluster size of 12?
(a) 3 km
(b) 2 km
(c) 1 km
(d) 500 m
(e) 200 m

Q2. A particular cellular system has the following characteristics: cluster size = 9, uniform cell size, user density = 100 users/sq. km, allocated frequency spectrum = 900–945 MHz, bit rate required per user = 10 kbps uplink and 10 kbps downlink, and the modulation code rate = 2 bps/Hz. What is the cell radius, approximately, assuming circular cells and FDMA/FDD?
(a) 1 km
(b) 2 km
(c) 0.5 km
(d) 712 m
(e) 792 m

Q3. A particular cellular system has the following characteristics: cluster size = 9, uniform cell size, user density = 100 users/sq. km, allocated frequency spectrum = 900–945 MHz, bit rate required per user = 10 kbps uplink and 10 kbps downlink, and the modulation code rate = 2 bps/Hz. If the available spectrum is divided into 100 channels and TDMA is employed within each channel, how many time slots are needed in a TDMA frame to fully utilize the channel bandwidth?

(a) 5

(b) 10

(c) 15

(d) 20

(e) 100

Q4. Which of the following cannot be a valid cluster size in cellular networks?

(a) 25

(b) 26

(c) 27

(d) 28

(e) 37

Q5. What would be the minimum distance between two co-channel cells if cell radius is 1 km and the reuse factor is one-third?

(a) 1 km

(b) 2 km

(c) 3 km

(d) 4 km

(e) 9 km

Q6. NxSxK notation defines the frequency distribution among sectors.

(a) True

(b) False

Q7. In fractional frequency re-use, more frequencies are available at the cell border than in the center.

(a) True

(b) False

Q8. The two dimensions of LTE resource allocation (resource block) includes:

(a) frequency and data rate

(b) frequency and time

(c) time and data rate

(d) frequency and cell size

(e) frequency and transmission power

Q9. In LTE, uplink and downlink slots are:
(a) 1 ms each
(b) 1 micro second each
(c) 500 micro second each
(d) 500 ms each
(e) 100 ms each

Q10. In LTE, the longer the Cyclic Prefix is, the smaller the number of symbols that can be transmitted within the 0.5 ms UL/DL slot.
(a) True
(b) False

References

[ASTELY 2009] D. Astely, E. Dahlman, A. Furuskär, Y. Jading, M. Lindström and S. Parkvall (April 2009). LTE: the evolution of mobile broadband. pp. 44–51. *In: IEEE Communications Magazine*, vol. 47, no. 4. doi: 10.1109/MCOM.2009.4907406.
[FCC 800 MHz] 800 MHz Cellular Service – FCC [accessed 22 October, 2001].
[Rappaport 2002] Theodore S. Rappaport (2002). *Wireless Communications: Principles and Practice*, Prentice Hall.

8
5G Networks

5G is the fifth and latest generation of cellular networks that had just started to roll out in 2019–2020. While the previous four generations mainly sought to improve the data rate and capacity of the cellular systems, 5G is designed to improve several other aspects of communications and connectivity beyond the data rates. This chapter discusses the new applications promised by 5G and the networking technologies behind them.

1. Key 5G Targets

5G promises to massively surpass 4G in the following three main categories:

1. **Data Rate:** While 4G offered the maximum data rate of 1 Gbps per user under ideal conditions, 5G promises 20 Gbps under the same conditions.

2. **Latency:** Radio contribution to latency between send and receive is an important metric for any wireless network. Latencies of cellular networks have been very high in the past; typically, about 100 ms with 3G and then improved to 30 ms in 4G. 5G promises latencies as low as 1 ms.

3. **Connection Density:** Number of devices per km^2 that can connect to a cellular base station becomes important as more and more devices need wireless connectivity. While 4G was able to connect only 100 thousand devices per km^2, 5G promises to increase that number to 1 million.

2. New Applications Enabled by 5G

Massive improvements in data rates, latency, and connection density are expected to enable new applications in the following key areas:

1. **Enhanced Broadband:** The huge data rates of 5G have made cellular networks a viable option for residential broadband, which is also referred to as fixed wireless. With fixed wireless, no cabling is required to

provision broadband service to the home. A home wireless router can simply be connected to the nearest 5G tower, using a SIM card. With high data rates, 5G mobile devices can enjoy new video standards, such as 4K streaming, augmented reality, virtual reality, and blazing fast photo uploads.

2. **Ultra-reliable Low Latency Communications:** Latencies below 1 ms will support real-time control of any devices, which will enable new applications, such as industrial robotics, autonomous driving, remote medical procedures, and so on.

3. **Massive Machine-to-Machine (M2M) and Internet of Things (IoT) Communications:** One million connections per sq. km will help support many M2M and IoT applications that involve connecting billions of devices at a scale not seen before. This has the potential to revolutionize almost all vertical markets, including agriculture, manufacturing, health, and defense.

3. 5G Technologies

To meet the massive capacity and data rate increase targets, enhancements will be made in three fundamental areas:

Increase bps/Hz or Spectral Efficiency: Develop new coding and modulation techniques as well as new spectrum-sharing methods to squeeze more bits out of the given spectrum. Enhancements in this sector of R&D will linearly increase the capacity. For example, increasing bps/Hz by a factor of 2 will directly double the capacity of a given cell.

Reduce Cell Radius or Increase Spectral Reuse: By reducing the cell size, the same spectrum can be reused many times in a given service area. This is the most effective method to increase capacity. Cell sizes have been consistently reduced over the 4 generations. 5G will continue to follow this trend.

Use New Spectrum: It has been known all along over the four generations that despite advancements in improving spectral efficient and spectral reuse, eventually we will need new spectrum to cope with the increasing demand for mobile traffic. 5G will be the first generation where new spectrum from the high frequency bands, notably millimeter wave bands, will be used.

Enhancements are also made in spectrum access techniques to address the aggressive new targets for low latency and massive connectivity. In the rest of this chapter, we discuss some of the key new developments in 5G to address these challenges.

4. Non-Orthogonal Multiple Access (NOMA)

NOMA [ALDA 2018] proposes to use the power as the fourth dimension for multiplexing. The previous generations used only orthogonal multiple access in the sense that the same communication resource could not be allocated to multiple users at the same time. Remember that initially, in 1G, only frequency was used to separate users using the so-called frequency division multiple access (FDMA). Then in 2G, time was used as the second dimension using the concept of time division multiple access (TDMA). In 3G, code was introduced in the form of code division multiple access (CDMA) as a third dimension to separate users who are using the same frequency at the same time. In 4G, OFDMA simply introduced highly flexible multiplexing techniques for the time and frequency dimensions. Use of power as a tool to separate users who are using the same frequency at the same time has not been implemented so far. With increasing handset computational powers, it has now become feasible to consider this.

In NOMA, multiple users' signals are superimposed at the transmitter side using different power coefficients for different users, based on their individual channel conditions. For example, a receiver closer to the transmitter is likely to be allocated higher power (due to higher channel coefficient) compared to the one located further away from the transmitter (lower channel coefficient). The superimposition of signals for N users can be mathematically described as follows:

$$X(f, t) = \sum_{i=1}^{N} \sqrt{a_i P}\, x_i(f, t) \tag{1}$$

where f is the frequency, $x_i(f,t)$ is the information signal for user i, P is the transmitter power, and a_i is the power coefficient for user i subjected to $\sum_{i=1}^{N} a_i = 1$ and $a_1 \geq a_2 \geq \cdots \geq a_N$ when channel gains are assumed to be ordered as $h_1 \leq h_2 \leq \cdots \leq h_N$.

At the receiver end, successive interference cancellation (SIC) is applied for decoding the signals one by one until the desired user's signal is obtained. SIC relies on the signal processing that allows a receiver to immediately decode the signal with the highest power by considering all other signals as noise. Once the signal with the highest power is decoded, it can be subtracted and removed from the combined signal. The signal with the second highest power now becomes the most powered signal in the residual superimposed signal; hence, can be decoded using the same technique. Thus, any receiver can use SIC to actually decode all the signals, but they stop decoding as soon as they receive their own signals.

The concept of NOMA and the associated SIC process is illustrated in Fig. 1, where a base station serves N users located at different distances from the base station. Using the same frequency, the base station transmits

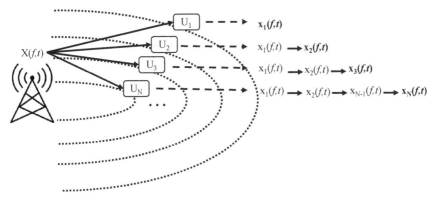

Fig. 1. Non-Orthogonal Multiple Access (NOMA).

a combined superimposed signal with the highest power allocated to the farthest user (the worst channel), U_1, and the lowest power to the closest one (the best channel), U_N. U_1 decodes the highest-powered signal easily and stops the decoding process because the decoded signal is addressed to it, i.e., it does not really carry out SIC. U_2 employs SIC once to remove the signal for U_1 before detecting its own signal, which is the second highest powered signal. U_3 has to repeat SIC twice and so on.

5. Full-duplex Wireless

Recall that for FDD, separate frequencies have to be allocated in uplink and downlink to achieve full-duplex communication. For a single frequency, full-duplex has not been possible so far due to the transmitter overwhelming the receiver causing too much interference, as illustrated in Fig. 2. Therefore, if single frequency is to be used for both DL and UL, then it would have to be half-duplex, like it is in TDD. In that case, when the frequency is used for DL, there is no traffic allowed in UL, and vice versa. Clearly, half-duplex reduces capacity and increases latency.

With advancements in DSP and processing powers, it is now contemplated to implement self-interference cancellation to realize full-duplex over the same frequency, so that simultaneous transmission and reception may be possible [FDUPLEX 2011]. Figure 3 illustrates how self-interference can be conceptually cancelled through additional signal processing and circuits implemented within the wireless radio. Basically, an attenuated and delayed transmit signal should be combined with the received signal to cancel the interference within the received signal that was caused by the over-the-air interference from the transmitting antenna. Such full-duplex communication would double the throughput, reduce end-to-end latency, and allow transmitters to monitor (estimate) the channel.

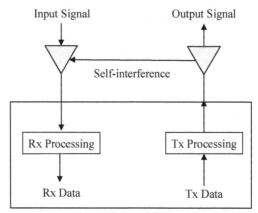

Fig. 2. The self-interference problem in wireless communications.

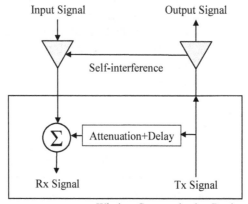

Fig. 3. Self-interference cancellation for full-duplex wireless communications.

6. Massive MIMO and 3D Beamforming

Most of the current radio towers use vertical sector antennas to focus energy in the 2D horizontal plane to serve people on the ground. Increasingly, people are now living in high rise apartments. With popularity of drones, cellular networks are also facing the issue of connecting devices that may fly above the ground. Thus, new mechanisms are required to reach devices that are spread in 3D.

5G is expected to serve users in 3D coverage spaces by using a new type of base stations that use massive MIMO and 3D beamforming [5G MIMO], as shown in Fig. 4. Instead of using a few vertical antennas to cover geographical sectors on the ground, 5G base stations are expected to deploy planar arrays

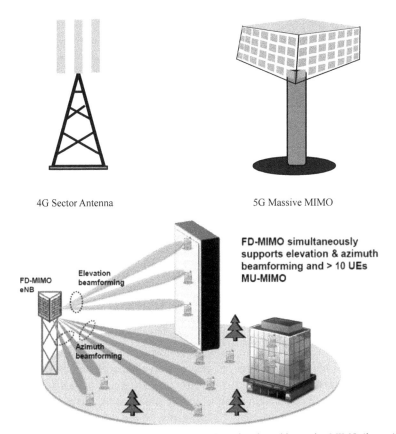

4G Sector Antenna   5G Massive MIMO

Fig. 4. Antenna shapes for 4G vs. 5G (*top*) and 3D beamforming with massive MIMO (*bottom*).

with many (> 100) antenna elements. By configuring the phase and amplitude coefficients of each elements, the base station can form many beams of different shapes in both vertical (elevation) and horizontal (azimuth) planes.

7. Mobile Edge Computing (MEC)

In future, mobile phones will need access to many computations that are not feasible to do in the handset; for example, speech recognition, augmented reality, and so on. However, sending these computation tasks to the cloud, which may be far away from the handset, would be costly and increase latency. Also to service IoT, where many machines may need some computing help from the cloud, the computation needs to come closer to the device. The idea behind MEC [MEC 2018] is to store such computing resources, a *micro cloud*, in every radio tower to make this very efficient. This concept is shown in Fig. 5.

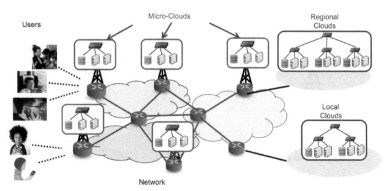

Fig. 5. Mobile Edge Computing (MEC).

8. New Spectrum

Finally we come to the point when we must discuss the opportunities for new spectrum. All those spectrum efficiency and spectrum reuse factor enhancements techniques we have discussed so far will help improving the capacity, but eventually we will need access to new spectrum to keep increasing the capacity.

While previous generations used frequencies in the highly congested bands below 6 GHz, there are plenty of spectrum available at higher frequencies, between 6–100 GHz, which is also referred to as high band. In this high band, 26 GHz and 28 GHz have emerged as two of the most important 5G spectrum bands [5G mmwave] as they can be utilized with the minimal user equipment complexity. These bands are also called millimeter wave (mmWave) bands as their wavelengths are close to 1 mm.

Use of mmWave bands will give 5G the much-needed spectrum boost to address the massive capacity increase targets. As the antenna size is proportional to the wavelength, the mmWave band will facilitate building massive MIMO base stations with hundreds of small antenna elements for efficient beam forming. However, signals at such high frequencies need line-of-sight for good performance, which will force 5G to exploit them for high-data rate short-distance communications.

9. Summary

1. 5G is being launched in 2020 promising to offer ultra-high data rates, ultralow latency, and massive connectivity for Internet of Things.
2. 5G will use NOMA as a new access technology that enables serving multiple users over the same frequency at the same time; NOMA uses power as a new dimension to differentiate users.

3. 5G promises full-duplex wireless communications where both the Tx and Rx antennas can function at the same time.

4. 5G base stations will use planar array antennas for massive MIMO and 3D beamforming.

5. 5G base stations will host computing and storage resources to reduce latency for applications requiring cloud support.

6. 5G will use new spectrum in the mmWave band.

Multiple Choice Test

Q1. Serving multiple users over the same frequency at the same time is facilitated by which of the following technology?
(a) NOMA
(b) Full duplex
(c) mmWave
(d) Edge Computing
(e) Massive MIMO

Q2. Which type of antennas are better suited to serve user equipment in 3D space?
(a) Sector antenna
(b) Planar array antenna
(c) Dish antenna
(d) Dipole antenna
(e) All of these

Q3. Which of the following scenarios can benefit from NOMA?
(a) There is always one user associated with the base station
(b) When users are experiencing different channel gains
(c) When all users experience identical channels
(d) None of these

Q4. Assume that a 5G base station is located at (0,0) and serving four users with the following locations: U1 = (0,1), U2 = (0,2), U3 = (0,3), and U4 = (0,4). Which user will be required to do the most computations to decode its packets if NOMA is used?
(a) U1
(b) U2
(c) U3
(d) U4

Q5. For self-interference cancellation, the Tx signal goes through an attenuation and delay circuit in the full duplex radio before being combined with the Rx signal because

   (a)   The Tx signal uses higher frequency than that used in Rx signal

   (b)   The interference signal is attenuated and delayed by the time it reaches to the Rx antenna due to the slight separation between the Tx and Rx antennas

   (c)   The Tx and the Rx signals use different waveforms

   (d)   The Rx signal is stronger than the Tx signal

References

[ALDA 2018] Mahmoud Aldababsa, Mesut Toka, Selahattin Gökçeli, Güneş Karabulut Kurt, Oğuz Kucur. A tutorial on nonorthogonal multiple access for 5G and beyond. *Wireless Communications and Mobile Computing*, vol. 2018, Article D 9713450, 24 pp., 2018. https://doi.org/10.1155/2018/9713450.

[FDUPLEX 2011] Jain et al. (2011). Practical, real-time, full duplex wireless. *ACM Mobicom*.

[5G MIMO] B. Yang, Z. Yu, J. Lan, R. Zhang, J. Zhou and W. Hong (July 2018). Digital beamforming-based massive MIMO transceiver for 5G millimeter-wave communications. pp. 3403–3418. *In: IEEE Transactions on Microwave Theory and Techniques*, vol. 66, no. 7. doi: 10.1109/TMTT.2018.2829702.

[5G mmwave] S. Sun, T. S. Rappaport, M. Shafi, P. Tang, J. Zhang and P. J. Smith (Sept. 2018). Propagation models and performance evaluation for 5G millimeter-wave bands. pp. 8422–8439. *In: IEEE Transactions on Vehicular Technology*, vol. 67, no. 9. doi: 10.1109/TVT.2018.2848208.

[MEC 2018] N. Abbas, Y. Zhang, A. Taherkordi and T. Skeie (Feb. 2018). Mobile edge computing: a survey. pp. 450–465. *In: IEEE Internet of Things Journal*, vol. 5, no. 1. doi: 10.1109/JIOT.2017.2750180.

Part V
Internet of Things

9
Internet of Things

◇◇◇

Internet of Things (IoT) is a new vision to connect all types of objects to the Internet, making it possible to digitize every phenomenon and processes of interest. IoT is arguably seen as the next Internet revolution promising unprecedented benefits in all socio-economic sectors. Currently there is a massive interest from industry, academia, and standards organizations in this topic. This chapter will provide an introduction to IoT, discussing the business opportunities and the recently standardized wireless networking technologies to support the need of IoT.

1. What are Things?

Internet has been there for more than four decades. It has connected all types of computers, such as servers, desktops, laptops, tablets, and smartphones from all over the world into a seamless gigantic virtual network. This seamless connectivity of the entire world made the Internet as one of the wonders of the modern era. People from anywhere in the world are now able to access, share, and contribute information at anytime.

IoT is the next evolution of the Internet. Instead of simply connecting computers, IoT promises to connect all types of *things*, such as wristbands, thermostats, cars, bikes, streetlamps, electric meters, washing machines, air conditioners, fridge, and the list goes on and on. This will enable not only humans, but also the *things* to access, share, and contribute information to take the automation to the next height. Besides the everyday objects, many types of environmental sensors are expected to be deployed and connected to the Internet for remote monitoring of agricultural fields, chemical plants, mining sites, and so on. Basically, things are any physical objects except the computers, as illustrated in Fig. 1. It is clear that there are more things to connect than computers and indeed we are at a pivotal point in the Internet history where more IoT are connected to the Internet than non-IoT.

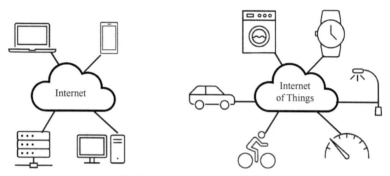

Fig. 1. Internet vs. Internet of Things.

Connecting things and objects to the Internet is not an entirely new concept. We have already connected many things to the Internet. We have fax machines, printers, security cameras, TV, etc., already connected to the Internet for remote access. With the emergence of new IoT standards and products, the IoT connections have already surpassed the total non-IoT connections. Despite this progress, at this moment, only a small fraction of all things is connected. With the rapid market uptake of IoT, the connectivity is expected to rise exponentially to hundreds of billions in the next few years as it will connect processes, data, things, people, and even animals, such as pets, farm animals, wildlife, etc. This dramatic shift in connectivity scale is what makes IoT the next big Internet evolution.

2. Why IoT Now?

The basic idea of IoT has been cultured for more than a decade, but why IoT is gaining this huge momentum now?

To answer this question, we need to look at the basic technical requirements of IoT, which are sensing, communication, and computation. Sensor technology has matured over the last 10–15 years. We can now buy all types of micro-sensors, such as temperature, moisture, pressure, air quality, and so on, dime a dozen. We now have various types of tags, such as radio frequency (RFID), Quick Response (QR) and so on, which can be readily attached to objects to track them over the Internet. We also have very low-power communication technologies, such as Bluetooth, NB-IoT, LoRaWAN, etc., which can meet the wireless communication needs of an object with a small battery. Micro-computing platforms, such as micro multi-core chips, Raspberry Pi, Intel Curie, etc., are available at less than $20. Cloud computing has become very affordable, making little or no local computing a possibility for the smart objects. Finally, we have open source micro operating systems, such as Tiny Core Linux, that can be easily ported to small objects. With all these developments in recent years, we suddenly have a new opportunity for realizing the vision of IoT on a grand scale.

3. IoT Applications and Business Opportunities

IoT is impacting all vertical sectors of the industry and all walks of life. For example, the power grid is now able to connect all of its power generation, supply, and consumption equipment to dramatically improve its efficiency in meeting its dynamic demands. Everyday wearable objects, such as shoes, watches, sunglasses, and even clothes can be connected to the Internet to constantly provide data about our daily fitness and health, making healthcare more precise, personalized, and affordable. Similarly, connected objects will make our homes, cities, industries much smarter and more efficient.

Basically, IoT helps digitize processes with unprecedented details, which in turn help achieve smarter products and services. To gain deeper insights into how IoT achieves this, let us a take a look at some of the real case studies of IoT from around the world.

3.1 Smart Whitegoods

Manufacturers of home appliances, such as washing machines, dishwashers, and refrigerators, are seeking cost-effective ways to monitor the distribution and usage of their products over time. China Telecom is aiming to use NB-IoT, a specialized cellular connectivity solution recently standardized by 3GPP to connect IoT devices at mass scale and low cost, to connect about 1.2 million whitegoods in schools and apartments in Beijing, Shanghai, Guangzhou, Shenzhen, and Chengdu [China-NBIOT]. The NB-IoT connectivity can be used to collect data from on-board sensors, such as a gyroscope, an accelerometer and temperature and humidity monitors to monitor the appliance's operational status, the environment in which it is located, and track fault information. The NB-IoT data transfer costs can be covered using a business model as follows: the whitegoods providers pay the first three years of data traffic fees to the mobile operators, after which the users can optionally continue the service and pay the connectivity bills themselves.

As we shall see later in the chapter, NB-IoT was designed for deep penetration to basements, underground car parks, and enclosed compartments within buildings, and it proves very useful to provide constant connectivity to whitegoods installed in basement laundries. The cost-effectiveness and coverage of NB-IoT has enabled appliance manufacturers to deploy machines that can be rented on a per-use basis. Together with a leading white goods maker and Huawei, China Telecom launched the Commercial Laundry Room at the Beijing University of Chemical Technology. After registering, using a QR code via WeChat, students and staff can make a laundry service reservation, pay, and then remotely follow the laundry cycle through an app.

3.2 Smart Smoke and Gas Detectors

As toxic gases and fires can kill people and ruin homes and workplaces, householders and businesses are increasingly looking to use innovative solutions for timely detection of smoke and gas with minimal cost. Connected smoke and gas detectors can act as automated sentries, able to detect smoke or gas leaks in real time and alert building residents as well as notify relevant fire-management platforms and any deployed actuators, such as sprinkler systems.

With NB-IoT, a large number of gas detectors from densely populated areas can be connected to a central management platform cost effectively and reliably. Once connected, the gas detectors can not only transmit sensing data to the management platform, they can also be updated remotely by pushing updated version of the firmware. Following successful trials, China Unicom plans to deploy 170,000 NB-IoT connected smoke detection and alarm devices in rental homes in Hangzhou [China-NBIOT]. The detectors will transmit data on smoke levels, power consumption, and network signal strength to a backend platform, which will enable constant monitoring of the gas level as well as the devices themselves. The deployment is expected to reduce the cost of fire monitoring and firefighting as well as minimize response times in the event of a fire.

China mobile operators are considering two different business models to support the connected smoke detectors. One model involves supplying the SIM card and connectivity to the smoke detector vendors and the other, purchasing the smoke detectors and supplying them to the residents as rental devices.

3.3 Smart Bikes

With improvements in battery technology, there has been a surge in the use of electric bikes. For example, there are about 3 million electric bikes in the city of Zhengzhou, China, alone. While increased use of electric bikes is helping citizens to move through the city conveniently without contributing to traffic congestion and pollution, they are causing higher risk of accidents, thefts, and fire hazards. To address these issues, Zhengzhou city administration has partnered with China Mobile and a local satellite positioning company to equip the electric bikes with NB-IoT-enabled positioning modules [China-NBIOT]. This has allowed the city administration to collect the position, speed, time, and temperature of an electric bicycle at regular intervals to a central bike management platform. Using this platform, the electric bike owners can register for a license and monitor the status of the bike in real-time to mitigate the risks of theft, accident, and fire.

3.4 Smart Waste Management

City of Canada Bay, located within the greater Sydney area of Australia, is using IoT technology to monitor garbage bin levels [CanadaBay]. City garbage bins are currently serviced, using a fixed schedule, which is proving very inefficient as different bins are filled at different rates. Using low-cost LoRaWAN, a new open-access IoT networking technology operating with unlicensed spectrum, city bins are fitted with sensors that can detect bin level and transmit the data periodically to a central garbage-management platform. The data is then used to infer how quickly bins are filling and when they need to be serviced, if more or less bins are required in a given area, if empty bins are serviced unnecessarily, and which bins need more frequent service. With low-power consumption of LoRaWAN, bins sensors are lasting three to five years without having to be replaced or recharged.

4. Wireless Standards for IoT

IoT poses new challenges for wireless communications not faced previously. Existing WiFi and cellular standards were designed for personal mobile devices to support high data rate applications, like web browsing, social media uploads, video streaming and so on. As a result, they were energy-hungry, requiring large batteries and frequent recharging. They also cannot reach devices located deep inside basements, forests, or in underground locations. Although Bluetooth was relatively low-power consuming, it could not reach objects beyond 10 meters.

For IoT, energy efficiency of the communication becomes a major issue as many of the small objects will be battery powered. Also, many objects are expected to be located in deep non-line-of-sight locations, such as in underground mines, deep forests, residential and industrial basements, in urban underground tunnels and so on. Connecting these devices at a scale with minimal infrastructure requires wireless standards that can reach long distances and difficult locations while consuming ultra-low power. Fortunately, IoT does not require high data rates as devices sleep most of the time and wake up only once in a while, to transmit a small message. Thus, all the major wireless technologies, i.e., Bluetooth, WiFi, and cellular, have released new extensions for IoT. Even completely new technologies dedicated entirely to IoT have emerged. A taxonomy of IoT connectivity solutions is

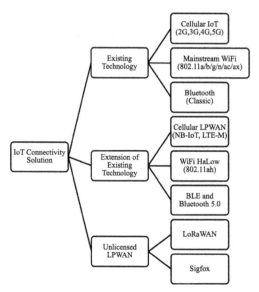

Fig. 2. Taxonomy of IoT connectivity solutions.

provided in Fig. 2 and the recent developments, including the extensions of existing technologies, is summarized below.

4.1 IoT Extensions for Bluetooth

The original Bluetooth, a.k.a. Bluetooth Classic, was designed for exchanging continuous, streaming data at close range. The typical use cases have been wireless headsets for talking or music streaming, wireless speakers, file transfer between two devices at close proximity, and so on. While these applications led to huge popularity of Bluetooth, many IoT applications require much lower power consumption and short message transfer capabilities at longer range.

Bluetooth Low Energy (BLE) was released in 2010 to meet these IoT demands. BLE was designed to sleep most of the time and wake up only to transmit a short message and then go back to sleep again. It extended the range and reduced the power consumption of Bluetooth significantly. BLE is incompatible with the classic version but addresses the need for many IoT sensors, which must operate for many years on a single coin battery. BLE is also known as Bluetooth 4.0. Typical applications of Bluetooth 4.0 include industrial monitoring sensors, data updates from wristbands to smartphones, targeted location-based advertising (e.g., iBeacon), etc.

Later, in 2016, Bluetooth 5.0 [BT5] was released to further extend the communication range of 4.0 without increasing the power consumption.

Version 5.0 can extend the range 4X (to ~ 250 m) compared to 4.0 (at ~ 50 m) at the expense of reducing the data rates to only a few hundred kbps, which suits IoT sensor data updates. Version 5.0 is compatible with 4.0. More details of all of these versions will be examined in a later chapter.

4.2 IoT Extensions for WiFi

WiFi was mainly designed for high speed wireless communications at short ranges typically within a building. This made WiFi a very popular wireless local area networking technology, but it consumes high power, cannot reach long distances or penetrate significant obstacles. Since IoT would require ultra-low power consumption with many sensors located in hard-to-reach places, new WiFi extensions were required for IoT.

As explained in Chapter 6, IEEE 802.11ah, a.k.a. HaLow, was released recently to address the IoT requirements. Specially, it achieved long range by shifting the frequency to 900 MHz, which not only can travel longer distances at low power but also can penetrate deep into buildings where many IoT devices may be located. The longer range can be achieved by reducing the data rates to as small as 150 kbps. Finally, the low data rate allows HaLow APs to connect four times more devices than existing WiFi, which is very important for densely-deployed IoT.

4.3 IoT Extensions for Cellular Networks

Cellular networks were already designed for connecting devices in a wide area and hence are inherently suitable to connect IoT devices and sensors deployed at city-scale. However, the conventional cellular networks, such as 2G, 3G, 4G, etc., were designed for sustained data transfers at high data rate from personal mobile devices, such as mobile phones. Cellular network connection therefore was considered most power-hungry compared to Bluetooth and WiFi.

Many IoT devices are 'meter reading' or 'status update' type of devices. These devices send only a small amount of data at some regular intervals and they are not delay sensitive. However, these devices are often deployed in places without power supply, thus making them necessary to run completely from a battery. As the battery replacement can be expensive for remote locations and due to the sheer number of these devices, the battery's lifetime often dictates the lifetime of the device. Low energy consumption therefore is a prime objective of any new cellular technology vying for the IoT market. In addition, the coverage has to be significantly higher than existing cellular technology because these devices are often deployed in hard to reach locations.

Also, due to the large numbers of these devices, they must be in the low-cost range, which means that any new cellular technology has to be much simpler than existing LTE for it to be IoT-friendly. Finally, to keep the cost low for the mobile operators, existing cellular infrastructure must be reused for any new services as much as possible.

To address the new market of large-scale IoT connectivity, 3GPP, i.e., the organization responsible for standardizing cellular networking, has recently introduced two new modes of cellular communications, namely NB-IoT (narrowband IoT) [NBIOT] and LTE-M (M represents machines) [LTEM]. These two modes are designed to support low data rate and low power intermitted data transfers from a large number of devices over a wide area of coverage using the same mobile towers and infrastructure. Due to their low-power consumption, these technologies are also referred to as Low Power WAN (LPWAN). The reuse of existing towers makes these services cost-effective for the mobile operators to support a new market. As these two services are offered by cellular network operators, they are also often referred to as Cellular LPWAN. It should be noted that unlike Bluetooth and WiFi, which use unlicensed spectrum, Cellular LPWAN uses licensed spectrum.

4.3.1 NB-IoT

NB-IoT is a fast-growing cellular LPWAN technology connecting a wide range of new IoT devices, including smart parking, utilities, wearables, and industrial solutions. Standardized by 3GPP in 2016, it is classified as a 5G technology. It has the following characteristics—enhanced coverage, massive connectivity (up to 50,000 per cell), low power consumption, low cost, reuse of installed LTE base.

Although IoT devices transmit a small amount of delay insensitive data, they can still overwhelm the cellular network with the signalling overhead due to the sheer number of them. Thus, many features of LTE, such as real-time handover, guaranteed bit rates, etc., which are essential for voice and video calls, are not available for NB-IoT. A different air-interface is therefore designed for NB-IoT. However, the existing cellular towers can still support both NB-IoT and normal user equipment by tagging the IoT devices with a new user equipment category as illustrated in Fig. 3.

Enhanced coverage of up to 28dB, compared to existing LTE, is achieved by using narrow band and allowing high number of retransmissions. NB-IoT uses the same framing and resource allocation structure of LTE, but it allocates only a single resource block (RB), which amounts to 180 kHz. A data frame is allowed to be retransmitted up to 128 times in the uplink. Such a high number of retransmissions can increase latency, but that is not an issue for NB-IoT devices.

New power classes are defined for NB-IoT devices, which allow them to operate with significantly low transmit power, suitable for coin cell batteries.

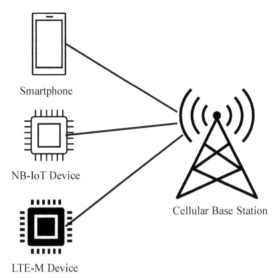

Smartphone

NB-IoT Device

LTE-M Device

Cellular Base Station

Fig. 3. Using different air interfaces, existing cellular towers can connect both traditional user equipment (e.g., a smartphone) as well as the new IoT devices fitted with NB-IoT and LTE-M connectivity modules.

Finally, NB-IoT defines new sleep modes that allow an IoT device to remain in complete sleep for an extended period of time when the base station cannot reach them. These sleep modes further help optimize the energy consumption and battery lifetime of NB-IoT devices.

4.3.2 LTE-M

Similar to NB-IoT, LTE-M also supports IoT devices that send small amounts of data infrequently and need to operate with low energy. However, unlike NB-IoT, LTE-M can support higher bandwidth, high-speed mobility, roaming between countries and operators, and efficient firmware updates. These services can be useful for applications, such as asset tracking where an asset typically moves from one country to another. LTE-M also has a lower latency than NB-IoT, which can be beneficial for connecting devices that have more delay-sensitive communication needs, such as an alarm or a self-driving car. Finally, LTE-M can also support voice. Clearly, LTE-M is more complex and costly than NB-IoT but filling a different segment within the IoT market.

4.4 New Unlicensed LPWAN Technologies

While the cellular industry deployed NB-IoT and LTE-M air interfaces to serve the IoT needs of the future through the licensed spectrum, parallel developments took place to solve the problem using unlicensed spectrum. The notable unlicensed LPWAN technologies include LoRaWAN [LORA] and Sigfox [SIGFOX]. Both need to set up their own infrastructures to roll out the service. Despite this, the unlicensed LPWAN has become equally competitive with their licensed counterpart. We examine LoRaWAN in detail in a later chapter.

5. Summary

1. IoT refers to connecting things that are not computers.

2. Only a small fraction of things is connected today and yet the number of connected IoT devices has surpassed the total number of traditional connected devices, i.e., mobile phones, laptops, data center computers, etc. The scale of IoT makes it the next big Internet evolution.

3. Advancements in sensor technology and low-cost computing platforms have worked as a catalyst for the IoT movement today.

4. There exist many different connectivity options for IoT. While early IoT deployments relied on the classical wireless networking, e.g., Bleutooth, WiFi, and cellular, specialized versions of these technologies are being created to better serve the IoT needs. Even new IoT networking technologies, e.g., LoRaWAN and Sigfox, have been designed and deployed from scratch.

Multiple Choice Questions

Q1. Which of the following device would be considered an IoT?
(a) Laptop
(b) Smart fridge
(c) Mobile phone
(d) Desktop computer
(e) iPad

Q2. Which of the following is an extension of WiFi designed to serve IoT?
(a) HaLoW
(b) WiFi 5
(c) BLE
(d) NB-IoT
(e) LoRaWAN

Q3. Which of the following is an extension of Bluetooth suitable for IoT?
(a) HaLoW
(b) WiFi 5
(c) BLE
(d) NB-IoT
(e) LoRaWAN

Q4. Which of the following is a 5G solution designed for IoT?
(a) HaLoW
(b) WiFi 5
(c) BLE
(d) NB-IoT
(e) LoRaWAN

Q5. Which of the following is an example of LPWAN that uses unlicensed spectrum?
(a) HaLoW
(b) WiFi 5
(c) BLE
(d) NB-IoT
(e) LoRaWAN

Q6. Which of the following is an example of LPWAN that uses licensed spectrum?
(a) HaLoW
(b) WiFi 5
(c) BLE
(d) NB-IoT
(e) LoRaWAN

Q7. Which of the following has the shortest range?
(a) HaLoW
(b) WiFi 5
(c) BLE
(d) NB-IoT
(e) LoRaWAN

Q8. Which of the following IoT technologies can support for both long-range and high-speed mobility?
(a) HaLoW
(b) WiFi 5
(c) BLE
(d) LTE-M
(e) LoRaWAN

Q9. Which of the following can support long range in unlicensed spectrum?
(a) BLE
(b) Bluetooth 5
(c) LTE-M
(d) NB-IoT
(e) Sigfox

Q10. Which of the following does not contribute toward low energy objective of LB-IoT?
(a) Narrow bandwidth
(b) Deep sleep modes
(c) New power class with lower transmit power
(d) New air interface

References

[BT5] Bluetooth 5.0. https://www.bluetooth.com/bluetooth-resources/bluetooth-5-go-faster-go-further/ (accessed 25 October 2021).

[China-NBIOT] NB-IoT Commercialization Case Study, How China Mobile, China Telecom and China Unicom Enable Million More IoT Devices. https://www.gsma.com/iot/wp-content/uploads/2019/08/201902_GSMA_NB-IoT_Commercialisation_CaseStudy.pdf [accessed 25 October 2021].

[CanadaBay] City of Canada Bay Bins Get Smart (10 October 2019). https://www.canadabay.nsw.gov.au/news/city-canada-bay-bins-get-smart [accessed 25 October 2021].

[LORA] LoRA Alliance. https://lora-alliance.org/.

[LTEM] R. Ratasuk, N. Mangalvedhe and A. Ghosh (2015). Overview of LTE enhancements for cellular IoT. 2015 IEEE 26th Annual International Symposium on Personal, Indoor, and Mobile Radio Communications (PIMRC), pp. 2293–2297. doi: 10.1109/PIMRC.2015.7343680.

[NBIOT] Y. D. Beyene et al. (June 2017). NB-IoT technology overview and experience from Cloud-RAN implementation. pp. 26–32. *In: IEEE Wireless Communications*, vol. 24, no. 3. doi: 10.1109/MWC.2017.1600418.

[SIGFOX] https://www.sigfox.com/en.

10
Bluetooth

Bluetooth is the oldest and the most pervasive technology to connect a wide range of devices and 'things' around us. Since its inauguration decades ago, it has gone through several upgrades and is continuing to play a dominant role in providing short-range connectivity for smart objects. In this chapter, we cover its history, markets, and applications, followed by the core technologies behind the three generations of Bluetooth.

1. Bluetooth History

The history of Bluetooth started with Ericsson's Bluetooth Project in 1994 for radio communication between cell phones over short distances [NIST-BT]. It was named after Danish king, Herald 'Blatand' Gormsson (AD 940–981). He was fondly called Blatand, which is 'blue tooth' in Danish, because of his dead tooth that looked blue [BT-SIG-ORG].

Intel, IBM, Nokia, Toshiba, and Ericsson formed Bluetooth SIG in May 1998 [NIST-BT, WIKI-BT]. Soon after, Version 1.0A of the specification came out in late 1999. IEEE 802.15.1, which was approved in early 2002 and was based on Bluetooth [NIST-BT]. However, all later versions of Bluetooth were handled by Bluetooth SIG directly.

The key features of the original Bluetooth were low power, low cost, and small form factor. Bluetooth now comes built-in with many systems on chip and microcomputer boards, such as Intel Curie, Raspberry Pi, Arduino, and so on.

2. Wireless Personal Area Networks

Figure 1 shows the IEEE networking technologies stacked according to their communication ranges. At the bottom, we have the networks that cover the last 10 m. These are collectively referred to as Wireless Personal Area Networks (WPANs) because historically these protocols were designed to serve devices

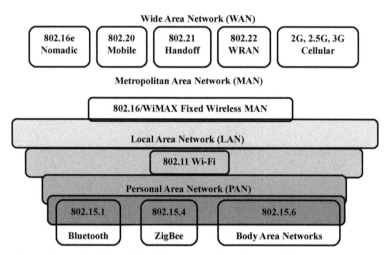

Fig. 1. Networking technologies with different communication range; 10 m or less technologies are at the bottom.

within the vicinity of the person. In the IoT era, with the growing dependence on machine-to-machine communications, the name 'personal' may not be very relevant for all scenarios, but the main criteria of 10 m coverage will remain. Within WPAN, we have several competing solutions, such as Bluetooth, Zigbee, and Body Area Networks (BANs). In this chapter, we will focus on Bluetooth.

All WPAN protocols follow a set of basic design principles:

Battery Powered: The devices run on coin cell batteries with a couple of hundred mAh capacity, which has to last for a few years. Maximizing the battery life therefore is one of the major challenges.

Dynamic Topologies: Because the devices have to conserve energy, they usually turn on for a short duration and then go back to sleep. For example, a temperature monitor may wake up every 10 seconds and connect with the WiFi AP to send the temperature reading and then it goes back to sleep again. Therefore, connections are very short.

No Infrastructure: They do not depend on any access point or base station.

Avoid Interference: These devices share the same ISM bands, such as 2.4 GHz, with the high-power LAN devices, such as WiFi. How to avoid interference with such high-power communications in the same area therefore is a major issue to tackle.

Simple and Extreme Interoperability: As there are billions of devices, we have more variety than LAN or MAN. The interoperability challenge therefore is more severe than LAN or MAN.

Low Cost: Communication technology must be affordable as many low-cost devices, such as a $2 electric bulb, may need such communication capabilities.

3. Bluetooth Market

According to a recent report from Bluetooth SIG [BT-SIG], 48 billion devices will be connected to the Internet by 2021, of those 30% are forecasted to include Bluetooth technology. This includes a wide range of market segments including cars, wearables, factory instruments, and smart home products. The forecast further shows that Bluetooth shipments are expected to grow at a rate of 8% CAGR, from 2019 to 2024.

4. Bluetooth Versions

Since the first release of Bluetooth 1.1 endorsed by the IEEE in 2002, there have been many updates over the years. The current version is 5.3. Table 1 provides a chronological list of Bluetooth versions and their capabilities [NIST-BT, BT-SIG]. Bluetooth versions prior to 4.0 are often referred to as Bluetooth Classic. Bluetooth 4.0 is also known as Bluetooth Smart and Bluetooth Low Energy (BLE).

Table 1. Chronological list of Bluetooth versions.

Bluetooth Version	Description
Bluetooth 1.1 (2002)	IEEE 802.15.1-2002. Classical.
Bluetooth 1.2 (2003)	Adaptive frequency hopping to avoid frequencies with interference.
Bluetooth 2.0 + (2004)	Enhanced Data Rate (EDR); 3 Mbps using DPSK; suitable for video applications; reduced power due to reduced duty cycle.
Bluetooth 4.0 (2010)	Low energy; smaller devices requiring longer battery life (several years); new incompatible PHY. A.k.a. Bluetooth Smart or BLE.
Bluetooth 5.0 (2016)	Make BLE go faster and farther.
Bluetooth 5.3 (2021)	Faster transitions between low and high duty cycle modes; enhanced key size control between host and controller; more efficient periodic advertisements, channel classification enhancement for arriving at more optimal channel map between peripheral and central devices.

5. Bluetooth Classic

We will start with Bluetooth 1.1 to understand the basic details of Bluetooth.

5.1 Bluetooth Piconet

A Bluetooth network is called a piconet, which is formed by a *master* device communicating with one or more *slave* devices [PRAVIN 2001]. Any

Bluetooth device can become a master. Basically, the device that initiates the communication becomes the master and the devices that respond to the initial call become the slaves. For example, when a computer is turned on, it may advertise a message looking for a Bluetooth keyboard. If a nearby keyboard responds and subsequently pairs with the computer, then the keyboard becomes a slave. Slaves can only transmit when requested by the master. Active slaves are polled by the master for transmissions. Slaves can only transmit/receive to/from the master, i.e., slaves cannot talk to another slave in the piconet. There can be up to seven *active* slaves per piconet at a time.

Beyond the active slaves within a piconet, Bluetooth allocates an 8-bit parked address to any device wishing to join the piconet at some time in the future. This allows up to 255 *parked* slaves per piconet that sleep most of the time but may join the piconet from time to time. All parked stations are then uniquely identifying, and they are usually referred to using some mnemonic identifiers for human use. Any parked stations can join the piconet in 2 ms and become active at any time. For other stations which are not parked yet, it usually takes much longer than 2 ms to join. Figure 2 shows examples of Bluetooth piconets with both active and parked slaves.

For more densely deployed IoT scenarios, Bluetooth can use a more complex network topology, called *scatternet*, to allow a device to participate in multiple piconets, as shown in Fig. 3. However, for a device to participate in multiple piconets, it has to timeshare and must synchronize to the master of the current piconet, i.e., it can *be active* in only one piconet and in *park* mode in the other.

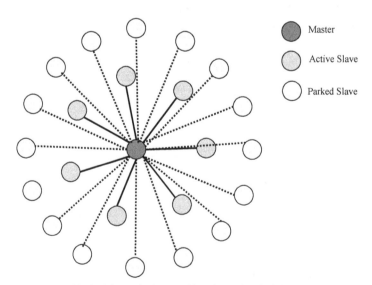

Fig. 2. Bluetooth piconet with active and parked slaves.

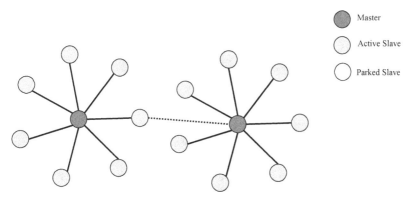

Fig. 3. Bluetooth scatternet.

Note that there is no routing protocol defined, so nodes can only talk to other nodes which are directly within the Bluetooth communication range of about 10 m.

5.2 *Bluetooth Spectrum and Channels*

Bluetooth operates in the same ISM band of 2.4 GHz as WiFi. Bluetooth classic divides the entire spectrum between 2402–2480 MHz (total 79 MHz) into 79 1-MHz channels, as shown in Fig. 4.

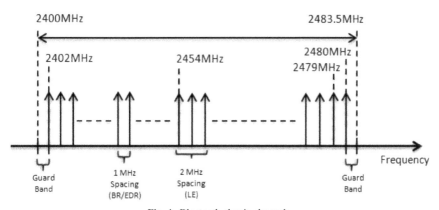

Fig. 4. Bluetooth classic channels.

5.3 *Modulation and Data Rates*

Modulation and data rates for Bluetooth classic are classified into two groups—basic rate (BR) and enhanced data rate (EDR).

For BR, it uses a binary frequency shift keying to achieve only 1 bit per symbol. Bluetooth uses a symbol duration of 1 µs, which gives 1 Mbps for the BR. The EDR also uses 1 μs symbols, but it supports more advanced modulations, namely μ/4-DQPSK with 2 bits/symbol and 8DPSK with 3 bits/symbol. Thus, under EDR, Bluetooth classic can deliver 2 Mbps and 3 Mbps data rates using μ/4-DQPSK and 8DPSK, respectively.

5.4 Frequency Hopping

Unlike WiFi, Bluetooth constantly switches channel within the same connection to avoid interference with other nearby WiFi or Bluetooth communications using the same 2.4 GHz band. Figure 5 shows how two Bluetooth networks can share the same frequency band without interfering with each other by hopping between channels (only four available channels are shown for illustration purposes). As we can see, the two networks are selecting different channels at each time slot, thus avoiding interference and collision.

So, how frequently Bluetooth switches the channel? Since it is rather complex to switch the channel within a packet transmission, Bluetooth only changes channels at packet boundaries effectively achieving a frequency hop per packet. No two successive packets are transmitted over the same channel. The effective frequency hopping rate therefore is a function of the packet duration.

In Bluetooth, time is slotted to 625 μs using a 3200 Hz clock, where 1 slot is determined by 2 clock ticks (1 clock tick = 312.5 μs for a 3200 Hz clock). Packet transmission can start only at the beginning of a time slot and it can last for 1, 3, or 5 slots. Other packet durations are not permitted.

The communication between the master and slave uses the entire frequency band, so both of them cannot transmit at the same time, i.e., full-duplex communication is not possible in Bluetooth. The master and the slave therefore alternate in using the channel, i.e., they implement half-duplex using time-division duplexing (TDD). Master-to-slave is called *downstream* and slave-to-master is called *upstream*. With TDD, downstream and upstream alternates in time.

The slots are numbered, starting at zero. Master starts communicating first in slot 0 and the slaves can transmit right after receiving a packet from the master. Given that the allowed packet lengths are only 1, 3, or

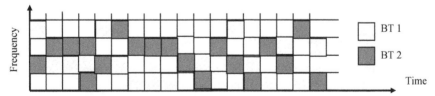

Fig. 5. Two close by Bluetooth piconets sharing the same frequencies without interference by hopping between channels; in this ideal hopping scenario, the same channel is never selected by both piconets.

5 slots, masters can only use the even numbered slots and the slaves, the odd numbered slots. Frequencies switch only at the start of the slot that starts after a packet transmission is completed, which may not align with slot boundaries. Finally, the packet lengths between the master and the slaves may not have to be symmetrical. For example, it is perfectly okay for a master to use a short 1-slot packet, while a slave transmits a 3-slot packet. Figure 6 shows such symmetric vs. asymmetric packet lengths. Figure 7 illustrates that the minimum and maximum frequency hopping rates in Bluetooth are 320 Hz (all packets are 5-slot) and 1600 Hz (all packets are 1-slot).

Example 1
Consider a Bluetooth link where the *master* always transmits 3-slot packets. The transmission from the master is always followed up by a single-slot transmission from a *slave*. Assuming 625 μs slots, what is the effective frequency hopping rate (# of hopping per second)?

Solution
Given that the frequency hopping cannot occur in the middle of a packet transmission, we only have 2 hops per 4 slots, or 1 hop per 2 slots.
The effective hopping rate = $1/(2\times625\times10^{-6})$ = 800 hops/s = 800 Hz

---

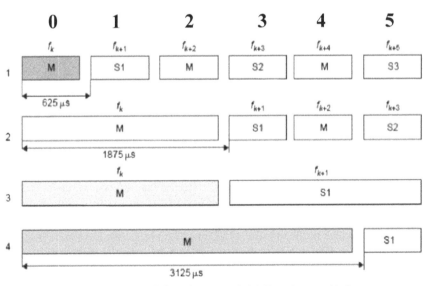

1. One-slot symmetrical; 2. Three-slot asymmetrical; 3. Three-slot symmetrical;
4. Five-slot asymmetrical

M=master, S = slave

Fig. 6. Frequency hopping for symmetric vs. asymmetric packet lengths.

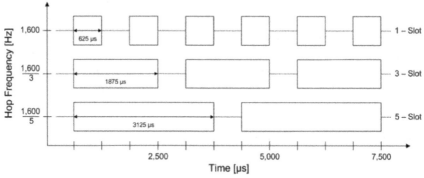

Fig. 7. Dependency of hopping rate on the packet length. The maximum and minimum hopping rates are 1600 Hz and 320 Hz, respectively [BT-RS].

Bluetooth is very popular for listening to music as well as for voice calls with earphones. Such traffic is synchronous, generating packets at fixed intervals, where the interval depends on the audio codecs. To support such synchronous traffic, Bluetooth reserves slots ahead of time. For asynchronous traffic, the master simply polls each active station. Note that there is no contention avoidance mechanism; all traffic is controlled by the master. If there are contentions, packets get lost, which are eventually retransmitted by the higher layer.

5.5 Bluetooth Packet Format and MAC Address

In Bluetooth, packets can be up to 5 slots long. Thus, with 625 μs slots, a packet is allowed to last for a maximum of $625 \times 5 = 3125$ μs. As BR and EDR have different data rates, their packet formats are also different. The packet format for BR is shown in Fig. 8, which has only three fields [BT-NI]: It has a 68/72b access code, 54b control header, and the rest is payload, which can be up to 2745b. The maximum size of a packet therefore can be 72+54+2745 = 2871b, which lasts for 2871 μs when data is transmitted at the rate of 1 Mbps.

There are three types of access codes: *Channel access code* (CAC) identifies the piconet, *device access code* (DAC) is used for paging requests and response, and *inquiry access code* (IAC) can be used to discover particular Bluetooth devices in the vicinity. CAC is 72 bits long, but DAC and IAC can be either 68 or 72 bits long. There is an 18-bit header comprising member address (3b), type code (4b), flow control (1b), ack/nack (1b), sequence number (1b), and header error check (8b). This 18b header is encoded using one-third rate coding resulting in 54b.

The packet format for EDR is more complex, which is shown in Fig. 9. A notable feature of an EDR packet is that the modulation changes within the packet. While GFSK is used for the access code and header fields, it switches

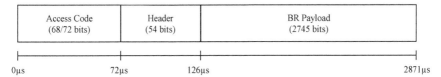

Fig. 8. Bluetooth classic packet format for BR.

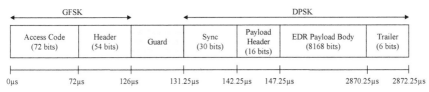

Fig. 9. Bluetooth classic packet format for EDR.

to DPSK (DQPSK for 2 Mbps and 8DPSK for 3 Mbps) after a guard interval lasting between 4.75 μs to 5.25 μs. EDR payload can accommodate more data than BR, but still fits within the maximum 5-slot due to higher data rates.

Example 2

How many slots are needed to transmit a Bluetooth Basic Rate packet if the payload is (a) 400 bits, (b) 512 bits, and (c) 2400 bits; assume that the non-payload portions do not change.

Solution

Bluetooth transmissions are 1, 3, or 5 slots (2, 4, 6, etc. not allowed)
Non-payload bits (max) = 54+72 = 126 bits
Each slot can carry 625 bits at most
(a) 400b payload results in 400+126 = 526b packet, which requires **1 slot**
(b) 512b payload results in 512+126 = 638b packet for which 2 slots would be sufficient, but will have to be padded for a **3-slot** transmission because 2-slot packets are not allowed
(c) 2400b payload results in 2400+126 = 2526b packet which fits in **5 slots**

Each Bluetooth device has a unique 48-bit MAC address included in the access code field of the packet header. As shown in Fig. 10, the most significant 24 bits represent the OUI (Organization Unique Identifier) or the Vendor ID. Typically, the vendors convert each 4b into a decimal number and show the MAC address as a string of 12 decimal digits. For example, Fig. 11 shows the label of a Bluetooth chip from Roving Networks with a MAC address of 000666422152 where 000666 would uniquely identify Roving Networks. Here, the decimal digits for the most significant bits are written from the left. While the main purpose of Bluetooth MAC address is identification and authentication,

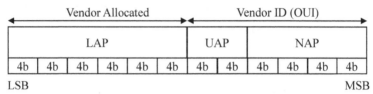

Fig. 10. Bluetooth MAC address format.

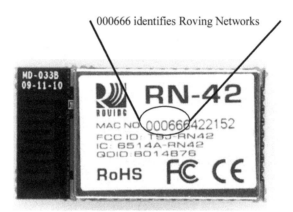

Fig. 11. Example of a real Bluetooth MAC.

specific parts of it are also used to seed the frequency hopping pseudorandom generator for synchronizing the master and slave clocks as well as to pair the devices at the beginning, which we shall examine shortly.

5.6 *Pseudorandom Frequency Hopping*

In Bluetooth Classic, frequency hopping is defined by a pseudorandom generating algorithm seeded with the following values from the master device: UAP and LAP of the MAC address, and bits 1–26 (27 bits) of the 28-bit Bluetooth clock. As the master communicates these values to the slaves during connection set-up, the master and the slaves generate the same frequency hopping patterns and switch to the same frequency values at every instant of the hop. As such, Bluetooth is both time and frequency synchronized at all times, as illustrated in Fig. 12.

Figure 13 shows an example trace of pseudorandom frequency hopping between a Bluetooth master and slave device that both use single-slot packets and use the first 16 channels for hopping. We can see that with single-slot packets, the master and slave take turns after every 612 μs and switch randomly to a new channel within the 16-channel set.

The pseudorandom pattern has a finite length and hence technically it would run out of the original pattern and then repeat itself. To be more precise,

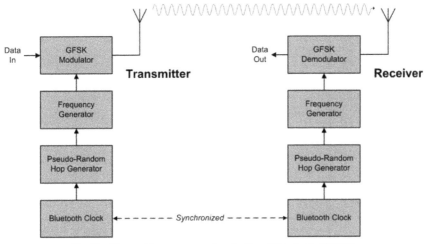

Fig. 12. Time and frequency synchronization of Bluetooth [BT-RS].

with 27 clock bits to define the pattern, Bluetooth pseudorandom pattern would repeat itself after 2^{27} hops, which would take at least 23.3 hours to repeat at the maximum hopping rate of 1600 Hz. In practice, the Bluetooth connections last much shorter than 23 hours, hence the pseudorandom sequence is not at the risk of being repeated.

5.7 Adaptive Frequency Hopping

Because Bluetooth operates in the free unlicensed ISM spectrum, it is likely to face interference from other wireless sources, such as a 2.4 GHz WiFi, sharing the same frequency of Bluetooth in the same time period. Especially, the interference from WiFi can be really harmful as WiFi uses much higher transmission power than Bluetooth. Therefore, some of the 79 channels can become unusable at certain times and should be avoided by Bluetooth during frequency hopping. This is illustrated in Fig. 14, where a WiFi transmission heavily interferes with the first 20 channels of Bluetooth. A Bluetooth device that always uses the 79 channels for hopping would end up transmitting some packets within those 20 interfered channels, at times causing packet and throughput loss.

The Adaptive Frequency Hopping (AFH) technique was proposed for Bluetooth to avoid hopping into channels that are experiencing interference. Basically, AFH requires a mechanism to measure channel states and mark interfering channels as bad channels when the interference is considered beyond certain threshold. How to implement this is left to the vendors, i.e., it is not part of the standard. Vendors usually measure metrics, such as received signal strength (RSS) and signal-to-noise ratio (SNR), etc., to decide whether

Time	Slot/Hop	Hopset															
10.000 ms	17 (TX)	▲TX															
9.375 ms	16 (RX)															▼RX	
8.750 ms	15 (TX)			▲TX													
8.125 ms	14 (RX)					▼RX											
7.500 ms	13 (TX)									▲TX							
6.875 ms	12 (RX)														▼RX		
6.250 ms	11 (TX)									▲TX							
5.625 ms	10 (RX)								▼RX								
5.000 ms	9 (TX)																▲TX
4.375 ms	8 (RX)								▼RX								
3.750 ms	7 (TX)									▲TX							
3.125 ms	6 (RX)						▼RX										
2.500 ms	5 (TX)			▲TX													
1.875 ms	4 (RX)																▼RX
1.250 ms	3 (TX)											▲TX					
0.625 ms	2 (RX)			▼RX													
0.000 ms	1 (TX)		▲TX														
	Bluetooth Channel	1	2	3	4	5	6	7	8	9	10	11	12	13	14	15	16
	Frequency	2402 MHz	2403 MHz	2404 MHz	2405 MHz	2406 MHz	2407 MHz	2408 MHz	2409 MHz	2410 MHz	2411 MHz	2412 MHz	2413 MHz	2414 MHz	2415 MHz	2416 MHz	2417 MHz

Fig. 13. An example trace of Bluetooth pseudorandom frequency hopping.

a channel is good or bad. Then, the hopping is constrained only within the good channels, as illustrated in Fig. 15. The standard specifies that a minimum of 20 channels are needed for hopping, i.e., a maximum of 59 channels can be marked as bad.

Because the interference can be dynamic, the set of good channels is likely to vary over time. Thus, the master maintains a channel map that marks good and bad channels and sends the map to the slave periodically.

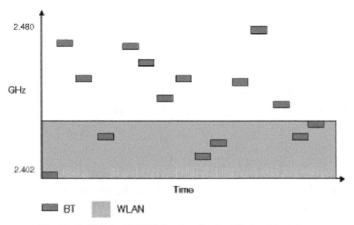

Fig. 14. Collision with WiFi for non-adaptive Bluetooth hopping.

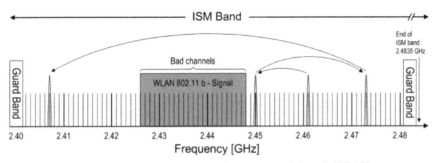

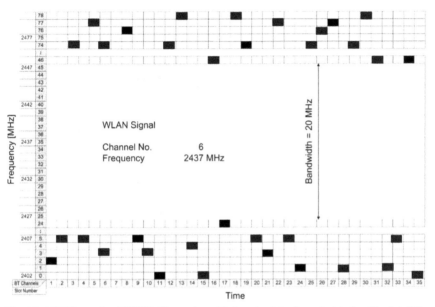

Fig. 15. AFH Illustration: hopping only between good channels [BT-RS].

Fig. 16. AFH Illustration [BT-RS]: Bluetooth avoids hopping into channels interfered by 2.4 GHz WiFi operating over WiFi channel 6.

Figure 16 illustrates AFH when a WiFi 2.4 GHz access point is operating over WiFi channel 6 nearby. Here the AFH successfully avoids hopping into any of the 25–45 Bluetooth channels which are marked as bad channels by the vendor's channel marker algorithm at that time.

5.8 Bluetooth Operational States

There is a total of eight distinct states as shown in Fig. 17. These are grouped into four high level states, Disconnected, Connecting, Active, and Low Power.

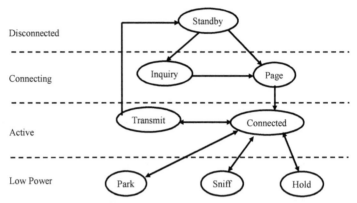

Fig. 17. Bluetooth operational state.

Standby is the initial state when the station is disconnected but may try to connect later. There are two types of inquiry that can be used when trying to connect. The first one is called Inquiry state and the other is called Paging.

In the Inquiry state, master broadcasts an inquiry packet. Slaves scan for inquiries and respond with their address and clock after a random delay to avoid collision among many potential slaves responding at the same time. Master computes the clock offset for this slave.

Master in Page state invites a slave to join the piconet. Slave enters *page response* state and sends *page response* to master, including its device access code if it detects the page message. Master informs slave about its clock and address so that the slave can participate in piconet. Slave computes the clock offset.

After the page state, it transitions to the Connected state where a short 3-bit logical address (member address within control header field) is assigned for the slave. After the address assignment, the devices move to the Transmit state where they can transmit and receive a packet.

5.9 Bluetooth Connection Establishment Procedure

The sequence of inquiry and paging messages exchanged between the master and the slave before the connection is established is shown in Fig. 18. Note that the hopping sequence is only known to the master and the slave after the connection is established, which means that the inquiry and page messages have to be successfully received without exactly knowing the frequency used by the other party. This means that the master and the slave will have to guess the frequencies and try again and again until successfully switching to the right frequencies. This makes the whole paging process indeterministic and could take several seconds before connection can be established. Let us take a closer look at how the frequency hopping is done during inquiry and paging.

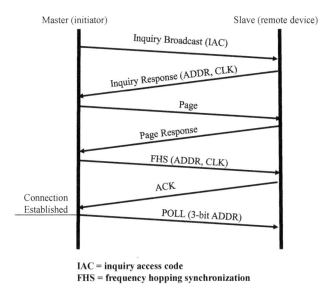

Master (initiator)   Slave (remote device)

IAC = inquiry access code
FHS = frequency hopping synchronization

Fig. 18. Bluetooth inquiry and paging flow diagram.

First, the hopping set is constrained over a subset of 32 instead of the full 79 channels to increase the possibility of a frequency match between the transmitter and the receiver. These 32 channels are further divided into two 16-channel *trains.* For inquiry, each train is repeated 256 times before *switching* to the other train and must complete 3 train switches, i.e., 1st to 2nd to 1st and then back to the 2nd. Thus, each train is effectively repeated 256 × 2 times.

Master sends two inquiry/page packets using two different frequencies per slot, i.e., it hops in the middle of the slot (which leads to hopping in 312.5 µs), and listens for responses in both frequencies in the following slots. Thus, eventually two frequencies are covered in two slots.

Now, let us try to derive the worst possible time that may be needed by the inquiry process. It takes 16 × 625 µs = 10 ms for completing a train once. The maximum possible inquiry time is then obtained as 256 × 4 × 10 ms = 10.24s. We should note that there would be an additional paging time before a connection is finally established.

5.10 Power Saving States

Bluetooth has three inactive states to manage power saving:

Hold: In this state, no asynchronous communication can take place, but synchronous communication can continue. This means audio will not be disrupted, but the node will not initiate any other traffic, such as file transfer, etc. Node can do something else though, such as scan, page or inquire. The station holds the 3-bit address as an active node of the piconet.

Sniff: It is a low-power mode to conserve energy. Slave does not continue with synchronous or asynchronous traffic but listens periodically after fixed sniff intervals. It keeps the 3-bit address.

Park: This is a very low-power mode. Slave gives up its 3-bit active member address and gets an 8-bit parked member address instead. It wakes up periodically and listens to the beacons broadcast by the master.

5.11 Bluetooth Protocol Stack

Being developed almost entirely outside IEEE, Bluetooth has a slightly different shape and terminology for its protocol stack (*see* Fig. 19). As we can see, it does not have a regular 'layer 2', 'layer 3', etc. stacked on top of each other. Rather, the application can access many different services from the lower layer. Also, because there is no routing (all connections are direct single-hop), we do not have a network layer.

The bottom-most layer, the RF layer, is the one that does frequency hopping. The actual bits are coded, using Gaussian Frequency Shift Keying, which is basically a FSK, but the shape of the pulse is Gaussian, as shown in Fig. 20.

Link manager negotiates parameters and sets up connections. Logical Link Control and Adaptation Protocol (L2CAP) is responsible for three tasks. It supports protocol multiplexing, such as multiplexing BNEP, TCS, RECOMM, and SDP onto the logical link layer. It implements segmentation

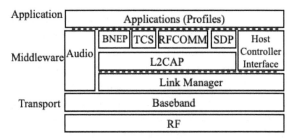

Fig. 19. Bluetooth protocol stack.

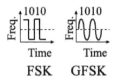

Fig. 20. PHY coding in Bluetooth. Gaussian Frequency Shift Keying is different than Frequency Shift Keying.

and reassembly. It also controls peak bandwidth, latency, and delay variation for different applications supporting quality of service for Bluetooth. Host Controller Interface is basically a hardware adaptation layer that enables the same software to run on different microchips.

When Bluetooth was designed, serial ports were major interfaces for many computers. Therefore, most chip manufacturers supported a serial interface to program their chips. RFCOMM layer presents a *virtual wireless* serial port capability for Bluetooth, so that it can be connected to another RFCOMM. Thus, two Bluetooth devices could in practice establish a serial port connection between them over the air. In the modern age, serial ports are hardly used but can be utilized if necessary.

Every Bluetooth device provides a service. A Bluetooth mouse provides a mouse service; a Bluetooth keyboard provides a keyboard service; a Bluetooth speaker provides a speaker service and so on. Service Discovery Protocol (SDP) provides a standard way for devices to find such available services and their parameters so that they can automatically connect to each other when turned on without human intervention.

Bluetooth can also be used to transmit standard IP data. The Bluetooth Network Encapsulation Protocol (BNEP) is used to encapsulate Ethernet/IP packets so that they can be transmitted over Bluetooth.

Bluetooth also supports telephone. All modern cars are equipped with Bluetooth telephone control, thus we can make or receive calls from our smartphone using buttons on the steering wheel. Telephony has audio as well as control signals. The telephony control is supported by the Telephony Control Specification (TCS) protocol. TCS support call control, including group management (multiple extensions, call forwarding, and group calls).

Finally, we come to the application profiles. In Bluetooth, each application has a strict set of actions that it is allowed to do. For example, all actions of a headset application are defined in *headset profile* (HSP). Such strict application profiling is the key to Bluetooth's success in global and pervasive interoperability. Today we can buy a Bluetooth headset from any airport in the world and it works just fine with any mobile device from any manufacturer in any part of the world. Similarly, we have human interface device (HID) profile to wirelessly connect a range of user input devices, such as mice, keyboards, joysticks, and even game controllers, such as Wii PS3 controllers. Figure 21 illustrates how HID profile is used within the Bluetooth protocol stack for connecting a wireless keyboard to the computer.

As Bluetooth became popular, the number of profiles it had to support grew dramatically over the last few years. Table 2 inspects some of the typical Bluetooth profiles used in many products and services. With IoT, this list is expected to grow rapidly in the coming years to support communication with many different objects. For example, if we wish to connect a coffee mug to the

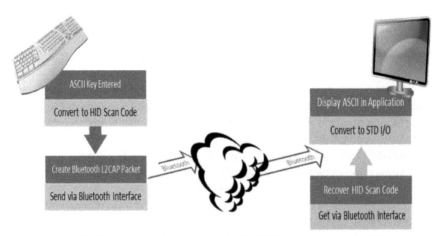

Fig. 21. Connecting a wireless keyboard with HID Bluetooth profile [BT-SF].

Table 2. Examples of commonly used Bluetooth application profiles.

Bluetooth Profile	Supporting Functions and Usage
Headset Profile (HSP)	Defines a mono audio connection (mainly to support telephone calls) between a Bluetooth audio gateway, like a mobile phone, and a headset or earpiece. It also supports a single button to start or end a call, and the use of a volume control.
Hands-Free Profile (HFP)	Allows more extensive control of the mobile phone, such as dial numbers and voice control. Cars use this profile to integrate a mobile phone to the vehicle's audio system.
Message Access Profile (MAP)	Allows a car to access the text messages from the mobile phone.
Advanced Audio Distribution Profile (A2DP)	Supports stereo and multi-channel audio.
Human Interface Device Profile (HID)	Supports low latency and low power wireless connectivity for input devices, such as mice, keyboards, joysticks, and game controllers.
AV Remote Control Profile (AVRCP)	Enables a smartphone to function as a remote control for computers and home theatre equipment.
File Transfer Profile (FTP)	Once paired, a device can browse, modify, and transfer files and folders of another nearby device.

Internet to detect object interactions for smart home residents of the future, then a coffee mug profile has to be defined.

6. Bluetooth Low Energy a.k.a. Bluetooth 4.0

BLE is also known as Bluetooth Smart or Bluetooth 4.0. To understand the motivation behind the development of BLE, we need to understand the new requirements imposed by IoT:

Low Energy: It needs to reduce the energy consumption to 1% to 50% of Bluetooth Classic, so tiny sensors can be powered for years from a small coin cell battery without needing replacements.

Short Broadcast Messages: Instead of file transfers and audio streams, it needs to broadcast very short messages containing body temperature, heart rate, etc., for wearable devices, industrial sensors, and so on. 1 Mbps data rate is required to quickly complete the transmission but throughput is not critical.

Simplicity: Star topology is good enough. There is no need for scatternets.

Low Cost: It must cost lower than Bluetooth Classic as thousands and millions of devices will have to have them.

To meet these new requirements, NOKIA came up with a completely new protocol called WiBree, which shares the same 2.4 GHz band with Bluetooth. Later this new protocol was accepted by the Bluetooth standard to be called Bluetooth Smart or BLE. Although both BLE and Bluetooth Classic share the same spectrum, they are not compatible. Many new Bluetooth chips are thus manufactured as dual-mode chips implementing both the Classic Bluetooth and the new protocol. All new smartphones support dual-mode Bluetooth. There are also Bluetooth chips that support only BLE at a much lower cost. These are used for devices, such as Bluetooth location beacons, which broadcast a packet announcing the current location. Other nodes receiving that broadcast can then work out their location.

6.1 BLE Channels

BLE has a much more simplified channel structure as shown in Fig. 22. Instead of using all 79 channels, it hops at every 2 MHz, which allows hopping over only 40 channels. Three channels, 37, 38, and 39, are reserved for advertising, while the rest, channels 0–36, can be used for data communications. The advertising channels are selected specially to avoid interference with popular WiFi channels, i.e., channels 1, 6, 11 as shown in Fig. 23. Use of only three

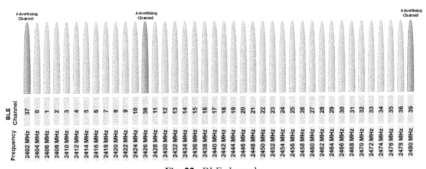

Fig. 22. BLE channels.

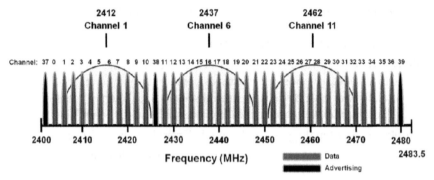

Fig. 23. Mapping between WiFi and BLE channels.

advertising channels significantly simplifies broadcasting and discovery for BLE compared to the complicated discovery process using 32 channels in BT Classic.

6.2 BLE Modulation and Data Rates

BLE uses binary GFSK over 2 MHz channel, which allows more significant frequency separations for '0' and '1' compared to Bluetooth Classic that uses only 1 MHz. The wider separation of frequencies allows longer range with low power. BLE transmits one million symbols per second, which yields 1 Mbps data rate for binary modulation.

6.3 BLE Frequency Hopping

In BLE, devices wake up periodically after every connection interval (CI) time; transmit some data (connection event) and then go back to sleep until the next connection event. A device sends a short blank packet if there is no data to send during a connection event but is allowed to send more than one packet during a connection event if data is pending. Connection interval time can vary from 7.5 ms to 4s and is negotiated during connection set up. The device hops frequency (switch to different data channel) at the start of each event. Figure 24 illustrates the frequency hopping for BLE.

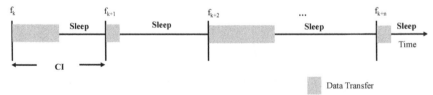

Fig. 24. BLE connection events and connection intervals.

BLE supports a simple frequency hopping algorithm, a.k.a. Algorithm #1, that hops a fixed number of channels instead of selecting a random hop as used in BT Classic. Given that data channels range from 0–36, BLE uses the following equation to derive the next channel:

$$f_{k+1} = (f_k + h) \bmod 37 \tag{1}$$

where h (hop increment) is a fixed value negotiated during connection setup.

Example 3

Assuming that two BLE devices negotiate a hop increment of 10 at the connection setup to generate the hopping frequencies during data transfers using Algorithm #1, what would be the BLE frequency selected after the fifth hop if Channel 0 was selected for the initial event?

Solution

Initial channel: 0
Channel after the first hop: (0+10) mod 37 = 10
Channel after the second hop: (10+10) mod 37 = 20
Channel after the third hop: (20+10) mod 37 = 30
Channel after the fourth hop: (30+10) mod 37 = 3
Channel after the fifth hop: (3+10) mod 37 = 13

6.4 BLE Services

The protocol stack for BLE has changed slightly from its predecessor Bluetooth Classic. The stack is shown in Fig. 25. As we can see, there are basically three main layers—Controller at the bottom, the Host in the middle, and then Application at the top. Many of the functions are similar though. A new function that we have is Generic Attribute Profile (GATT).

Recall that in Bluetooth Classic, the application profiles were very narrow and specific to a particular application, such as a headset or a keyboard and so on. It was adequate at the time because they had to define only a limited number of profiles. If we follow the same approach with IoT, we will have to define thousands of different profiles, which will not scale. This is why, the profile has to be more generic.

Instead of defining specific profiles for specific applications, GATT introduces an The BLE attributes protocol that can define data formats and interfaces to suit any application. This is a major change in BLE that enables it to support a large number of different objects and sensors in an efficient and scalable manner.

Specifically, GATT uses a two-level hierarchy to structure the discovery and accessing BLE services. The first level is called *service*, which is

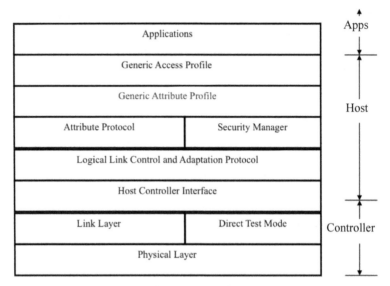

Fig. 25. BLE protocol stack.

uniquely identified by a 16-bit universally unique ID (UUID) standardized by Bluetooth SIG. A set of sensor measurements, called *characteristics*, are then defined under each service. Characteristics are also uniquely defined, using UUID. Both service and characteristic UUIDs are 16-bit numbers expressed in hexadecimal. This means in excess of 65,000 distinct services can be defined each with the capacity to define 65,000 characteristics. Table 3 shows some BLE services and characteristics, for example, 0×1756

Table 3. Example of BLE GATT services and characteristics.

Service	Characteristic	Format
Environmental Sensing Service (ESS) UUID = 0×1756	Temperature (2A1C)	16-bit little endian value representing the measured temperature. Unit: 0.01 deg C
	Humidity (2A6F)	16-bit little endian value representing the measured relative humidity. Unit: 0.01%
	Pressure (2A6D)	32-bit little endian value representing the measured pressure. Unit: 0.1 Pa (0.001 hPa)
Heart Rate Service (HRS) UUID = 0×180D	Hear Rate Measurement (2A37)	1–2B integer representing BPM
	Body Sensor Location (2A38)	1B integer as a code for standard locations on the body, e.g., 0×02 for WRIST.
Battery Service (BAS) (UUID = 0×180F)	Battery Level (2A19)	1B integer with the battery level as a percentage (takes a value between 0–100)

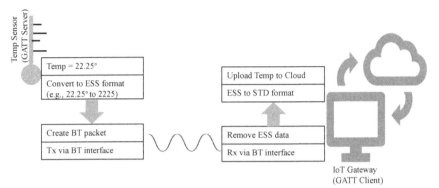

Fig. 26. Temperature sensing using BLE environmental sensing service profile.

defines the environmental sensing service (ESS), which can measure temperature, humidity, pressure, etc.

The sensors or peripheral devices are called GATT servers. They advertise the services they implement, so a GATT client, such as a mobile phone or a home IoT gateway, can scan and identify the sensors of interest in the vicinity to collect data. Bluetooth SIG defines standard representations for exchanging sensing measurements between products from different manufacturers. Figure 26 illustrates how an IoT gateway can collect temperature data from a nearby sensor, using BLE that implements the GATT ESS service.

6.5 Bluetooth Gateway Devices

In WiFi, the devices talk directly to the Internet, but in Bluetooth, small sensors may talk to some intermediate devices, which can help forward requests or data to the cloud servers. Example of these intermediate devices, which become Bluetooth gateways, can be a smartphone for supporting fitness bands or smart watches, as shown in Fig. 27. Tablets, laptops, desktops, or any dedicated computer that has Bluetooth can act as a gateway.

Fig. 27. Bluetooth gateway devices.

6.6 BLE Applications

There are many new BLE applications emerging. We discuss some of them here:

Proximity and Location Contexts: This BLE application helps users discover their location contexts; for example, it can detect that the user is in the car, or in a specific room, or in a shopping mall near a perfume shop, etc.

Object Tracking: Small BLE tags can be attached to objects and animals to track them; for example, this application can help find keys, watches, phones, dogs, cats, children, and so on.

Health Devices: Heart rate monitors, physical activities monitor, thermometer, etc. can all use BLE chips to send periodic measurements to a central server.

Sensors: Many sensors are used in industry and vehicles to constantly monitor the status of many critical components of the system for better management and improving efficiency, such as fuel efficiency of a car. For example, it can monitor temperature, battery status, tire pressure, and so on. BLE can help these sensors to send the data to a nearby controller without having to lay out complicated wiring.

Remote Control: Many new types of remote controls are appearing in the market; for example, it can be used to open/close locks, turn on lights or change the color of LED lights in the house, turn on the swimming pool heating from a nearby gateway connected to the Internet, etc.

Object Interaction Detection: For monitoring activities of elderly in home care, many objects, such as medicine box, toaster, shower tap, etc., can be fitted with Bluetooth Smart and sensors so that when these objects are used by the person, a status is updated in the central server, which can be later analyzed to figure out what activities were completed by the person.

6.7 Bluetooth Beacons

Bluetooth Smart advertising by the peripherals was initially designed for connecting keyboards to the computer, headsets to the phone, phone to the car and so on. Now there is a new use for it in marketing.

When the Bluetooth is turned on, it starts to advertise its presence on the advertising channels. Any other device in proximity then can pick up the signal and will detect the presence of the device. Now if the device happens to be your smartphone, then as soon as you walk into a store, the store server will immediately detect your presence. From the MAC address, it can also find out whether you previously visited the store and bought something. Then it can send you some advertisements and coupons, as shown in Fig. 28.

Fig. 28. Bluetooth coupons during shopping.

Advertising packets consist of a header and a maximum of 27B of payload with multiple TLV-encoded data items. It may also include signal strength and distance to help you find out your precise location; for example, after some measurements, if it is established that a particular signal strength is received at a particular distance from the Bluetooth transmitter, then the receiving device will know from the signal strength whether it is at that distance from the transmitter. And if the transmitter also encodes its current location, then the receiver can find out its location. Such location beacons, also known as BLE beacons, are now installed in many buildings to help people identify their position in an indoor map.

Beacons are also used for verification in electronic payments, such as PayPal. Geofencing is another use of the beacon. New smartphones support this application, which allows to draw a perimeter on the map. When the dog or the child goes outside the perimeter, an alarm is turned to warn you.

7. Bluetooth 5

BLE (Bluetooth 4) was a major advancement compared to BT Classic in terms of reducing energy consumption and extending battery life. BLE, however, could not support high data rate applications, such as audio and file transfer (e.g., quick firmware updates), and the range was still limited for some new IoT applications. Bluetooth 5 extends BLE to realize a faster (2x) and longer range (4x) without compromising the battery life. Advertising and frequency hopping are also improved. Bluetooth 5 is seen as a significant new milestone in the evolution of Bluetooth, which is expected to support many new IoT markets at home and industrial automation, health and fitness tracking and so on.

7.1 Bluetooth 5 PHY

Bluetooth 5 [BT-SIG] introduces two new PHYs, one to support 2x data rate improvement and the other to provide 4x communication range compared to

BLE. The PHY that provides 2x data rate increase is called 2M and the PHY providing extended range is known as Coded.

PHY 2M: The symbol duration is reduced to 55ns, which is half of BLE. This yields 2 million symbols per second, which can support 2 Mbps with binary modulation. It uses the same GFSK modulation, but with higher frequency deviation to combat inter-symbol interference arising from shorter symbols. Specifically, it has frequency deviation of 370 kHz (c.f. 180 kHz in BLE 4) from the central frequency to denote '1' or '0' in FSK.

PHY Coded: It uses one million symbols per sec, the same as in BLE 4. However, to increase the range, data is coded with FEC. Two coding rates are used. The ½ rate cuts the data rate by half to 500 Kbps but provides 2x range increase against BLE 4. The rate ¼ supports only 250 Kbps, but achieves 4x range increase. Note that BLE 4 and BT Classic do not employ any FEC, i.e., they are not *coded*.

7.2 Advertising Extensions

Bluetooth beacon is considered a major advertising use case for future smart cities and smart environments. Bluetooth 4, however, has limited advertising capabilities. Specifically, BLE allows just ID or URL to be advertised in the beacon due to limited advertising packet size (31 bytes). BLE also suffers from heavy load on its three advertising channels as every beacon has to be transmitted on all three channels. Bluetooth 5 proposes three advertising extensions to address the limitations of Bluetooth 4.

Packet Payload Extension: The first extension that Bluetooth 5 proposes is to allow advertising packets up to 255B payload, enabling smart devices and products to advertise many more things and status, such as a fridge can advertise its contents, temperature, expiry dates of sensitive items, etc.

Channel Offload: With this extension, only the header is transmitted over advertising channels and the actual payload is offloaded to a data channel. Note that Bluetooth 4 reserves data channels only for data transfers during connection events when connections are established. Channel offload allows Bluetooth 5 to use data channels in connectionless manner. Channel offloading is illustrated in Fig. 29.

Packet Chaining: Bluetooth 5 allows chaining multiple 255B packets together to carry a very large advertising message. The packet chaining is illustrated in Fig. 30.

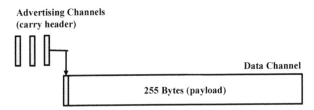

Fig. 29. Advertising channel offload in Bluetooth 5.

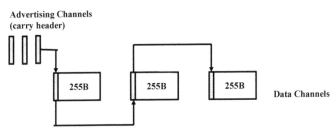

Fig. 30. Advertising packet chaining in Bluetooth 5.

7.3 Frequency Hopping Extension

Bluetooth 4 supports only a simple hopping algorithm, called Algorithm #1, which uses only a fixed hopping increment to switch channels. Fixed hopping increment limits the number of possible sequences to choose from. Bluetooth 5 supports pseudorandom hopping, like the BT Classic, using an algorithm called Algorithm #2, which allows a large number of options for channel switching sequences.

8. Bluetooth 5.3

In 2021, the following new features were added to Bluetooth [BT-SIG] to further improve latency, battery life, security, and protection against interference.

Fast Adjustment of Duty Cycling: As we have studied earlier in this chapter, Bluetooth version 4.0 introduced a parameter, called Connection Interval (CI) to duty cycle the device for improved battery life. Given the inherent trade-off between low duty cycling (good battery life) and high throughput (lower latency), version 4.0 allowed the CI parameter to be selected from 7.5 ms to 4s to address the needs of different applications. However, the CI value could only be negotiated during connection set up, which made it difficult to switch between different duty cycling modes quickly.

In many applications, the devices need to change duty cycling rates to optimize the trade-off between battery life and latency or response time; for example, an environment monitor may start with a very low duty cycling rate to conserve battery, but when an event of interest is detected, it would like to switch to a high duty cycling rate to transfer the event-related data at a faster rate to the server for immediate analysis of the event. Bluetooth 5.3 has added a parameter that now enables a device to change the CI value as a multiple of some base values within the connection. This allows devices to rapidly change duty cycling for better battery life as well as latency.

Peripheral Input to Adaptive Frequency Hopping: Before Bluetooth 5.3, only the central (master) device could decide the eligible list of frequencies (channel map) for adaptive hopping, based on its own experience of interference. However, with longer ranges allowed by version 5.0, the peripheral devices (slaves) may experience different interferences than the central device depending on the locations and environments. To achieve improved protection against all interferences affecting the communication between the master and the slave, Bluetooth 5.3 includes protocol enhancement for the master to consult with the slave for deciding the final channel map to be used in frequency hopping.

Encryption Key Size Control Enhancement: With home and commercial building automation, Bluetooth is being used by a central controller to communicate with many peripheral devices, such as door-locks, privacy curtains, lights, and so on. As peripherals have better knowledge about the security needs of the application, it is desirable for these devices to efficiently negotiate with the central controller about the size of the encryption keys. The new enhancement in version 5.3 allows a peripheral to convey minimum key lengths to the central controller. While this enhancement sounds trivial, it is designed to increase the competitiveness of Bluetooth in the competing market for automation.

More Meta Information for Periodic Advertising: Periodic advertising is one of the key applications of Bluetooth, where sensors and things fitted with a Bluetooth chip periodically broadcast their sensing data, such as temperature, pressure, etc., which are received and processed by nearby Bluetooth hosts to infer actionable information. In many cases, such periodic advertisements contain the same data (if there is no change in the status of the thing or environment from the last broadcast), which creates unnecessary processing load on the host. To address this situation, Bluetooth 5.3 adds a separate field in the advertising packet header to contain more meta information about the content of the advertising packet. Specifically, this header can be used by the thing or sensor to indicate whether the packet content is the same as the previous one. Thus, the host can stop processing the rest of the packet as soon as the header says that it is a repeat information.

9. Summary

1. Bluetooth Classic uses frequency hopping over 79 1-MHz channels with 1, 3, and 5-slot packets.
2. Bluetooth 4 is designed for short broadcasts by sensors. 40 2-MHz channels are used with three channels reserved for advertising and 37 used for data transfers.
3. BT Classic uses flat application profiles to support different types of communication services, which require different application profiles to be defined for different types of sensing and communications.
4. BLE has a hierarchical service structure to group many sensing measurements into a given service type, which scales for large variety of devices and services expected in the IoT era.
5. Bluetooth 5 extends BLE to support higher data rate and longer-range. It also has an improved advertising structure that allows advertisement of more comprehensive information and contents.
6. Bluetooth 5.3 was released in 2021 to further improve latency, battery life, security, and protection against interference.

Multiple Choice Questions

Q1. Protocol A has four times the data rate of Protocol B but consumes three times as much power. Which protocol has less energy consumption per MB (megabyte)?
(a) Protocol A
(b) Protocol B
(c) Both protocols have the same energy consumption

Q2. If 2-slot packets were allowed in Bluetooth, we could not guarantee
(a) that the master starts in even numbered slots only
(b) that the slave starts in even numbered slots only
(c) interference-free communication
(d) error-free communication

Q3. In Bluetooth, only masters are allowed to transmit 5-slot packets.
(a) True
(b) False

Q4. In Bluetooth, the 3b member address is used to identify the
(a) Parked devices
(b) Active devices
(c) Both active and parked devices
(d) Piconet
(e) Scatternet

Q5. Bluetooth employs frequency hopping to
  (a) Detect communication errors
  (b) Correct communication errors
  (c) Avoid interference with other networks operating in the 2.4 GHz band
  (d) Avoid interference with all types of WiFi networks
  (e) Recover from packet loss

Q6. With Gaussian FSK,
  (a) Frequencies do not change
  (b) Frequencies switch rather smoothly
  (c) A large number of frequencies are used, which have a Gaussian distribution
  (d) Both amplitude and frequency are used for modulation
  (e) Both phase and amplitude are used for modulation

Q7. Bluetooth LE uses
  (a) Less number of channels than Bluetooth 5
  (b) Less number of channels than Bluetooth Classic
  (c) Less number of channels than WiFi
  (d) Three data channels and 37 advertising channels
  (e) A different spectrum than Bluetooth 5

Q8. What would be the maximum total number of non-payload bits in a Bluetooth packet if the header was encoded with two-third rate FEC?
  (a) 84
  (b) 86
  (c) 89
  (d) 95
  (e) 99

Q9. Which Bluetooth LE channel will have less likelihood of interference with wireless LAN?
  (a) 1,2,35
  (b) 32,33,34
  (c) 33,34,35
  (d) 36,37,38
  (e) 37,38,39

Q10. Bluetooth 5 achieves longer range by
  (a) using error detection and correction, which reduces the effective data rate
  (b) using higher transmission powers
  (c) using a more sensitive receiver circuit that can decode symbols at a much lower received power
  (d) using a wider channel bandwidth
  (e) using a narrower channel bandwidth

References

[BT-SIG-ORG] 'Origin of the Bluetooth name', Bluetooth Special Interest Group, https://www.bluetooth.com/about-us/bluetooth-origin/ [accessed 26 October 2021].

[BT-SIG] Bluetooth Special Interest Group. https://www.bluetooth.com/.

[BT-NI] Introduction to Bluetooth Device Testing: From Theory to Transmitter and Receiver Measurements. National Instruments. https://download.ni.com/evaluation/rf/intro_to_bluetooth_test.pdf [accessed 26 October 2021].

[BT-RS] Bluetooth Adaptive Frequency Hopping on an R&S CMW Application Note. Rohde Schwarz. https://scdn.rohde-schwarz.com/ur/pws/dl_downloads/dl_application/application_notes/1c108/1C108_0e_Bluetooth_BR_EDR_AFH.pdf [accessed 26 October 2021].

[BT-SF] Bluetooth HID Profile user Manual. Sparkfun. https://cdn.sparkfun.com/datasheets/Wireless/Bluetooth/RN-HID-User-Guide-v1.0r.pdf [accessed 26 October 2021].

[NIST-BT] (August 2012). Security of Bluetooth Systems and Devices. NIST. https://csrc.nist.gov/csrc/media/publications/shared/documents/itl-bulletin/itlbul2012-08.pdf [accessed 26 October 2021].

[PRAVIN2001] P. Bhagwat (May-June 2001). Bluetooth: Technology for short-range wireless apps. pp. 96–103. *In*: *IEEE Internet Computing*, vol. 5, no. 3. doi: 10.1109/4236.935183.

[WIKI-BT] Bluetooth Special Interest Group, Wikipedia. https://en.wikipedia.org/wiki/Bluetooth_Special_Interest_Group [accessed 26 October 2021].

11
LoRa and LoRaWAN

Pervasive IoT deployments demand low-power wide-area networking (LPWAN) solutions that can connect hundreds of thousands of sensors and 'things' over a large area with minimal infrastructure cost. The low-power solution is needed to ensure that the battery-powered sensors can last for many years with a tiny battery. While Bluetooth is certainly low-powered, it works only for short ranges. Cellular networks are designed for wide area coverage, but they consume too much power which requires large batteries and frequent battery recharging for the end nodes. Consequently, there is a significant momentum in standardizing new networking solutions for LPWAN. New developments are emerging from both cellular and WiFi standard bodies, i.e., from the 3 GPP and IEEE/WiFi Alliance, respectively, to fill this gap, but there is a third momentum that is proving very successful. It is called LoRa Alliance (LoRa stands for *long range*), which is an industry alliance committed to accelerate the development and deployment of LPWAN networks. In this chapter, we shall study the details of the LoRa technology.

1. LoRa

LoRa is a proprietary and patented PHY technology originally developed by a small company, called Cycleo in France [SEMTECH-BLOG]. Later it was acquired by Semtech Corporation, which formed the **LoRa Alliance** [LORA-ALLIANCE]. Now LoRa Alliance has 500+ members. The first version, LoRa, was released to public in July 2015. Since then, it enjoyed rapid adoption with many different types of products selling fast. For long-range IoT, this is at the moment the major choice in the market currently implemented in over 100 million devices.

The main advantage of LoRa is the support for extremely long-range connectivity. It supports communications up to 5 kms in urban areas depending on how deep within indoor the sensors are located, and up to 15 kms or more in rural areas with line of sight [LORA-SEMTECH]. Such long distances are supported with extremely low power and low cost. These advantages are gained by trading off the data rate. LoRa supports very low rates on the order of only a few kbps. However, these rates are sufficient for the targeted IoT applications which only need to upload a small message once in a while.

2. LoRa Frequencies

Like 802.11ah, LoRa also uses sub-GHz ISM license-exempt bands to reach long distances at low power. Different regions have different restrictions on the use of LoRa frequencies. The following bands are specified in LoRa developers' guide from SEMTECH [LORA-SEMTECH]:

- 915 MHz in US. Power limit. No duty cycle limit.
- 868/433 MHz in Europe. 1% and 10% duty cycle limit
- 430 MHz in Asia

Note that there is a power limit in the US, but no duty cycle. It means devices can be awake all the time and transmit as often as they like. However, in Europe, devices have to implement 10% duty cycle, which means they can be up only 10% of the time on an average. Limiting the duty cycle enables more devices to be connected to the LoRa network with minimum infrastructure at the expense of slightly higher latency.

LoRa uses channels with significantly smaller bandwidths compared to Bluetooth, WiFi, or cellular networks. Specifically, LoRa channels are either 125 kHz or 500 kHz wide [LORA-SEMTECH]. For example, in the US, 125 kHz channels can be used only for the uplink (end device to gateway), whereas 500 kHz can be used for both uplink and downlink.

3. LoRa Modulation: Chirp Spread Spectrum

Supporting long-range communication with low power is challenging because the receiver will be required to demodulate a signal that can be very weak and even below the noise floor, i.e., demodulation with negative signal-to-noise ratio (SNR) would be required. To achieve this objective, LoRa adopts a specific form of chirp spread spectrum that spreads the signal power to all frequencies over the entire channel bandwidth by continuously increasing or decreasing the frequency during the symbol transmission. This allows the receiver to combine samples from many frequencies to reconstruct the signal despite low signal power. The chirp phenomenon with linear frequency increasing or decreasing rates is illustrated in Fig. 1.

Chirps with increasing frequency are called up-chirps and the ones with decreasing frequency are called down-chirps. In time-frequency graphs,

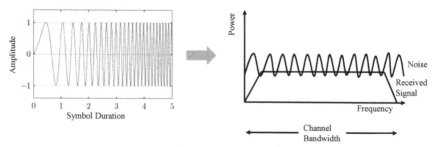

Fig. 1. Frequency domain representation of a linearly increasing chirp symbol. The power is spread over the entire channel bandwidth and the received signal power is below the noise floor.

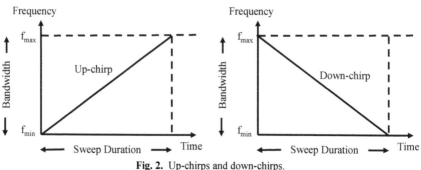

Fig. 2. Up-chirps and down-chirps.

these up-chirps and down-chirps are shown as straight lines with positive and negative slopes, respectively (*see* Fig. 2).

As we can see in Fig. 2, the chirps sweep the entire bandwidth, from the minimum frequency to the maximum frequency, within a specified chirp sweep duration. The sweeping speed, k, is thus obtained as:

$$k = \frac{B}{T_s} Hz / sec \qquad (1)$$

where B is the bandwidth in Hz and T_s is the chirp sweeping duration in second.

So, how does LoRa encode information with chirps? Clearly, these chirps need to be modulated in some ways to convey data. In LoRa, data bits are encoded with either up-chirps or down-chirps, depending on the direction of communication, i.e., uplink vs. downlink. Each chirp represents one symbol, which means that the symbol duration is equivalent to the chirp duration, T_s.

LoRa shifts the starting frequency of the chirp to produce different symbol patterns [LORA-SYMBOL]. The amount of frequency shift is then used to code the symbol, which represents the data bits carried by that symbol. Figure 3 illustrates an example of 4-ary modulation that uses four possible frequency shifts, including zero shift, to create four different symbol patterns.

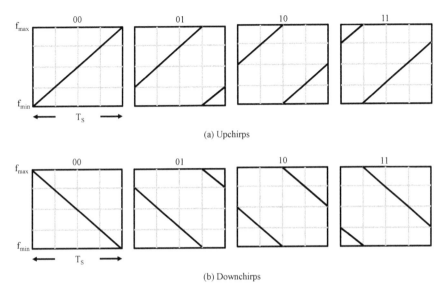

(a) Upchirps

(b) Downchirps

Fig. 3. LoRa symbol patterns for 4-ary modulation.

Note that for the non-zero shifts, the chirp is 'broken' into two pieces because it reaches the maximum (for up-chirp) or minimum (for down-chirp) frequency sooner than the symbol duration. The second piece of the chirp then starts from the minimum (for up-chirp) or maximum (for down-chirp) frequency and continues the frequency sweep until the end of the symbol duration.

Example 1

A LoRa transmitter configured with SF = 8 can send how many bits per symbol?

Solution

8 bits. SF = 8 means there are 2^8 different symbol patterns, thus each symbol can be coded with an 8-bit pattern.

A striking difference between LoRa and the conventional wireless networks is that the symbol duration in LoRa is not fixed but is a function of the modulation order. The larger the modulation order, the longer the symbol duration, and vice versa. Both the modulation order and the symbol duration are controlled by the parameter called spreading factor (SF). For M-ary modulation, SF = $\log_2(M)$ and Ts = $2^{SF}/B$ seconds, where B is in Hz. This means that by increasing SF by 1 would not only double the modulation order (increase bits per symbol by 1), but also double the symbol duration. The relationship between SF, modulation order, and the symbol duration is illustrated in Fig. 4 for up-chirps.

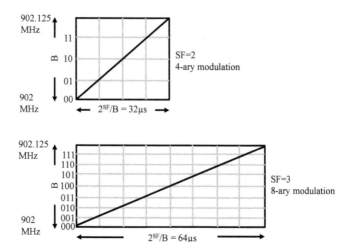

Fig. 4. Relationship between SF, modulation order, and symbol duration.

Example 2

How long a LoRa transmitter configured with SF = 10 would take to transmit one symbol over a 125 kHz channel?

Solution

$Ts = 2^{SF}/B = 2^{10}/125 \text{ ms} = 8.192 \text{ ms}$

LoRa increases the symbol duration to increase the communication range, as longer symbols help decode the signal at the receiver despite weak receptions. Hence SF is adaptively adjusted, based on the received signal strength. By choosing to exponentially increase both the modulation order and the symbol duration, LoRa seeks to achieve orthogonality between signals of different SF. Thus, two signals from two transmitters would not interfere or collide at the receiver even if they are transmitted on the same channel at the same time if they use different SFs [LORA-SEMTECH].

A major consequence of exponentially increasing the symbol duration with increase in SF is that the symbol rate, i.e., the number of symbols per second, is reduced exponentially as well. This means that instead of increasing the data rate with increasing modulation order, the data rate is actually reduced with increasing SF. This can be clearly seen in the following universal equation that derives data rate as a function of the modulation rate (bits per symbol),

symbol rate, and the coding rate (CR) that reflects the forward error correction (FEC) overhead:

Data rate = bits per symbol × symbol rate × coding rate

$$= SF \times \frac{B}{2^{SF}} \times CR\, bps. \tag{2}$$

where B is in Hz and CR is the FEC ratio between actual data bits and the total encoded bits. In LoRa, CR can technically take values from 4/5, 4/6, 4/7, and 4/8, although the default value of 4/5 is often used. As can be seen from Eq. (2), data rate would be reduced nearly exponentially by increasing the SF. Thus, SF is the main control knob used by LoRa to trade-off between data rate and range. A total of six spreading factors, SF = 7 to SF = 12, are supported by LoRa [LORA-SEMTECH].

Example 3
A LoRa sensor is allocated a 125 kHz uplink channel. What would be its effective data rate if it is forced to use a spreading factor of 10 and 50% redundancy for forward error correction?

Solution
SF = 10; 2^{SF} = 1024; CR = 0.5
Symbol rate = $B/2^{SF}$ sym/s = 125,000/1024 sym/s
Effective data rate = 10 × 125000/1024 × 0.5 = ~ 610 bps

Energy is another important parameter affected by the choice of SF. For a given message, the total energy consumed is proportional to the airtime of the message, i.e., the amount of time the LoRa module needs to be active and consume power. The higher the data rate, the shorter is the airtime and vice-versa. Thus, shorter SF would reduce the energy consumption and vice versa. That is why LoRa implements adaptive data rate (ADR), which tries to select the minimum possible SF. For example, devices closer to the gateway would be using shorter SF (due to good quality link) and enjoy a longer battery life compared to the ones located further from the gateway.

4. LoRa Networking with LoRaWAN

LoRa actually refers to only the PHY layer of the LoRa network protocol stack as shown in Fig. 5. The PHY is available for all frequency bands available in different regions of the world. The MAC layer is called LoRaWAN, which is an open standard. The MAC supports connecting LoRa end devices to the LoRa gateways, which in turn are connected to the network servers in the backbone. The end-to-end LoRa network system is illustrated in Fig. 6.

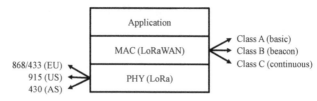

Fig. 5. LoRa network protocol stack.

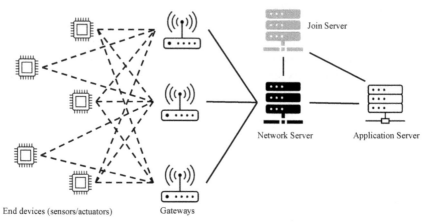

Fig. 6. End-to-end LoRa network system [LORA-SEMTECH].

The gateways are like the base stations in cellular networks. Many gateways are controlled by a central network server. However, unlike cellular networks, LoRa end devices do not associate with a single gateway; instead, all gateways within range receive and process the messages transmitted by all the end devices. The gateways work only at the PHY layer. They only check data integrity if CRC is present. The message is dropped, if CRC is incorrect. They pass the LoRa message to the network server only if the CRC is correct along with some metadata, such as received signal strength (RSSI) and timestamp. The network server actually runs the MAC and makes all networking decisions. It assigns each device a frequency, spreading code, eliminates duplicate receptions, and schedules acknowledgements. If requested by the end device, the network server also implements the adaptive data rate (ADR) for that device by dynamically controlling its transmitters' parameters, such as its SF, bandwidth, and transmit power.

LoRa supports scalable and flexible deployment of networks by provisioning for cost-optimized gateways. For small networks, very simple gateways made from Raspberry Pi can be used with a limited number of channels. For carrier-grade networks run by city municipalities, more heavy-duty gateways with a large number of channels (up to 64 channels in the US) can be used to deploy on the rooftop of high-rise buildings, cellular towers, etc.

LoRa supports bidirectional communications. This allows the sensors (LoRa end devices) to upload data to the server and the server to send acknowledgements or update software/firmware on the sensors. Gateways listen to multiple transmissions on multiple channels, all gateways listen to all transmissions, which provide antenna diversity and improved reliability for the simple Aloha protocol. For example, if one gateway could not receive it because of collision, another gateway may receive it and forward it to the server. The server selects one gateway for the downlink ACK to the device.

LoRa frame format is shown in Fig. 7 [HAX2017]. The preamble, which uses a series of up-chirps followed by a few down-chirps, is used to synchronize the transmitter and receiver clocks. An optional header is used before the payload to automate the configuration of several important parameters, namely the payload length, coding rate, and the use of CRC. When the header is not used (to save transmission energy), these parameters must be configured manually before the start of the session. Finally, the payload is optionally followed by a CRC field to detect errors in the payload.

Application Servers are ultimately responsible for processing and interpreting the received LoRa payload data. They also generate the appropriate payload for the downlink messages.

Join Servers are used to facilitate over-the-air activation of LoRa end devices. A join server processes an uplink *join-request* message from an end device and a downlink *join-accept* message. It also informs the network server about the application server a particular end-device should be connected to. Thus, with join servers in place, users can connect their LoRa sensors and actuators by simply turning them on.

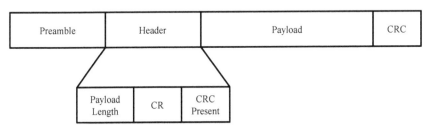

Fig. 7. Lora packet format.

5. LoRa Device Classes

LoRaWAN supports three classes of devices—A, B, and C [LORA-SEMTECH]. Class A is the most basic mode of operation, which must be supported by any device. Class B devices must also support Class A option. Finally, Class C devices must have the option to operate in either of the three classes. Let us take a look at the operational features of each of these classes.

Class A: These are the lowest power and lowest traffic LoRa devices which mostly sleep and wake up once in a while to transmit data if a monitoring event is detected. For each uplink (end device to gateway) transmission, the device will be allowed to receive up to two short downlink (gateway to end device) transmissions. One may be for ACK, but another can be used for the other kind of information, such as an actuation signal triggered by the application based on the uplink information. Examples of these devices include various environmental sensors and monitors with limited actuation capabilities.

The device cannot receive anything else until it transmits again. When it does, again it gets two credits for downlink communication. This cycle repeats. Class A devices are very simple and they use Pure Aloha for channel access, which is basically contention-based. Pure Aloha performs well under light traffic, but struggles under heavy load. Its performance under sustained heavy load approaches 1/2e or approximately 18.4%.

Class B: This is basically Class A plus extra receive window at scheduled time following the periodic beacons from Gateway, i.e., the beacon contains reserved slots for the stations. This class is for stations which need to receive more frequent traffic from the network or server. All gateways transmit beacons every 2^n seconds ($n = 0…7$) to provide plenty of opportunity for the network to synchronize with Class B end devices. All gateways are synchronized using GPS, so that they all can align to the exact beacon timing.

Class C: These are the most powerful stations typically connected to mains power and almost always awake. They can receive anytime, unless transmitting. As such, the server enjoys the lowest latency in reaching a Class C device compared to the other classes. Class C devices include things, such as streetlights, electrical meters, etc., which can be constantly monitored and controlled by a server. Figure 8 illustrates and compares the operations of the three classes.

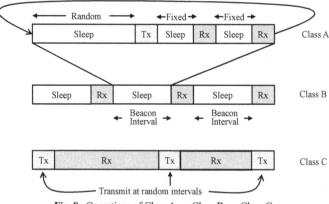

Fig. 8. Operations of Class A vs. Class B vs. Class C.

6. Summary

The main aspects of LoRa can be summarized as follows:

1. LoRa is designed to work with narrow bandwidth channels, long symbols, and low data rates; data rate is sacrificed for longer range.

2. LoRa modulation is a variation of chirp spread spectrum where the modulation order as well as the frequency sweeping speed of the chirp is modulated by an integer variable, called spreading factor (SF).

3. For a given bandwidth B Hz and spreading factor SF, modulation order = 2^{SF} and symbol duration = $2^{SF}/B$ sec. As a result, contrary to typical wireless communications, increasing the modulation order actually decreases the data rate in LoRa.

4. For a given bandwidth, the larger the SF, the longer the symbol duration and longer the range at the expense of reduced data rates.

5. Orthogonality of the SF enables transmission of multiple LoRa chirps at the same frequency channel and at the same time slot.

6. There are six valid SF values in LoRa: 7 to 12.

7. LoRa data contains either all up-chirps or all down-chirps, depending on the direction of communication (uplink vs. downlink); up-chirps and down-chirps are never mixed within the same LoRa packet except for the preamble field.

8. LoRa end devices broadcast to all gateways within a range. The gateway with the best connectivity replies back.

9. LoRa gateways are only PHY-layer devices; all MAC processing is done at the network server.

10. LoRa supports three classes of devices. Class A devices can sleep most of the time to conserve energy but allow most restricted access from the network. Class B devices can be accessed more frequently by the network at the expense of higher energy consumption. Class C devices are usually powered by the mains; they never sleep and hence can be reached by the network at any time without delay.

Multiple Choice Test

Q1. Which of the following layers in LoRa protocol stack is based on proprietary technology?
(a) PHY
(b) MAC
(c) Network
(d) Application

Q2. Duty cycle limit is imposed for LoRa end devices to
(a) save the energy cost of network servers
(b) save the energy cost of application servers
(c) save the energy cost of gateways
(d) increase the capacity of LoRa networks

Q3. LoRa gatways can decode the signals even if the received power is below the noise floor because
(a) LoRa gatways are produced from novel materials with exceptional electromagnetic properties
(b) LoRa uses ultra-wide bandwidth channels
(c) LoRa spreads the power over all frequencies within the channel bandwidth as well as transmits the symbol over a long duration
(d) LoRa uses high transmission power

Q4. For a 500 kHz channel, the frequency sweeping speed of a LoRa transmitter configured with SF = 7 can exceed
(a) 1 GHz/s
(b) 2 GHz/s
(c) 3 GHz/s
(d) 4 GHz/s

Q5. For a 125 kHz channel, a LoRa transmitter configured with SF = 8 can send
(a) ~ 1024 sym/s
(b) ~ 512 sym/s
(c) ~ 488 sym/s
(d) ~ 390 sym/s

Q6. Which of the following statements is incorrect?
(a) Header is optional in LoRa packets
(b) CRC is optional in LoRa packets
(c) LoRa gateways are responsible for medium access control
(d) LoRa network server is responsible for medium access control
(e) None of these

Q7. Which of the following statements is correct?
    (a) Each LoRa chirp represents one or more symbols
    (b) Up-chirps and down-chirps are often mixed in a given LoRa payload
    (c) LoRa preamble contains both up-chirps and down-chirps
    (d) In LoRa chirps, frequency increases exponentially
    (e) LoRa chirps always start from the lowest frequency of the channel

Q8. If SF is downgraded from 12 to 10,
    (a) symbol duration is increased by a factor of 2
    (b) symbol duration is decreased by a factor of 4
    (c) data rate is increased by a factor of 2
    (d) data rate is increased by a factor of 4
    (e) frequency sweeping speed is increased by a factor of 2

Q9. If SF is upgraded from 7 to 10,
    (a) symbol duration is increased by a factor of 8
    (b) power consumption of the client device is reduced significantly
    (c) message air-time is reduced significantly
    (d) data rate is increased by a factor of 8
    (e) data rate is decreased by a factor of 8

Q10. With SF = 10, LoRa symbols for 500 kHz channels would be
    (a) shorter than 2 ms
    (b) longer than 2 ms
    (c) exactly 2 ms
    (d) longer than 3 ms
    (e) exactly 3 ms

References

[HAX2017] J. Haxhibeqiri, A. Karaagac, F. Van den Abeele, W. Joseph, I. Moerman and J. Hoebeke (2017). LoRa indoor coverage and performance in an industrial environment: Case study. *2017 22nd IEEE International Conference on Emerging Technologies and Factory Automation (ETFA)*, pp. 1–8. doi: 10.1109/ETFA.2017.8247601.

[LORA-ALLIANCE] https://lora-alliance.org/.

[LORA-SEMTECH] (December 2019). LoRa and LoRaWAN: A Technical Overview. Semtech Corporation. https://lora-developers.semtech.com/documentation/tech-papers-and-guides/lora-and-lorawan/ [accessed 26 October 2021].

[LORA-SYMBOL] N. E. Rachkidy, A. Guitton and M. Kaneko (2018). Decoding Superposed LoRa Signals. *2018 IEEE 43rd Conference on Local Computer Networks (LCN)*, pp. 184–190. doi: 10.1109/LCN.2018.8638253.

[SEMTECH-BLOG] A Brief History of LoRa®: Three Inventors Share Their Personal Story at The Things Conference. Semtech Blog. https://blog.semtech.com/a-brief-history-of-lora-three-inventors-share-their-personal-story-at-the-things-conference [accessed 26 October 2021].

Part VI

Next Frontiers in Wireless Networking

12
Artificial Intelligence-assisted Wireless Networking

Artificial intelligence (AI) has emerged as a crucial tool to combat many complex decision-making tasks across a wide variety of domains. As wireless networks get more and more complex to deal with the ever-growing demand for capacity and quality of service, AI is eagerly explored as a potential aid to wireless networking in the future. This chapter examines the what, why, and how questions for AI in wireless.

1. What is AI?

AI is a computation paradigm for machines to learn and make decisions like humans. AI is a broad umbrella that covers many techniques, such as knowledge acquisition, knowledge representation, expert systems, evolutionary algorithms, and machine learning (ML). ML empowers a machine or process to automatically learn useful information from the observed events or data and make decisions without being explicitly programmed. Deep learning (DL) is a special branch of ML that tries to mimic the way the complex network of neurons works inside the human brain.

1.1 Machine Learning

ML algorithms can be categorized into two fundamental methods—supervised learning and unsupervised learning [Sammut 2011]. In supervised learning, a ML model is trained by examining data samples from a historical dataset for which the correct outputs, called labels, are known. First, some specific features are computed from the raw input sample, which are fed to the ML model to produce an output. The model is then adjusted repeatedly with each input sample, based on the observed loss or error, i.e., the difference between the model output and the label. With sufficient training, the model learns to

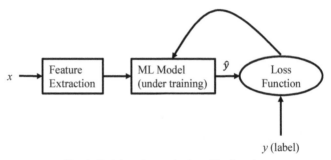

Fig. 1. Training of supervised machine learning.

predict the label accurately and gets ready to be deployed in the real field for decision making on unlabelled input. The training and testing processes of ML are illustrated in Fig. 1. Supervised learning is typically used for applications where historical data can predict the likely future events; for example, trained on sufficient historical data, ML can predict whether a home loan customer is likely to default. Typical supervised ML algorithms include Support Vector Machine (SVM), k-Nearest Neighbour (k-NN), Random Forest, Neural Network and so on.

Unsupervised ML refers to learning based on unlabelled data. Here the goal of learning is to identify some structure in the data; for example, unsupervised ML can separate all customers into some distinct groups, which can be treated for some targeted campaigns.

ML can also work for some applications when there is no historical data, but a machine or process must learn the right policy or decision from trials and errors. This can be very useful for robots trying to learn walking, for example. This type of learning is called reinforcement learning, which has three primary components: (1) the **agent** that tries to learn the best policy, (2) the **environment** with which the agent interacts, and (3) the **actions** that the agent is allowed to perform. The agent should be able to observe the outcome of an action and its objective is to choose the action that maximizes the expected reward over a certain period. The question is—which action to choose given a particular observation? This is called the policy. A good policy will lead to a better reward. Hence the goal of reinforcement learning is to learn the best policy.

1.2 Deep Learning

Conventional ML has several limitations. First, it requires expertise and manual effort to design or engineer the features that must be extracted from the raw data for training the model. Second, its accuracy plateaus after using certain volume of data, i.e., the accuracy cannot be improved further even if more data is made available.

DL is a special type of ML in which a model learns to perform classification tasks directly from raw input data without having to engineer features manually [DL-GOOD]. DL implicitly learns the optimal features for maximum accuracy as more data is fed to the model during training. As illustrated in Fig. 2, this property allows DL to increase accuracy potentially unboundedly, if large datasets and computing resources are available for training.

DL is usually implemented using a neural network architecture with many layers, as shown in Fig. 3, which is inspired by the complex network of neurons in the human brain. There is an input layer, an output layer, and an unlimited number of hidden layers, which cannot be directly accessed or manipulated by the programmer. Each layer has a certain number of nodes or neurons and different layers are interconnected to each other by connecting

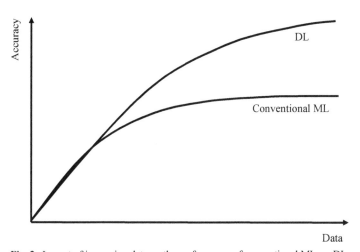

Fig. 2. Impact of increasing data on the performance of conventional ML vs. DL.

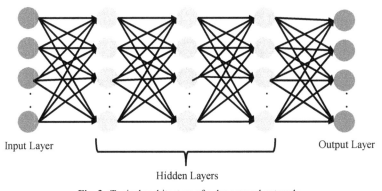

Fig. 3. Typical architecture of a deep neural network.

the output of the neurons from the previous layer to the input of the next layer. The term 'deep' refers to the number of hidden layers in the network—the more the layers, the deeper the network. Traditional neural networks, which are also sometimes used by conventional ML, contain only two or three hidden layers at most, while deep neural networks can have hundreds.

Recall that DL learns features automatically directly from the raw data. Each hidden layer helps in extracting some fine-grained features of the data and in improving the classification accuracy at the output layer. Thus, a deeper network with more layers can potentially improve the accuracy further, but it would require more training data to learn. DL, therefore, is more data- and resource-hungry as compared to conventional ML.

With development of sensor and IoT technology, large volumes of data are often available in many applications' domain. Also, with the help of crowdsourcing, massive labelled datasets are now publicly available; for example, the publicly available ImageNet database contains over 14 million labelled images for any researcher to download and use in their DL research. With advancements in Graphical Processing Units (GPUs), it is now possible to efficiently compute many layers within a short period of time. Most cloud services now offer DL programming platforms and GPU resources at competitive prices for tailored training activities with DL.

The combination of data and computing resource availability has sparked a massive interest in applying DL to solve complex problems in vision, natural language processing, automated text processing, and in many other fields where precise mathematical models are not readily available. Indeed, DL has advanced to the point where they can outperform humans at winning chess and GO and classifying images as shown in Fig. 4.

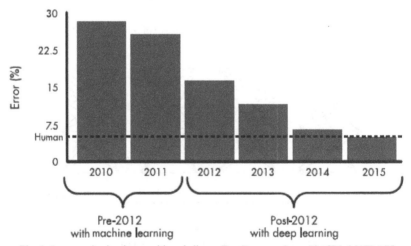

Fig. 4. Large-scale visual recognition challenge Top-5 error on ImageNet [DL-MATLAB].

2. Why AI in Wireless Networks?

DL has shown remarkable performance improvement in vision, natural language processing, and in many other domains. Would AI also be useful in wireless communication?

We should note that a key difference between other AI-dominated domains, such as vision, and wireless communications is that the systems that are used for wireless communication are completely man-made. As such, many things in wireless systems are known or we could design it in a way that we can solve it optimally. Unlike vision, where a robot may be asked to identify an arbitrary scene encountered in nature, a wireless receiver is asked to detect signals that are designed by humans. Thus, the problem domain in wireless communication is different than those in vision or natural language processing. As a matter of fact, for most problems in wireless communications, there exist known algorithms or signal-processing techniques that provide the optimal solutions. As such, until recently, AI received little attention in wireless networking.

However, future wireless systems are facing major challenges arising from the growing demand for higher capacity and quality of service. To address this future need, wireless systems are increasingly required to solve much more complex problems in real-time without compromising on accuracy. The rising complexity is motivating recent interest in exploring AI and DL as an additional aid to design future wireless systems.

3. Applications of DL in Wireless Networks

Recall that there already exist a large suit of optimization and signal processing techniques to deal with problems in wireless system design. As such, a wireless engineer has to carefully identify problems where DL can potentially offer better or more efficient alternatives. In the following, we discuss some scenarios where AI and DL can bring performance benefits in wireless networks.

Scenario-1: Avoid execution of complex algorithms, thereby reducing latency, power consumption, and computation requirements: Many known optimal algorithms are highly complex and take too long to converge. Although optimal solutions are known, the complexity may cause excessive delay in arriving at the optimal solution, which is not desirable for real-time ultra-low-latency applications envisioned in next-generation wireless systems. In this case, a DL can be trained with a large input dataset, where the labels (ground truths) can be generated, using the conventional optimal algorithm. Then after the training is over, the trained DL can be used in production systems, which can estimate the output very quickly. This

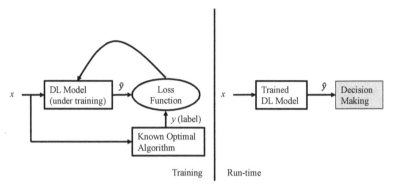

Fig. 5. Application of DL to reduce latency in wireless communications.

application is illustrated in Fig. 5. Examples of such DL applications would include power control for massive MIMO, beamforming phase computations for large antenna array systems, complex signal detection at the receiver, and so on [Bjornsson 2020], where the size of the problem increases complexity and convergence time exponentially. It is important to note that such gains not only reduce latency, but also significantly reduce power consumption and computational requirements for wireless devices, which become very important for the IoT era.

Scenario-2: Mitigation of the effects of hardware distortion. In wireless communication systems, generated signals pass through several hardware components in its end-to-end path before being finally used by a decoding algorithm at the receiver. Often, these hardware components introduce some non-linear distortions in the signal along the way, which can propagate through other system components amplifying the net distortion and error at the decoder. Conventional signal processing solution to this problem attempts to approximate the hardware distortion and then applies corrective signals at the output of the hardware to mitigate the distortion. However, due to the non-linearity of the distortion, the performance of such signal processing remains low. Recent studies have shown [Bjornsson 2020] that DL can effectively learn to reverse the effect of the hardware and reconstruct the original signal through a low-overhead training process that does not require separate processes to generate labels.

The training process of signal reversal is illustrated in Fig. 6. The generated signal x is distorted to y when it passes through a hardware, such as the transmitter. A DL model is trained with y as input and the same x as the ground truth label, so it adjusts itself to reproduce x as accurately as possible. Because the labels are basically the generated signals, there is no cost here for producing the labels. As such, it is possible to train the DL with large training dataset to achieve good accuracy.

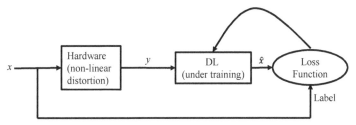

Fig. 6. Application of DL to address hardware-induced signal distortion in wireless communications.

4. Combating Pitfalls of Deep Learning

DL has some specific pitfalls that wireless engineers must be aware of. Here we discuss some of these pitfalls and their potential remedies.

4.1 Mitigating the Training Overhead with Transfer Learning

For high accuracy, DL requires large training datasets. The deeper the neural network, the more data is required to converge. In some applications, acquisition of labels can be extremely time consuming; for example, DL applications that need to run a complex known algorithm to derive each label, as illustrated earlier in Fig. 5, training effort can be significant. In contrast, no training is involved when conventional algorithms are used.

There are some specific methods that can be used to reduce the training effort. **Transfer learning** [TLSURVEY 2010] is one such method that allows use of already available trained ML models that were trained for another related task. In this case, the available pre-trained model can be trained specifically for the task at hand with a very small amount of training data, which drastically reduce the training effort. For example, as illustrated in Fig. 7, a model trained

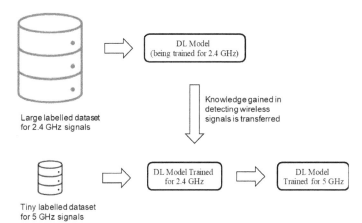

Fig. 7. Illustration of transfer learning.

to classify 2.4 GHz signals using a large dataset of labelled 2.4 GHz signals could be later trained to classify 5 GHz signals with a small amount of labelled 5 GHz samples. It should be noted though that there does not exit a one-size-fit-all transfer learning methods that can be used for all problems. Often one has to spend time to identify an effective transfer learning method that works for the problem at hand.

4.2 Overcoming Communication Constraints with Federated Learning

For many expected applications of future wireless networks, data may be distributed over multiple mobile devices. Spectrum sharing by two co-existing wireless services, such as radar and cellular (or WiFi), is one such example where devices could benefit from machine learning to predict spectrum availability and make intelligent decisions about their spectrum usage. Machine learning in this case requires all individual radar and cellular/WiFi devices to upload their detailed radio usage data, including frequency, timings of data transmissions, etc., to a central node where an appropriate machine learning model can be trained with the aggregate data. Unfortunately, bringing these distributed data to a central entity faces important communication constraints, such as privacy, bandwidth, and energy consumption.

Originally introduced by Google, **federated learning** [FL 2020] is an emerging distributed machine learning approach to address the afore-mentioned challenges of privacy and resource constraints of mobile devices. It utilizes the on-device processing power and the emerging low-power neuromorphic circuits, such as IBM's TrueNorth and Qualcomm's Snapdragon, to perform the model training in a distributed manner, as illustrated in Fig. 8. With federated learning, the private data therefore never leaves the end device; only the parameters of the locally-trained models are transmitted to the central node. In the central node, the local models are aggregated to train a global model, which is eventually fed back to the individual local learners for their use.

Federated learning saves bandwidth and energy consumption of mobile devices by transmitting only a small amount of data related to their local models instead of sending huge volumes of raw data. The privacy is inherently protected by not disclosing the raw data to the central node. To further protect against the possibility of any information leakage through model parameters, the devices could transmit only encrypted versions of their models, which could still be aggregated using a class of secure multi-party computation to train the global model without having to decrypt them [MADI 2021].

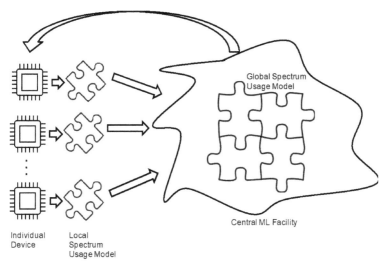

Fig. 8. Illustration of federated learning for spectrum sharing applications.

5. Summary

1. AI is a computation paradigm for machines to learn and make decisions like humans. ML is a branch of AI that empowers a machine to automatically learn useful information from the observed events or data. DL is a special branch of ML that tries to mimic the way the complex network of neurons works inside the human brain.

2. DL has a much higher training overhead and requires much more data to learn, compared to conventional ML. The main benefits of DL are that it can learn directly from the raw data and potentially increase accuracy unboundedly if large datasets and computing resources are available for training.

3. The combination of data and computing resource availability has sparked a massive interest in applying DL to solve complex problems in a growing number of domains. The rising complexity of future wireless systems is motivating recent interest in exploring AI and DL as an additional aid to solve wireless communication problems.

4. DL can potentially offer a fast approximation solution for some complex wireless algorithms that are computationally intensive. In such scenarios, DL can practically reduce latency and energy consumption in wireless communications.

5. DL can provide an efficient solution to address hardware distortion in wireless communications.

6. Transfer learning is a special learning technique that can help reduce the training overhead of DL.

7. Federated learning is an emerging learning paradigm that allows learning from data distributed across individual wireless devices without violating data privacy. It also reduces bandwidth and energy consumption of distributed learning by allowing the individual devices to learn locally and transmit only the learned model to the central learning node instead of transmitting the large volume of raw data.

Multiple Choice Questions

Q1. Which of the following statements is true?
(a) ML is a special branch of DL
(b) DL is a special branch of ML
(c) AI is a special branch of DL
(d) AI is a special branch of ML

Q2. An DL network has
(a) many input layers
(b) many output layers
(c) one or more hidden layers
(d) a single hidden layer

Q3. Which of the following statements is true?
(a) DL usually takes longer to train compared to conventional ML
(b) Conventional ML usually takes longer to train compared to DL
(c) DL can learn using only a small amount of data
(d) Conventional ML requires an enormous amount of data to train

Q4. Which of the following is motivating the current interest in DL?
(a) The fact that DL can turn a machine to think like a human
(b) DL can classify very accurately and that access to both large datasets and computational resources are becoming affordable
(c) DL can solve any problem
(d) DL has low training overhead

Q5. What is the utility of low-power neuromorphic circuits?
(a) They can speed up AI computations in large data centers
(b) They can accurately classify wireless signals
(c) They can allow local training and learning within small mobile devices
(d) They can reduce power consumption of wireless communications

Q6. Which of the following statements is true?
   (a) DL can provide a better alternative for solving all wireless communication problems.
   (b) DL can provide a better alternative for specific problems in wireless communications.
   (c) DL is expected to replace the existing signal processing tools used for designing wireless communications systems.
   (d) DL is unlikely to be used as a designing aid in wireless communications due to its high training overhead.

Q7. The main benefit of approximating a computationally-intensive optimal algorithm with DL is
   (a) faster execution and decision making
   (b) reduction of design time and effort
   (c) reduction of device manufacturing cost
   (d) enhanced accuracy

Q8. Which of the following statements is true?
   (a) Label generation is always costly for ML in wireless communications.
   (b) Label generation can be very easy for some ML applications in wireless communications.
   (c) Labels are not required in some ML applications in wireless communications.
   (d) Labels must be generated manually for ML applications in wireless communications.

Q9. Transfer learning can
   (a) always learn effectively from any available trained ML model
   (b) potentially learn significant knowledge from an available model pre-trained for a similar task
   (c) eliminate the need for training
   (d) improve accuracy compared to the case when the new model is trained from scratch with an equally large dataset for the new task

Q10. Federated learning
   (a) requires wireless devices to send their data to a central ML training node
   (b) requires wireless devices to train locally on the local data and only send the local model to a central ML training node
   (c) reduces computational burden on the wireless devices
   (d) increases bandwidth requirement for distributed ML

References

[Bjornsson 2020] E. Bjornson and P. Giselsson (Sept. 2020). Two applications of deep learning in the physical layer of communication systems [Lecture Notes]. pp. 134–140. *In*: *IEEE Signal Processing Magazine*, vol. 37, no. 5. doi: 10.1109/ MSP.2020.2996545.

[DL-GOOD] Ian Goodfellow, Yoshua Bengio, Aaron Courville (2016). *Deep Learning*, MIT Press.

[DL-MATLAB] *Introducing Deep Learning with MATLAB*, by MathWorks. https://www. mathworks.com/campaigns/offers/deep-learning-with-matlab.html [accessed 27 October 2021].

[FL 2020] T. Li, A. K. Sahu, A. Talwalkar and V. Smith (May 2020). Federated learning: challenges, methods, and future directions. pp. 50–60. *In*: *IEEE Signal Processing Magazine*, vol. 37, no. 3. doi: 10.1109/MSP.2020.2975749.

[MADI 2021] A. Madi, O. Stan, A. Mayoue, A. Grivet-Sébert, C. Gouy-Pailler and R. Sirdey (2021). A secure federated learning framework using homomorphic encryption and verifiable computing. *2021 Reconciling Data Analytics, Automation, Privacy, and Security: A Big Data Challenge (RDAAPS)*, pp. 1–8. doi: 10.1109/ RDAAPS48126.2021.9452005.

[Sammut 2011] Claude Sammut and Geoffrey I. Webb (Ed.). (2011). *Encyclopedia of Machine Learning*, Springer Science & Business Media.

[TLSURVEY 2010] S. J. Pan and Q. Yang (Oct. 2010). A survey on transfer learning. pp. 1345–1359. *In*: *IEEE Transactions on Knowledge and Data Engineering*, vol. 22, no. 10. doi: 10.1109/TKDE.2009.191.

13
Wireless Sensing

While wireless has revolutionized mobile data communications, it has also played a major role as a sensing technology. Meteorologists routinely use wireless signals to scan the atmosphere for weather forecasts, astronomers use radio to probe deep space, geologists use radio frequencies for remotely sensing various Earth phenomenon, and airport authorities are increasingly using wireless signals at security gates to detect prohibited materials concealed by passengers. Recently, scientists are discovering techniques to monitor human activities and even vital signs, such as heart and breathing rates, simply by analyzing the wireless signals reflected by the human body. These advancements have created the potential for wireless to penetrate the growing mobile- and IoT-sensing market. This chapter explains the working principles of the popular wireless sensing tools and techniques targeted at the IoT market.

1. Motivation for Wireless Sensing

Sensing is fast becoming an indispensable technology for modern living. There is a push to integrate various types of sensors in the environment for seamlessly detecting human contexts, to realize more natural and effortless living. For example, sensors embedded into wearable devices, such as wrist bands, can continuously monitor the user's activity levels and vital signs, offering 24×7 low-cost health and fitness care for many groups of citizens, including high-risk individuals. Low-cost cameras can be deployed in aged care facilities to help detect diagnostic movements or falls of elderly occupants.

While wearable sensors and cameras can be very effective for sensing human contexts in smart environments, they have several disadvantages. Wearable sensors are not always convenient to carry or wear and they need to be regularly recharged, adding additional maintenance burden on the user. Cameras on the other hand free the user from such burdens but they intrude user privacy and do not work without line-of-sight. As radio signals can penetrate walls; they offer more ubiquitous sensing than cameras and unlike the cameras, they do not record privacy details. Wireless sensing can work with ambient radio signals and hence eliminate the need to wear sensors on the body. Due to these distinct advantages, wireless sensing is fast becoming a critical technology in smart living.

2. Principle of Wireless Sensing

Figure 1 illustrates the overall working principle of wireless sensing [COMST 2021]. The human body reflects wireless signals. As such, human activities cause changes in wireless signal reflections, which in turn cause variations in received signals, e.g., the amplitude and phase of the signal. Carefully-designed algorithms therefore can distinguish one human activity or state from another by measuring and analyzing various features, such as received signal strength, time of flight, etc., of the received signals.

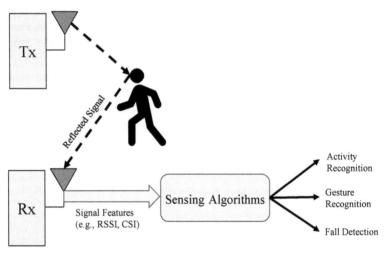

Fig. 1. Principle of wireless sensing.

3. Types of Sensing Signals

There are two dominant types of wireless signals that are currently used for mobile sensing: WiFi and radar. The actual techniques of sensing are different for these two types of signals. While WiFi sensing can sense humans and the environment directly from the existing signals used for communications, radars use signals specifically designed and dedicated for sensing. These two types of mobile sensing are explained in the remaining part of this chapter.

4. WiFi Sensing

WiFi sensing refers to systems that try to detect human states from the WiFi signals reflected from the human body. Working principle of WiFi sensing system is illustrated in Fig. 2 where an existing access point (AP) or WiFi router transmits WiFi packets, while a receiver, such as a laptop, extracts specific signal information for sensing. RSS and channel state information (CSI) are dominant signal informations currently used for WiFi sensing.

Fig. 2. WiFi sensing using existing WiFi infrastructure.

4.1 Sensing with RSS

RSS is a single scaler power value in dBm reported for the entire wireless channel, irrespective of the number of OFDM subcarriers within the channel. Humans can affect RSS in different ways; they can block the LoS between the transmitter and the receiver, or they can act as an additional source of reflection. Blocking of LoS would directly reduce the signal strength, while the reflection would cause variations in the overall received signal power as all reflected rays are combined at the receiver to produce the received signal. Thus, the presence, location, and activities of the human would create distinct patterns in RSS time series, which can be detected using appropriate algorithms.

Figure 3 shows an example of hand gesture detection using WiFi RSS. It shows that raw RSS data is very noisy due to complex propagation and interaction of the signals with surrounding objects. Raw RSS time series therefore is 'denoised' or 'smoothed' first before gesture patterns can be detected.

The major advantage of using RSS for sensing is that it is widely and readily available as most mobile devices measure and report RSS for all received WiFi packets. Thus, no special hardware/software is needed for WiFi sensing with RSS. The downside is that commodity WiFi chips provide low

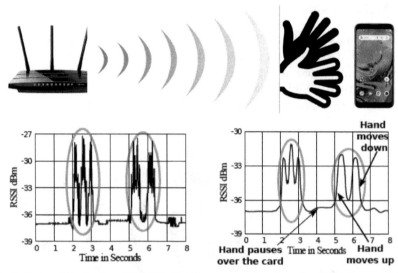

Fig. 3. Gesture detection from WiFi RSS. Hand gestures conducted near a mobile phone receiving WiFi packets from an AP (*top*). Raw (*bottom left*) and denoised RSS (*bottom right*) time series for moving a hand up and down over the mobile phone [YOUSSEF 2015].

RSS resolutions, hence only coarse activities can be detected with limited accuracies. For example, RSS can be used to detect a few hand gestures, but it is not good for detecting more fine-grained activities, such as detecting gestures of sign language or detecting daily activities of the residents.

4.2 Sensing with Channel State Information (CSI)

In wireless communications, the received signals are never the exact replicas of their transmitted counterparts. Factors, such as distance-related path loss, atmospheric absorption, reflection and scattering from various objects, etc., affect the amplitude and phase of the signal during its travel from the transmitter to the receiver. Conceptually, it is said that the signal travels through a wireless channel, h, which has a particular channel frequency response (CFR) function, $h(f)$, which determines the amplitude and phase response for each individual frequency, f, contained within the signal. This concept is illustrated in Fig. 4. The received signal for frequency f at any time instant, t, is obtained by multiplying the CFR with the transmitted signal as follows:

$$y(f, t) = h(f, t) \times x(f, t) + n \tag{1}$$

where n is the receiver noise independent of the transmitted frequencies. The CFR, $h(f,t)$, expresses the amplitude and phase changes using the complex number, $Ae^{j\theta}$, where A and θ, respectively, represent the changes in amplitude

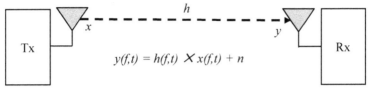

Fig. 4. Channel frequency response for wireless communications.

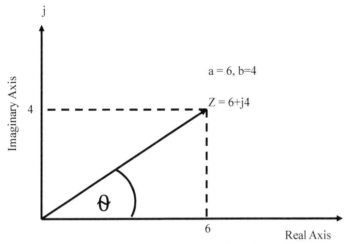

Fig. 5. Geometric plot of the complex CSI. The x-axis plots the real part while the y-axis plots the imaginary part of the complex CSI number.

and phase, and $j = \sqrt{-1}$. A is often measured in dB and θ in radians. As illustrated in Fig. 5, $Ae^{j\theta}$ can be geometrically plotted in a 2D graph as $(a+jb)$, where $A = \sqrt{a^2 + b^2}$ and $\theta = \tan^{-1}\frac{b}{a}$.

The complex number, $Ae^{j\theta}$, is also known as the channel state information (CSI), which is used to estimate the wireless channel between the transmitter and the receiver. CSI estimation is a very important function at the physical layer of wireless communication systems because it helps the system to adjust the changes inflicted by the channel on the transmitted signal. For example, in WiFi, the packet preamble contains known signals, which are compared with the received signals to estimate CSI at the receiver; the receiver then uses the CSI to decode data symbols in the packet payload. The receiver may also provide CSI feedback to the transmitter, e.g., in 802.11n, so the transmitter can adjust the data rates (modulation and coding) or configure the power and phase parameters of the MIMO transmission more precisely.

In most commercial devices, CSI is produced and consumed inside the WiFi chip at the physical layer and cannot be accessed at user or application layer, which limits CSI-based WiFi sensing to some extent. However, some commercial WiFi chips, such as Intel 5300 and Atheros 9390, do provide CSI for selected subcarriers, usually for 30 subcarriers which are adequate for fine-grained sensing.

By configuring a WiFi transmitter to transmit packets at a fixed rate, a receiver can obtain a CSI time series for **each subcarrier** at a target sampling rate, e.g., 100 packets/s leads to CSI sampling at 100 Hz for each of the N time series, where N is the number of subcarriers for which CSI is estimated. For receiving devices with multiple (M) antennas, each antenna produces N CSI time series for a given transmitting antenna.

While CSI time series provides more detailed frequency-dependent channel information, it becomes overwhelming to detect patterns from so many individual time series. Often, some **dimensionality reduction**, such as Principle Component Analysis (PCA), is performed on the large number of CSI time series to produce a **single CSI time series** [WIDANCE 2017], which is then used to detect patterns for human activities. The dimensionality reduction pre-processing is illustrated in Fig. 6.

While CSI provides both amplitude and phase values, the phase values are typically very noisy due to frequency drifts in oscillators. This phenomenon is particularly pronounced in WiFi receivers due to low-cost electronics compared to cellular (3G, 4G, etc.) receivers. Therefore, phase values of the WiFi CSI are often ignored and sensing is performed using CSI amplitudes only. Future

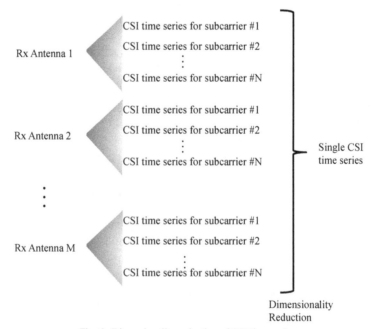

Fig. 6. Dimensionality reduction of CSI time series.

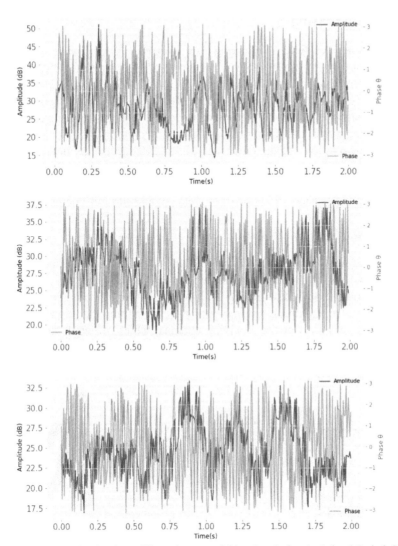

Fig. 7. CSI time series for three different human activities; Leg Swing (*top*), hand Push & Pull (*middle*), and Hand Swipe (*bottom*). The amplitude (blue) shows distinct patterns while the phase (yellow) is too noisy to be useful.

generations of WiFi radios designed to work with very high modulations, such as 4096 QAM in the proposed 802.11be, are expected to provide cleaner phase values as they will require stricter phase noise control for correctly detecting very small phase differences between symbols. Figure 7 shows examples of CSI amplitude and phase time series collected from a 802.11n WiFi receiver for different human activities. We can see that different activities have distinct amplitude patterns while the phase values are too noisy.

5. Radar Sensing

Radar stands for **RA**dio **D**etecting **A**nd **R**anging. As the name suggests, it is a technology to detect objects and estimate the range of the object, i.e., how far the object is from the transmitter, using radio signals. Traditionally, radars have been used to detect and track objects at long ranges, such as aircraft, ships, and cars as well detecting rains. With advancements in low-power electronics and miniaturizations, radar technology is now penetrating the mobile and IoT consumer market, giving these consumer devices greater sensing capability to realize the vision of smart living [TI-RADAR]. These compact radars have much enhanced sensing capabilities than WiFi; they can sense distance, speed, direction of movement, and sub-millimeter motions.

5.1 Principle of Radar Sensing

The fundamental principle of radar is illustrated in Fig. 8. Radar uses a single device instrumented with a transmitting and a receiving antenna synchronized by the same clock. It works by transmitting a directional wireless signal through the transmitting antenna and then measuring the signal reflected by the target object at the receiving antenna, which allows it to accurately compute the time of flight (ToF). The range is then computed by multiplying the ToF by the speed of light.

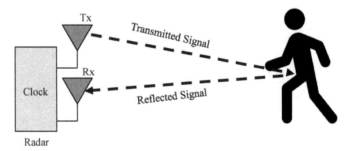

Fig. 8. Fundamental principle of radar.

5.2 Range and Resolution

The range of a radar refers to the detection or coverage range, i.e., the maximum distance from which a radar can reliably detect and estimate the range of an object. Range therefore basically relates to 'how **far** the radar can see'. Resolution, on the other hand, refers to its ability to separate two or more targets at different ranges within the same bearing. Resolution therefore relates to 'how **clearly** the radar can see'. Usually, longer-range radars have lower resolution and vice-versa. The concepts of range and resolution of a

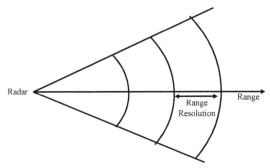

Fig. 9. Illustration of range and resolution of radar.

radar are illustrated in Fig. 9. We note that both the range and the resolution are measured in units of distance, such as in meters or millimeters.

Fundamentally, the resolution directly depends on the bandwidth of the radar signal as follows [RADAR-NATURE]:

$$\text{Resolution} = \frac{c}{2B} \text{meter} \tag{2}$$

where c is the speed of light in m/s and B is the bandwidth in Hz.

5.3 Types of Radar Signals

Radars are specifically designed for sensing and cannot be generally used as communication devices. This contrasts with WiFi sensing, which can sense with commodity WiFi devices and signals designed for data communications.

There are two major types of radar signals: **Pulse** vs. **FMCW.** Pulse radars are usually used for long-range detections; they are bulky, power hungry and used by large infrastructure, such as weather stations, aircraft control tower, cars, and so on. FMCW is lightweight, energy-efficient and used in mobile devices, such as mobile phones and IoTs.

5.4 Pulsed Radars

A pulse is a very short signal on the order of μs or ns, which is transmitted with very high peak power on the order of kW or MW. These high-power pulses are suitable for long-range applications, e.g., aircraft detection and tracking. Radar antennas are highly **directional** and usually rotate continuously to provide 360° coverage for applications, such as aircraft detection in control towers.

Pulses are transmitted periodically with tens or hundreds of pulses per sec, while the transmitter remains completely silent in between pulse transmissions. As pulse durations are extremely short, compared to the silence periods, the average power consumption of pulsed radars is considerably lower than the

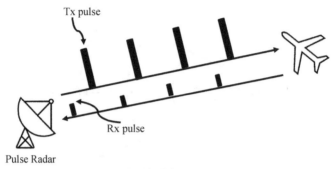

Pulse Radar

Fig. 10. Pulsed radar.

peak pulse power. While the transmitted pulse powers are high, the received pulses are very weak as illustrated in Fig. 10.

Wider pulses contain more energy; hence they provide longer detection range, but echoes from multiple objects can overlap, yielding low resolution. Since B is inversely proportional to pulse width, the resolution of pulsed radars can be obtained as:

$$Resolution = \frac{c \times \omega}{2} meter \tag{3}$$

where ω is the pulse width in meter. Thus, narrower pulses have higher resolution at the expense of shorter range and higher bandwidth requirements.

With advanced signal processing, it is possible to measure the frequency of the received pulses, which enable Doppler shift calculations. Thus, radars can also calculate the radial **velocity** of the target and detect whether the target is moving closer or farther from the radar.

For large objects, such as aircraft, pulses get reflected by different parts of the object body. With advanced signal processing, it is then possible to detect the **shape** of the target and identify it.

5.5 FMCW Radars

FMCW stands for Frequency Modulated Continuous Wave. As the name suggests, unlike narrow pulses, FMCW transmits continuous signals, but it modulates the frequency of the transmitted signal in a special way that helps detect the ToF [TI-RADAR]. Basically, the frequency modulation follows a linear chirp, as shown in Fig. 11(a), where the frequency is increased at a constant speed over time. In the time-frequency representation, as shown in Fig. 11(b), the chirp appears as a straight line. As we can see, the chirp sweeps the entire bandwidth, from the minimum frequency to the maximum

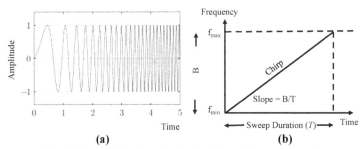

Fig. 11. Linear chirp in amplitude-time (a) and frequency-time (b).

frequency, within a specified chirp sweep duration. The sweeping speed is basically given by the slope, S, as:

$$S = \frac{B}{T} \tag{4}$$

where B is the bandwidth in Hz and T is the chirp sweeping duration in second.

So, how does a chirp transmission help FMCW radar measure the ToF? As shown in Fig. 12, this is achieved by measuring the instantaneous frequency difference, Δf, between the transmitted chirp and the received chirp. The reason that there exists a frequency difference at any given time instant between these two signals is because there is a time delay, ToF, between them. Given that the frequency difference is basically the product of the slope of the chirp and the ToF, we have:

$$ToF = \frac{\Delta f}{S} \tag{5}$$

The range is then obtained as:

$$Range = ToF \times c = \frac{\Delta f \times c}{S} \tag{6}$$

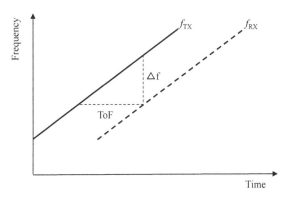

Fig. 12. Principle of FMCW radar.

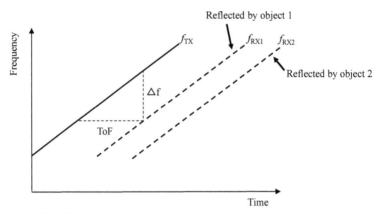

Fig. 13. Transmitted and received chirps in the presence of two objects.

Using the same chirp concepts, FMCW radars can detect two or more objects located at different distances but at the same bearing. This is possible as each object reflects the chirp with slight delays from each other. Figure 13 shows the chirp transmissions and receptions at the radar when two objects are located at the same bearing but at different distances.

Let us now derive the resolution of FMCW radars by considering two objects along the same bearing but with a difference of Δd meters from each other. If we denote the instantaneous frequency difference between the received chirps from these two objects with Δf, then we have:

$$\frac{\Delta f}{2\Delta d/c} = S = \frac{B}{T} \tag{7}$$

where $2\Delta d/c$ is the difference between the round-trip times of the two objects. According to the frequency detection principle, which relates to Fast Fourier Transform, two frequencies within a signal can be distinguished if $\Delta f > 1/T$, where T is the observation time of the signal. Thus, replacing Δf with $1/T$ in Eq. (7), we obtain:

$$\Delta d = \frac{c}{2B} \tag{8}$$

It is interesting to note that the resolution of FMCW radar obtained in Eq. (8) is identical to the resolution of the pulsed radar, which depends only on the bandwidth. This means that FMCW resolution does not depend on the slope of the chirp.

Example 1

Q1. What is the resolution of a 24 GHz FMCW radar operating within the ISM band from 24 GHz to 24.25 GHz?

Solution

Bandwidth (B) = 24.25 − 24 = 0.25 GHz

Speed of light (c) = 3×10^8 m/s

Resolution = c/2B = $(3 \times 10^8)/(2 \times 0.25 \times 10^9)$ = 60 cm

6. Summary

1. Wireless signals are good for both communication and sensing.
2. Two major types of wireless sensing: WiFi sensing and radar sensing.
3. Using RSS and CSI, WiFi can be used for many human sensing and monitoring applications.
4. RSS is readily available, but cannot provide fine-grain sensing.
5. CSI can provide fine-grain sensing, but modifications are required to access CSI in commodity WiFi devices.
6. Radar can provide accurate range and motion information; more sophisticated sensing applications are possible with radars, but they require dedicated infrastructure for sensing.
7. Millimeter-wave FMCW radars have emerged as a popular low-cost, small form-factor IoT-sensing device with applications in many IoT domains: health, smart home, smart industry, smart transport, etc.

Multiple Choice Questions

Q1. What is the resolution of an FMCW radar utilizing the frequency band 77 GHz–81 GHz?
(a) 7.5 cm
(b) 3.75 cm
(c) 30 cm
(d) 60 cm
(e) 90 cm

Q2. What is the resolution of pulse radar operating with 100ns pulses?
(a) 5 m
(b) 10 m
(c) 15 m
(d) 20 m
(e) 100 m

Q3. A 60 GHz radar is likely to
  (a) have better resolution than a 24 GHz radar
  (b) have worse resolution than a 24 GHz radar
  (c) have better resolution than a 77 GHz radar
  (d) have a resolution on the order of a few μm
  (e) none of these

Q4. For a CSI = 5+j5, the phase shift is
  (a) 90 degree
  (b) 60 degree
  (c) 45 degree
  (d) 30 degree
  (e) 10 degree

Q5. More subcarriers per channel mean
  (a) more CSI values available per packet
  (b) more RSS values available per packet
  (c) more CSI and more RSS values available per packet
  (d) more RSS values but less CSI values available per packet
  (e) more CSI values but less RSS values available per packet

Q6. Which of the following statements is true?
  (a) Pulse radars transmit signals continuously
  (b) FMCW radars estimate range by transmitting down-chirps
  (c) FMCW radars estimate range by transmitting chirps
  (d) FMCW radars estimate range by transmitting modulated pulse
  (e) Pulse radars are widely used in small-form factor IoT devices

Q7. An UWB radar operating in the band 1.5 GHz–2.5 GHz can separate two objects along the same bearing if
  (a) the difference of distances of the two objects from the radar is 10 cm
  (b) the difference of distances of the two objects from the radar is 12 cm
  (c) the difference of distances of the two objects from the radar is 16 cm
  (d) the difference of distances of the two objects from the radar is less than 15 cm
  (e) the difference of distances of the two objects from the radar is less than 10 cm

Q8. Radars are often used for both communication and sensing.
  (a) True
  (b) False

Q9. RSS can detect more fine-grained human activities compared to CSI
  (a) True
  (b) False

Q10. CSI is used by radars to detect and estimate the range of target objects.
(a) True
(b) False

References

[COMST 2021] I. Nirmal, A. Khamis, M. Hassan, W. Hu and X. Zhu (second quarter 2021). Deep learning for radio-based human sensing: recent advances and future directions. pp. 995–1019. *In*: *IEEE Communications Surveys & Tutorials*, vol. 23, no. 2. doi: 10.1109/COMST.2021.3058333.

[RADAR-NATURE] R. Komissarov, V. Kozlov, D. Filonov et al. (2019). Partially coherent radar unties range resolution from bandwidth limitations. *Nature Communications* 10: 1423. https://doi.org/10.1038/s41467-019-09380-x.

[TI-RADAR] mmWave Radar Sensor. Texas Instrument. https://www.ti.com/sensors/mmwave-radar/overview.html [accessed 28 October 2021].

[WIDANCE 2017] Kun Qian, Chenshu Wu, Zimu Zhou, Yue Zheng, Zheng Yang, Yunhao Liu. (2017). Inferring Motion Direction using Commodity Wi-Fi for Interactive Exergames. CHI.

[YOUSSEF 2015] H. Abdelnasser, M. Youssef and K. A. Harras. (2015). WiGest: A ubiquitous WiFi-based gesture recognition system. *2015 IEEE Conference on Computer Communications (INFOCOM)*, pp. 1472–1480. doi: 10.1109/INFOCOM.2015.7218525.

14

Aerial Wireless Networks

◇◇

Miniaturization of electronics has created an opportunity to fit wireless communications equipment into the payload of various aerial platforms, such as drones and aerostats. Aerial wireless networks can be deployed quickly and cost-effectively to provide coverage in remote areas where terrestrial infrastructure is difficult to build, in disaster zones with damaged cellular towers, and even in urban areas to absorb sudden peaks in data traffic. Aerial wireless networks are currently being investigated as a promising new dimension for the next generation communication networks. This chapter examines options, characteristics, and design considerations for such aerial networks.

1. Non-terrestrial Networks

Figure 1 illustrates the basic categories of non-terrestrial networks based on their altitudes. Satellite networks deploy communications infrastructure in the space well above the Earth's atmosphere. While satellite networks can provide ubiquitous coverage for the entire Earth surface, they are costly to deploy and suffer from extended latency due to the long distance. Additionally, they are not suitable for direct communication with small IoT sensors on the ground due to the high transmission powers required to reach satellites.

Aerial networks refer to networks that use platforms within the Earth's atmosphere. As such, they are low-cost and low-latency networks that can be quickly deployed to provide coverage at specific regions of interest. Aerial networks can directly connect small user equipment and IoT devices on the ground. There are two major categories of aerial networks based on their altitudes. High Altitude Platform Station (HAPS) uses platforms like aerostats floating in the stratosphere 20 kms from Earth's surface [HAPS-SOFTBANK]. HAPS can provide coverage to a large area and the platform can be practically powered by solar power. In contrast, Unmanned Aerial

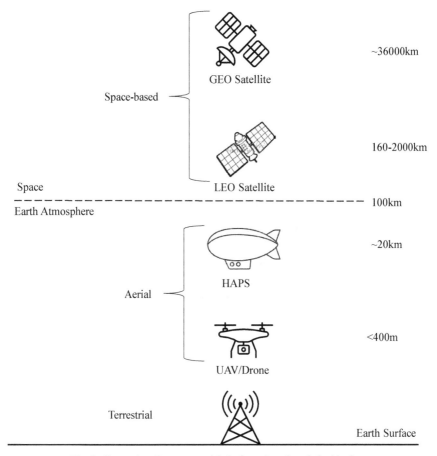

Fig. 1. Categories of non-terrestrial platforms based on their altitudes.

Vehicles (UAVs), also commonly known as drones, fly at a very low altitude, often restricted below 400 m by regulation [FOTOUHI 2019].

UAVs have several advantages compared to HAPS. UAVs are very low-cost equipment that can be deployed much more quickly than any other aerial platforms. As such, they are especially suitable for unexpected and limited duration events, such as disasters and dynamic hotspots. The low altitude of UAVs can help establish short-range line-of-sight (LoS) communication links with ground users offering significant performance gain. Finally, the manoeuvrability of UAVs offers opportunities to dynamically adjusting their location or mobility to best suit the communication environment. These benefits of UAVs make them a promising new addition to the future wireless system that must support communications to more diverse scenarios [MOZ 2019].

2. Air-to-ground Propagation and Path Loss

We have seen in Chapter 3 that in terrestrial networks, the signal propagates through the urban environment where it experiences reflections and scattering from man-made and other structures. Path loss for terrestrial networks is thus simply modelled following the d^{-n} law, where d is the Tx-Rx distance and n is a path loss exponent, which vary for different environments.

Path loss in aerial networks, however, is modelled differently. It is directly affected by the **elevation angle**, θ, which is obtained as **arctan(h/r)**, as illustrated in Fig. 2, where h is the height of the aerial BS and r is the ground distance between the mobile device and the centre of the BS's ground coverage. It is clear that θ decreases as the mobile device moves away from centre of the coverage, and vice versa.

Now let us examine why and how the elevation angle influences the path loss in aerial networks. Figure 3 illustrates the air-to-ground (A2G) propagation experienced by a signal travelling from a drone to a receiver on the ground [HOURANI 2016]. The signal experiences free-space path loss until it enters the urban environment where it is subject to reflections and scattering. A2G path loss, L_{A2G}, therefore has two components—the free space path loss, L_{FS}, plus an additional path loss, L_{SC}, which is caused by the scattering within the urban environment:

$$L_{A2G}(dB) = L_{FS}(dB) + L_{SC}(dB) \tag{1}$$

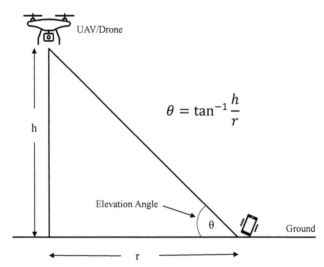

Fig. 2. Elevation angle in aerial wireless networks.

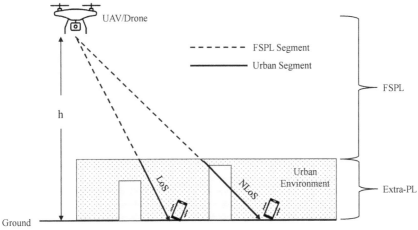

Fig. 3. Air-to-ground radio propagation in aerial wireless networks.

L_{FS} can be derived directly using the well-known Frii's law (discussed in Chapter 3) as follows:

$$L_{FS}(dB) = 20log_{10}(d) + 20log_{10}(f) + 20log_{10}\left(\frac{4\pi}{c}\right) \tag{2}$$

where d is the distance from the drone to the ground receiver, i.e., $d = \sqrt{h^2 + r^2}$. L_{SC}, however, depends on whether the receiver has a LoS with the drone or not. L_{SC} is very small when there is LoS, but is significantly higher for a NLoS link. That is, if L_{SC}^{LoS} and L_{SC}^{NLoS} represent the scattering loss for LoS and NLoS links, respectively, then we have $L_{SC}^{NLoS} \gg L_{SC}^{LoS}$. In order to derive the A2G path loss, we therefore need to know the probabilities of LoS and NLoS for the ground receiver.

Critical analysis and modelling show that the probability of LoS can be obtained as follows [HOURANI 2014]:

$$P(LoS,\theta) = \frac{1}{1 + e^{b(a-\theta)}} \tag{3}$$

where a and b are environment parameters which assume different values for the four types of urban environments, namely Suburban, urban, Dense Urban, and Highrise Urban.

It is further assumed that if a link is not LoS, then it is NLoS. The probability of NLoS is therefore simply obtained as:

$$P(NLoS, \theta) = 1 - P(LoS, \theta) \tag{4}$$

The expected A2G path loss thus can be obtained as:

$$\overline{L_{A2G}}(dB) = L_{FS}(dB) + L_{SC}^{LoS}(dB) \times P(LoS, \theta) + L_{SC}^{NLoS}(dB) \times P(NLoS, \theta) \tag{5}$$

It is interesting to note that the higher the aerial BS, the higher the LoS probability but higher the free space path loss due to longer distance. Thus, for any given urban environment, there is an optimal height for the aerial BS. However, in practice, the optimal height of the aerial BS may be constrained by regulation.

3. HAPS-based Aerial Networks

3.1 HAPS Platforms

There are two main categories of HAPS platforms—lighter-than-air and heavier-than-air [HAPS 1997]. The former type uses some sort of lifting gas, such as hydrogen or helium, to float in the air without requiring external sources of power. Examples are aerostats or dirigible balloons that can float over a fixed location for months. It needs a small amount of power to maintain its position against occasional wind bursts in the stratosphere.

Heavier-than-air category refers to aircraft built from composite materials and require external power to fly. With large wingspans, these aircraft can be powered by solar energy to keep them at the stratosphere for many days. Unlike the lighter-than-air platforms, they are unable to stay at a fixed location, hence they are flown in circles to provide coverage over a given area.

3.2 Network Architecture

A typical HAPS-based aerial network architecture is shown in Fig. 4 [HAPS-SOFTBANK] where the platform is placed on top of the intended coverage area. To achieve frequency reuse, like the terrestrial cellular networks, the HAPS would emit multiple beams to the coverage area to form a cellular network. Sophisticated phase array antennas can be used to electronically form these beams but even simple parabolic antennas, with mechanical steering, could also do the job. HAPS BSs can be back hauled either via satellite links or through terrestrial cellular towers.

High antenna gains are necessary to compensate for the high path loss arising from high altitude of the platforms. This means the beams need to be adequately narrow, which would limit the size of the cells on the ground. A key challenge is to keep the beams sticking to the same position (keep

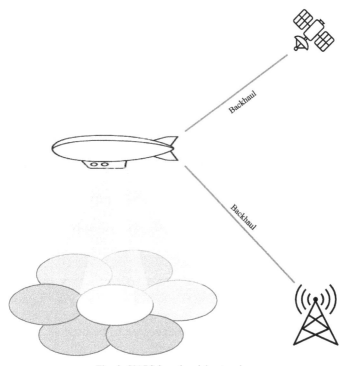

Fig. 4. HAPS-based aerial networks.

the cells stationary) on the ground to avoid unnecessary handoffs for ground receivers from beams to beams. This would require sophisticated mechanical and electronic means to address HAPS movements due to sudden wind bursts or the circling motion in the case of heavier-than-air platforms.

4. UAV-based Aerial Networks

4.1 UAV Platforms

Based on the flying mechanism used, UAV platforms can be categorized into two broad classes—wing-based and rotor-based (*see* Fig. 5). Wing-based UAVs use fixed wings to glide through the air, which helps them move faster and save energy at the same time. The downside of fixed-wing UAVs is that they need a runway to take-off and land and cannot hover over a fixed location. Rotor-based UAVs, on the other hand, can take-off and land vertically from any location, which makes them easy to deploy at urban locations. They are also capable of hovering above a fixed location, which makes them suitable for providing continuous wireless coverage over specific locations with high precision. However, rotor-based flying consumes more energy as it has to

Rotor-based UAV   Wing-based UAV

Fig. 5. Rotor vs. wing-based UAVs.

fight against gravity at all time. Hybrid UAVs featuring both wings and rotors are commercially available at a higher cost.

4.2 Network Architecture

Possible deployment scenarios for UAV aerial networks are illustrated in Fig. 6. Due to small payloads and energy restrictions, UAVs are expected to use only a single antenna or beam to provide coverage for a single cell when used as an aerial BS. UAVs are also expected to be used as aerial relays to improve cell-edge coverage for macro cells, off-load traffic from a hot-spot, or extend the coverage to difficult-to-reach locations. Unlike HAPS, UAVs have limited coverage. Therefore, multiple UAVs would be needed if coverage is required for a large area. UAVs are expected to be back hauled through nearby macro cell towers.

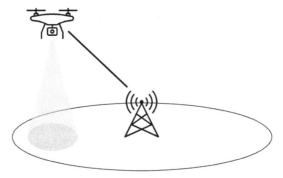

Fig. 6. UAV aerial network.

4.3 Mobility of UAV Base Stations

The fundamental advantage of a UAV BS compared to a terrestrial one is that it can dynamically change its location in the sky to maintain optimal coverage

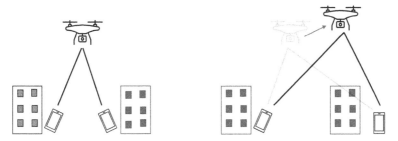

Fig. 7. UAV aerial BS moves to a new location to achieve line-of-sight.

and network performance at all times despite changes in user locations and demands on the ground. Using a simple scenario involving two ground users, Fig. 7 illustrates the benefit of repositioning a UAV BS as one of the users move. This means that such aerial networks must be empowered with intelligent BS mobility-control algorithms that can sense network changes and reposition the UAVs accordingly [DRONE-CELL].

4.4 Backhaul Connectivity for UAV Base Stations

The mobility of UAV BSs, however, would make it more challenging to maintain the wireless backhaul links. This is particularly challenging if sharp mm-wave beams are used to back haul the UAV as any movement would require rapid adjustment of the narrow beam. Any movement of the UAV BS therefore must be jointly considered with the potential impact on the backhaul performance.

4.5 Endurance Time of UAV Base Stations

As UAVs are powered by batteries, they suffer from short endurance time in the sky. A UAV base station or relay therefore must return to a charging station when battery runs low. Unfortunately, opportunities to carry large batteries onboard is limited due to small payloads offered in UAVs. Energy harvesting from solar, RF, or laser sources could be viable to extend the battery lifetime to some extent, but due to significant mechanical power consumption of flying UAVs, alternative solutions are required to provide long-term coverage with flying base stations. We discuss a couple of such alternative options:

Replacement UAVs: Fully-charged spare UAVs can be organized to take over a flying UAV experiencing battery depletion. This is analogous to player replacement in soccer matches where tired players are replaced by new players who wait in the side lines. Existing user associations can be gracefully handed over from the departing UAVs to the arriving UAVs using established handover concepts. However, this would require installing UAV charging stations near the coverage area with autonomous algorithms precisely orchestrating UAV replacements to avoid any service disruption.

Tethered UAVs: UAVs can be tethered to a ground station with cables [DRONE-TETHER]. The cables can supply both power and data, thus solving the endurance and back haul problems of UAV-based aerial networks simultaneously. The trade-off of tethering would obviously be limited mobility for the UAV BS, which would limit the opportunities to optimize its placement for network performance maximization.

5. Summary

1. Aerial network is a specific category of non-terrestrial network that resides within the Earth's atmosphere, i.e., below the space.

2. There are two main categories of aerial networks – HAPS at the altitude of ~ 20 km and UAV flying below 400 m.

3. Path loss models in aerial networks are different than those experienced in terrestrial networks.

4. HAPS can float for months whereas UAVs have a very limited flying lifetime, lasting on the order of hours at best.

Multiple Choice Questions

Q1. HAPS platforms float
   (a) in the space
   (b) at stratosphere
   (c) below 400 m
   (d) by burning liquid fuel
   (e) on the water

Q2. UAVs fly
   (a) in the space
   (b) at the stratosphere
   (c) below 400 m
   (d) above 100 km
   (e) below the radar

Q3. Non-terrestrial networks refer to networks deployed
   (a) underwater
   (b) in the space
   (c) above 400 m in the sky
   (d) within aeroplanes
   (e) in the air or space

Q4. Probability of LoS in aerial networks increases with increasing platform height
(a) True
(b) False

Q5. Aerostat is
(a) a UAV platform
(b) a HAPS platform
(c) heavier than air
(d) floats in the space
(e) cannot float at a fixed location

References

[DRONE-CELL] Azade Fotouhi, Ming Ding and Mahbub Hassan. (2021). Drone cells: Improving spectral efficiency using drone-mounted flying base stations. *Journal of Network and Computer Applications*, vol. 174.

[DRONE-TETHER] M. Kishk, A. Bader and M. -S. Alouini. (Dec. 2020). Aerial base station deployment in 6G cellular networks using tethered drones: the mobility and endurance tradeoff. pp. 103–111. *In: IEEE Vehicular Technology Magazine*, vol. 15, no. 4. doi: 10.1109/MVT.2020.3017885.

[FOTOUHI 2019] A. Fotouhi et al. (fourth quarter 2019). Survey on UAV cellular communications: practical aspects, standardization advancements, regulation, and security challenges. pp. 3417–3442. *In: IEEE Communications Surveys & Tutorials*, vol. 21, no. 4. doi: 10.1109/COMST.2019.2906228.

[HAPS 1997] G. M. Djuknic, J. Freidenfelds and Y. Okunev. (Sept. 1997). Establishing wireless communications services via high-altitude aeronautical platforms: a concept whose time has come? pp. 128–135. *In: IEEE Communications Magazine*, vol. 35, no. 9. doi: 10.1109/35.620534.

[HAPS-SOFTBANK] Y. Shibata, N. Kanazawa, M. Konishi, K. Hoshino, Y. Ohta and A. Nagate. (2020). System design of gigabit HAPS mobile communications. pp. 157995–158007. *In: IEEE Access*, vol. 8. doi: 10.1109/ACCESS.2020.3019820.

[HOURANI 2016] S. Chandrasekharan et al. (May 2016). Designing and implementing future aerial communication networks. pp. 26–34. *In: IEEE Communications Magazine*, vol. 54, no. 5. doi: 10.1109/MCOM.2016.7470932.

[HOURANI 2014] A. Al-Hourani, S. Kandeepan and S. Lardner. (Dec. 2014). Optimal LAP altitude for maximum coverage. pp. 569–572. *In: IEEE Wireless Communications Letters*, vol. 3, no. 6. doi: 10.1109/LWC.2014.2342736.

[MOZ 2019] M. Mozaffari, W. Saad, M. Bennis, Y. -H. Nam and M. Debbah (third quarter 2019). A tutorial on UAVs for wireless networks: applications, challenges, and open problems. pp. 2334–2360. *In: IEEE Communications Surveys & Tutorials*, vol. 21, no. 3. doi: 10.1109/COMST.2019.2902862.

Index

◇◇

2-ray model 39, 45, 46, 54
802.11af 104, 105, 108, 110–113, 134, 135
802.11ah 104, 113–121, 134, 135

A

Adaptive Frequency Hopping 189, 197, 214
Aerial wireless networks 260, 262, 263
amplitude 11–14, 16, 21, 23, 34
Amplitude Shift Keying (ASK) 21
Announcement Time (AT) 127
antenna 35–37, 40, 41, 46, 48, 50, 53–56
Artificial intelligence (AI) 233, 237, 241, 242
Association Beamforming Time (A-BFT) 127, 132

B

Backoff Count 67, 70
base stations 142
Basic Channel Unit (BCU) 112
basic rate 191, 195
Baud rate 21
beacon 67, 74
beam forming 48
Beam Refinement Procedure 131
Bidirectional Transmit 118
Bluetooth Classic 189, 190, 192, 195, 196, 205–207, 215, 216
Bluetooth Low Energy (BLE) 189, 204–212, 215
Bluetooth SIG 187, 189, 208, 209
Bluetooth Smart 189, 204, 205, 210

C

carrier sense multiple access (CSMA) 66
Cell on Wheels 142, 143
Channel Bonding 82, 85, 87, 88, 90, 100
channel modeling 38
Channel Schedule Management (CSM) 110
channel state information (CSI) 90, 246–251, 257–259

chirp spread spectrum 219, 227
chirp sweep duration 220
clear-to-send (CTS) 65
co-channel cells 145–147, 161, 162
code division multiple access (CDMA) 27
Coherence time 31, 33
collision avoidance 65, 75
collision detection 64, 65
constellation diagram 23
contention-based period (CBP) 127, 128
contention-free period (CFP) 67
Contention Window 67

D

Data rate 11, 21, 23–25, 33, 34
Data Transfer Time (DTT) 127
dB 19, 20, 25, 32–34
dBm 19, 20, 32–34
decibel 19, 20
Deep learning (DL) 233–239, 241–243
delay spread 44, 55, 81, 87, 94, 100
Delivery TIM (DTIM) 119, 120
Diffraction 37, 38
Digital Dividend 106, 107
directional antenna 35, 54, 55
Direct-Sequence Spread Spectrum (DSSS) 29
Distributed Coordination Function (DCF) 66
diversity gain 49
Doppler effect 30, 33
Doppler shift 30, 31, 33
Doppler spread 30, 31, 33
drones 260, 261

E

electromagnetic waves 11, 14, 17, 18, 32
elevation angle 262
enhanced data rate 189, 191
Enhanced Distributed Control Function (EDCF) 83

F

Fast Fourier Transform (FFT) 17
federated learning 240–243
FMCW 253–258
Fourier transform 16, 17
fractional frequency reuse 149, 150
frame aggregation 85, 89, 90
frame bursting 84
frequency 11–18, 21, 26, 28–34
Frequency Division Duplexing (FDD) 32, 142, 158, 161
frequency division multiple access (FDMA) 26
frequency domains 15
Frequency Hopping 189, 192, 193, 196–198, 200–202, 206, 207, 211, 213–216
frequency hopping spread spectrum (FHSS) 28
Frequency Modulated Continuous Wave 254
frequency reuse 144–146, 148–150
Frequency Shift Keying (FSK) 21
Frii's law 39–41

G

Gaussian Frequency Shift Keying 202
Geofencing 211
geolocation database (GDB) 108, 111
Geolocation Database Dependent 108
GSM 152–157, 161
guard interval 80–82, 85–88, 92, 94, 95, 100, 101

H

HaLow 113, 114
Hamming distance 25, 26
hidden node problem 64, 65
Hierarchical Association Identifier 116, 120
High Altitude Platform Station 260
High Frequency 105, 113, 124, 135
High Throughput Control (HTC) 90
Hybrid Coordination Function (HCF) 83

I

IETF 108, 111
inter-frame space (IFS) 66
Internet of Things (IoT) 175–185
inter-symbol interference 43, 44, 51, 54, 55
Inverse FFT (IFFT) 17
ISM bands 61, 62
isotropic antenna 35, 36, 54

L

license-exempt 61, 62
line-of-sight 37, 50
Long Term Evolution (LTE) 152, 153, 157–163
LoRa Alliance 218
low-power wide-area networking (LPWAN) 182–185, 218
LTE Advanced 153, 157
LTE-A 157
LTE-M 182, 183, 185

M

machine learning (ML) 233–236, 240–243
medium access control 26
mmWave bands 170
Multi-AP Coordination 99
multiband communication 99
multipath 39, 42–47, 50, 54, 55
multiplexing gain 49

N

narrowband IoT 182
NB-IoT 176–178, 182–185
Network Allocation Vector (NAV) 67
Non-Orthogonal Multiple Access (NOMA) 167, 167, 170, 171
non-terrestrial networks 260, 268
Null Data Packets 116, 134
Nyquist's Theorem 24, 25, 32

O

Orthogonal Frequency Division Multiple Access (OFDMA) 51
Orthogonal Frequency Division Multiplexing (OFDM) 51, 64, 75
OUI (Organization Unique Identifier) 195, 196

P

particular channel frequency response (CFR) 248
path loss 39–42, 45, 47, 48, 54
PAWS 108, 111, 112, 134
PBSS Central Point (PCP) 127–129, 132, 133, 136
Personal BSS (PBSS) 127, 133
phase 11–13, 21–23, 34
Phase Shift Keying (PSK) 21
Physical Resource Block 159

Piconet 189, 190, 194, 200, 202, 215
Point Coordination Function (PCF) 66, 83
power management 62, 74, 76
protocol data unit (PDU) 89
pseudorandom hopping 213

Q

Quadrature Amplitude and Phase Modulation
(QAM) 23

R

Radar 246, 252–258
radio channel 35, 38
RAdio Detecting And Ranging 252
radio towers 142
ready-to-send (RTS) 64, 65
Receiver sensitivity 41, 42, 55
Reflection 37, 38, 45, 46
Registered Location Query Protocol (RLQP)
108, 110
Registered Location Secure Server (RLSS) 108
reinforcement learning 234
Response Indication Deferral (RID) 119
restricted access window (RAW) 118, 120–122,
134
reuse factor 145, 146, 162
reuse ratio 146
RSS 247, 248, 257, 258

S

scattering 37, 38, 55
Scatternet 190, 191, 215
service data unit (SDU) 89
service period (SP) 127, 128
Shannon's Theorem 25
short IFS (SIFS) 66
short message service (SMS) 157
signal-to-noise (SNR) 20
small-scale fading 46, 47, 50
spatial diversity 48, 49
spatial frequency sharing (SFS) 128, 133, 134
spatial multiplexing 48, 49

spectrum 17, 18, 28, 29, 33, 34
Speed Frame Exchange 116–118, 120, 134
Spread spectrum 28, 29, 33
spreading factor (SF) 221–223, 227–229
Subscriber Identity Module (SIM) 154, 155
successive interference cancellation (SIC) 166,
167
Super-Fi 105
supervised learning 233, 234
sweeping speed 220, 227–229
Symbol 21, 23, 24, 34
symbol duration 21

T

target wake time (TWT) 116, 120, 122, 123
Time Division Duplexing (TDD) 32, 158
time division multiple access (TDMA) 26
Traffic Indication Map (TIM) 74, 118, 119,
121, 122
Transfer learning 239, 240, 242, 243
transmission opportunity (TXOP) 84
TVWS databases 108, 135

U

Ultra High Frequency (UHF) 105, 107
Unmanned Aerial Vehicles (UAVs) 261,
265–268
unsupervised learning 233

V

Very High Frequency (VHF) 105, 135
virtual carrier sensing 69, 75

W

White Space 105–111, 134, 135
white space map (WSM) 110
White-Fi 105, 134, 135
wireless LANs 59, 62, 63, 65
Wireless Personal Area Networks (WPANs)
187

Ingram Content Group UK Ltd.
Milton Keynes UK
UKHW020616070423
419735UK00001B/1